INDIA
THE ROAD AHEAD

INDIA
THE ROAD AHEAD

MARK TULLY

LONDON · SYDNEY · AUCKLAND · JOHANNESBURG

1 3 5 7 9 10 8 6 4 2

Published in 2011 by Rider, an imprint of Ebury Publishing
A Random House Group Company

The Random House Group Limited Reg. No. 954009

Addresses for companies within the Random House Group can be found at
www.randomhouse.co.uk

A CIP catalogue record for this book is available from the British Library

The Random House Group Limited supports the Forest Stewardship Council® (FSC®),
the leading international forest certification organisation. All our titles that are
printed on Greenpeace approved FSC® certified paper carry the FSC® logo.
Our paper procurement policy can be found at
www.randomhouse.co.uk/environment

Printed and bound in Great Britain by CPI Mackays, Chatham ME5 8TD

ISBN 9781846041617

Copies are available at special rates for bulk orders. Contact the sales development
team on 020 7840 8487 for more information.

To buy books by your favourite authors and register for offers, visit:
www.randomhouse.co.uk

CONTENTS

ACKNOWLEDGEMENTS

Paying adequate tribute to each of those who gave their time to talk to me, and often travel with me, during the writing of this book, would require many pages and that might become rather tedious too. So I hope that they will find their roles in the stories in which they appear a recognition of my gratitude. Without their willingness to give their time and share their knowledge there would be no stories.

Two people read some of the chapters and offered invaluable advice. Both are former colleagues from my days as the BBC's Delhi Correspondent, Ramdutt Tripathi from Lucknow, and Subir Bhaumik from Kolkata. The economist and translator Bibek Debroy does not appear in the book but he gave me invaluable advice. The radio producer Matt Thompson willingly gave me permission to use the some of the recordings we made when making a programme together on tiger poaching. Mandeep Singh Bajwa generously helped my research in Punjab. I am deeply indebted to my editors, Judith Kendra and Sue Lascelles from Random House in London and Ravi Singh from Penguin India. They helped me overcome the difficulties a broadcasting journalist, used to writing short snappy reports, faces when he has to write a coherent book. Lastly I am profoundly grateful to my partner, and my companion on many of the journeys I have described in this book, Gillian Wright. As well as companionship, she provided a critical eye, drive when enthusiasm was flagging, and an awful lot of hard work.

INTRODUCTION

Yamunanagar is a town in the northern Indian state of Haryana. It's dusty and slightly down at heel – not the sort of place pilgrims driving to the historic Sikh gurudwara, or temple, of Paonta Sahib, or tourists travelling to the foothills of the Himalayas, would normally stop at unless obliged to by the railway crossing in the centre of town. In the eighties I was obliged to stop there because I had crashed into the back of a tractor that was driving in the dark without lights on a country road. I had been driving an Ambassador, a version of the late forties British Morris Oxford which had few rivals then, and survives today although it now does face fierce competition. The Ambassador had limped to the nearest village where a puncture repairer managed to separate the fan and radiator from the rest of the engine with a crowbar. He also sprinkled turmeric powder into the radiator, saying that it would stop the leaks temporarily but that I should go to Yamunanagar to get the radiator welded.

While the welder was at work the level crossing gates closed and I watched the traffic build up. Queues formed in both the left and the right lanes on either side of the gates and grew longer and longer. Eventually a seemingly endless coal train rumbled slowly by. After some time the gatekeeper leisurely opened the crossing. Vehicles from both directions in the left and right lanes moved forward a few yards until they met head on in the middle of the track. There wasn't a policeman in sight. Every driver seemed to think that merely by blowing the horn the traffic would move. Amidst this cacophony a pony in the shafts of a cart reared in alarm, spilling sacks of grain on the road. Frustrated truck drivers revved their engines futilely and noxious black fumes poured from their exhausts. At first it looked as though no one was going to give way, but then slowly by a process of reluctant mutual give and take, the traffic started to crawl across the railway track.

I asked the welder whether this happened every time the level crossing gates closed. 'Oh yes,' he replied.

'Well, why doesn't someone do something to stop the build-up of traffic on both sides of the road?' I asked.

'Arre,' he said impatiently, as though that was a stupid question, 'who does anything about anything in this country? Why are we Indians religious people? Because we know that this country only runs because God runs it. It's all *jugaar*.' *Jugaar* could loosely be translated as muddling through, or making do. Putting turmeric in a leaky radiator was a classic example of the principle.

More than twenty years later things have changed dramatically in India and so there may well be a bridge built over the railway line in Yamunanagar. I haven't been to back to see, but I have seen many elsewhere. There may even by a bypass. If there are traffic jams it's far less likely now that horse-drawn vehicles will be caught up in them. The relentless expansion of the motor industry has seen to that. But *jugaar* still flourishes.

The word came into prominence in 2010 when the preparations for the Commonwealth Games were so behind schedule and so slip-shod that some countries threatened to pull out their teams. There was particular concern about the accommodation for the athletes. However, almost miraculously everything was all right on the day. This miracle was widely attributed to India's talent for *jugaar*, rather than God, and it prompted a debate on that peculiar phenomenon's merits and demerits. In an article in *The Times of India*, the economist Swaminathan S. Anklesaria Aiyar put a positive spin on the word, attributing to it India and Indians' ability to innovate. He quoted a survey showing that 81 per cent of Indian businessmen said *jugaar* was the reason for their success. A week later in

The Times of India the journalist Swapan Dasgupta came back with an attack on *jugaar*, saying, 'It's bleeding you,' and going on to maintain, '*Jugaar* has prompted a celebration of expediency, shortcuts and shoddiness, a penchant for taking a winding course where a straight road would survive ... *jugaar* has become an obstacle to India reaching its true potential.'

I would still support the view of that welder. To me *jugaar* seems to mean a talent for muddling through. This is undoubtedly a valuable talent. It has seen India through numerous crises which could have destabilised a country that was less adaptable – four wars, for example.

So with this meaning, *jugaar* could be seen to have served India well. But it has a downside. It has, in my view, led to a dangerous complacency, the belief that India has muddled through so many crises that there is no need for urgency in tackling the problems it faces. In 1984 there would have been no need for Indira Gandhi to send the army into the Sikhs' most sacred shrine, the Golden Temple in Amritsar, if action had been taken against the Sikh separatist leader Sant Jarnail Singh Bhindranwale before he occupied and fortified the temple complex. That delay in taking a decision led to mutinies by Sikh soldiers in the Indian army, and cost Indira Gandhi her life. She was assassinated by two of her Sikh bodyguards. The assassination sparked off massacres in Delhi in which thousands of Sikhs were brutally killed.

Looking back over the years since 1991, and looking forward too, all this *jugaar* raises the question, is India still muddling through, and if so how does that affect its much-touted prospects of becoming an economic super-power? There is a simplistic but widely publicised view of India's history over the last twenty years which would have us believe that this unwieldy country with its vast population will definitely be very near the top of the economic league, if not right at the top, by 2050.

According to this version of history, India was held back by a particularly virulent form of socialist central planning that tied up the economy in red tape. This was known as the Licence-Permit Raj. The licences and permits were intended to ensure that investment and trade were controlled by the government in what it claimed was the national interest. In fact the interests served were in the main the politicians' and bureaucrats' who issued the licences and permits, and those of the members of the business community who paid for them. Hence the system also became known as the Neta-Babu Raj, or politician and bureaucrat raj. Then in 1991 India found itself on the brink of bankruptcy. The government had even been forced to sell gold, a devastating blow to the self-respect of a nation where possession of that shining metal is the ultimate status symbol. To complete the humiliation it was reported that the truck carrying the gold to the airport broke down.

The Congress Party returned to power shortly after the gold was sold. The Prime Minister was Narasimha Rao, an elderly politician with a reputation for indecisiveness. He was in a weak position – heading a minority government and not being a member of the Gandhi-Nehru family which had dominated the Congress Party since independence. But Narasimha Rao and his Finance Minister the economist Dr Manmohan Singh, who is the current Prime Minister, saw an opportunity in this crisis. They relaxed the controls on private sector investment, liberalised the trade rules, accepted that market economics had their validity, and heavily devalued the rupee. From then on, according to this simplistic history of the last twenty years, India started on the path to rapid economic growth with dramatic results and is now set to grow and grow.

But what do economists make of this view of India's prospects? There is no shortage of economists in India or of Indian economists teaching and working abroad. They come from the left, the right, and the centre of the spectrum. One of them is Ram Gopal Agarwala who worked on econometric models of the British and Canadian economies before joining the

World Bank and working there for twenty-five years. I would describe him as in the centre. He's certainly no market economy fundamentalist. He does see a role for the government, but he is not a leftist either. I sat with this small, earnest economist on the lawn of Delhi's India International Centre, a club which likes to be called an institution and describes itself as 'a place for the exchange of new ideas and knowledge in the spirit of international cooperation'. Ram kept apologising for talking too much although talk was exactly what I wanted him to do.

When I asked whether the standard history of the last twenty years was simplistic, Ram replied eagerly, 'Oh yes. People forget, or don't know, that India's economy started to speed up in the nineteen eighties and it did not accelerate as fast in the nineties. And by the time Rajiv Gandhi, the son of Indira Gandhi, became Prime Minister in 1984 cracks had already started to appear in the Licence-Permit Raj.' Rajiv was Prime Minister for five years, before he was assassinated in 1991.

Ram went on, 'Rajiv's rule was far less gloomy than it's usually made out to have been. For instance the telecom revolution, the precursor to the IT revolution that has done so much to boost India's economy and its reputation, took place then. There was also some relaxation of the Licence-Permit Raj, and plans to relax its grip further had been drawn up too. Rajiv himself was very keen on technology and modernising India.'

'But surely industry started to expand rapidly as a result of the 1991 reforms?' I suggested.

'I don't think it's as simple as that,' Ram replied. 'Liberalisation was largely about industrial policy and there was no acceleration in the growth rate of industry in the nineties. It's IT which is really providing the spark in the economy and the foundations for that were laid before 1991.'

Nevertheless Ram was reasonably optimistic about the future, and he reeled off a large number of reasons for this. They included India's young labour force, which he felt could expand further if more women came into it. When I suggested that unless the labour force was educated most of the man- and womanpower would be of little or no value, he maintained that education was indeed improving. Ram also listed India's high savings rate, its need for massive investment in housing and infrastructure, which could attract Asian investment, and the services it could now export because of the internet.

India had a bad image for environmental protection and so I was interested to hear that Ram believed its carbon emission level was low.

'Yes, it is,' he said eagerly. 'We will not find our growth is restrained by having to limit our carbon emissions in the way that China will have to.'

But perhaps the most interesting reason for Ram's optimism was what he called Indians' ability to conceptualise. When I asked what he meant by that Ram said, 'We Indians are good at thinking, conceiving concepts and handling them, while the Chinese are good at doing. This will favour us because we are going to live more and more in a knowledge economy.' When I asked him if he could put some numbers behind his optimistic view of the Indian economy, he replied wistfully, 'I would rather not. From my long and painful experience of econometric forecasting I have learnt that it is better to be vaguely right than precisely wrong.'

'So what would you say to the person who said to me we have licked the growth problem, now we only have to get the distribution of the wealth we produce more balanced?'

Ram laughed and said, 'Oh that's nonsense. It's far too definite. Growth is possible but cannot be taken for granted. There have been far too many surprises in the past. One should be cautious in making long-term forecasts.'

But no such restraint held back the British economist Jim O'Neill of the investment bank Goldman Sachs, who wrote what is known as the BRIC report in 2003. BRIC stands for Brazil, Russia, India and China. The report confidently predicts those countries will dominate the world's economy. It had such an influence in the BRIC countries that they formed themselves into an economic group. According to the report, India's economy will grow faster than that of any other major country between 2015 and 2050, and that includes China. However, in his book *India: The Emerging Giant*, the Indian economist Arvind Panagariya, who teaches in the United States, has said that '... such long-term predictions have no more validity than astrological predictions'. He pointed out that in the jubilation that greeted the BRIC report everyone forgot that in the 1950s it had been forecast that India and Africa would be the powerful economies and East Asia would be left behind, but in fact the opposite had happened. But Arvind Panagariya did not put a question mark after his title *India: The Emerging Giant*.

Another distinguished Indian economist teaching in America, Pranab Bardhan, wrote a book with a title that did raise a question about India and China's economic prospects. That title is *Awakening Giants, Feet of Clay*. Although he doesn't use the word *jugaar*, Bardhan does quote an example of that phenomenon when he says: '... infrastructure has been for many years the bottleneck in Indian economic growth'. That had been obvious for all those years. In the late nineties the then Prime Minister Atal Bihari Vajpayee remarked, with his trademark humour, 'Our roads don't have a few potholes. Our potholes have a few roads.' He did introduce a plan to link the major cities of India with a road system called the Golden Quadrilateral, and this system is at last almost complete. The railways, however, still muddle on under the burden of archaic management practices, political interference, and lack of capital.

Although the weight of opinion among economists, with one or two notable exceptions, is cautious optimism about India's prospects, the business community both in India and internationally is bullish. One of the most prominent Indian businessmen, Nandan Nilekani, a founder of Infosys, India's second largest IT company, wrote a book called *Imagining India: Ideas for the New Century*. In it he described India as 'the luckiest country of the twenty-first century'. Explaining this remarkable claim, Nilekani wrote, 'India's unique combination of IT skills, its labour advantages, capital flows, and pool of ambitious, outward-looking companies is giving it a massive triple-play advantage across sectors – in manufacturing, services and agriculture.' By triple play he meant growth in the domestic market, and growth in the world economy through migration, as well as the rise of the outsourcing industry.

However, another leading businessman, William Nanda Bissell, in his recent book *Making India Work*, warned against 'a culture of short-sighted optimism both at home and abroad'. He went on, 'From the glowing references in Tom Friedman's bestseller *The World is Flat* to the *new* India to the gushing adulation heaped on its businesses by the Western media, India is constantly fed by an establishment drunk on visions of grandeur.' William Bissell heads the retailer Fabindia, which buys its stock of clothes, furniture, and handicrafts from rural entrepreneurs, and so he knows how bemused villagers would be by Nandan Nilekani's vision of their country.

The danger of the Nilekani view is that India will continue to rely on the belief that the winds are so favourable it can simply sail ahead. That is not to say there isn't room for optimism. I firmly believe with my friend Ram Agarwala that India has a lot going for it, and if it fulfils its potential it will become an economic super-power. In this book I tell stories which will, I hope, leave the reader optimistic too, but at the same time I raise the questions which make my optimism conditional.

Whether India grows faster than any other major country, as the BRIC report prophesied, or not isn't really relevant. What does matter is that India's economy should grow sufficiently fast and in such a way that Indians of all classes, castes, and creeds have the wealth, health, and education needed to fulfil their potential, and make their country prosperous. That matters not just to Indians but to everyone who realises the threat that poverty anywhere poses.

For all the hype about India's economic miracle it is still a very poor country. According to a survey published in 2010 by Oxford University, based on a new index which takes in more indications of poverty than previous ones, if you take one dollar a day as the minimum income someone needs to be above the poverty line, 42 per cent of Indians are poor. If you take two dollars per day the figure rises to 76 per cent. Poverty like this creates problems for everyone, not just for the poor. There is the risk of disease that can spread way beyond the boundaries of the country in which the poor live. The poor try to migrate to areas of their own countries or other countries where opportunities are better. Illegal migration is a problem, to put it no stronger than that, in almost all wealthy countries, and in India migration to the national and state capital is swamping them. Reduced to despair the poor can all too easily fall victim to religious fundamentalism or decide that crime is the way out of their dire circumstances, and crime does not recognise international borders.

There is an economic reason for caring about India's future too. Over the last twenty years there has been a sea change in international companies' interest in India. That is because it has become a market and a supplier, particularly of services. Investors see it as a growing market too and therefore a good place to put their money. The larger the Indian economy becomes the more opportunities it will provide for investment and for trade.

Perhaps most important of all, if India prospers it will be a triumph for democracy and all that democracy stands for.

One of the reasons, other than those Ram Agarwala gave, for being optimistic about India, is that all the institutions essential for a democracy to function are in place. There are legislatures right down to the village level; elections, as I have said, are held regularly; there is a civil service; there are courts; the press is free. Furthermore there are politicians, bureaucrats, lawyers and journalists who know exactly what their responsibilities should be, and how their institutions should function.

There is also a great appetite for democracy, as Indira Gandhi discovered when she temporarily snuffed it out by declaring a state of emergency. But that is not to say that democracy is functioning well in India.

Here I have to be careful because there is, as Ram Agarwala pointed out to me, a temptation to blame all India's problems on bad governance alone. He believed Indians were chronically critical of their governments because they had been ruled by foreigners for so long they considered any government alien. Having lived in India for more than forty years I have become affected by the widespread cynicism about governments and governance in this country.

The chapters in this book are all stories of my travels with my partner Gillian Wright; they are not analyses. During these travels we found plenty of evidence to suggest that governance is a major problem and that there is a need for the institutions to be reformed. In the chapter 'Caste Overturned', about Dalits or former Untouchables, both the police and the courts are shown up. In the chapter 'Building Communities', set in the desert state of Rajasthan, India is described as 'a flailing state' because of the government's weak policy implementation. The link between bad governance and India's endemic corruption is highlighted in the chapter about the success of Indian companies called 'Entrepreneurship Unleashed'.

Speaking in a debate on allegations that members of his own party had bribed opposition MPs to vote for the government in a crucial Parliamentary motion, the Prime Minister Dr Manmohan Singh, while denying the allegations, admitted that India did need to deal with 'the malice of corruption and improve governance'. But here again Ram warned me against over-simplification:

'You know, you can't just look at corruption as a problem of governance. It has to be seen in a wider context. The private sector is often as much a partner in corruption as the public sector. Mere liberalisation, and reducing the government's role in the economy, does not reduce corruption. We've seen that here. Society as a whole needs a moral compass to make a difference in the level of corruption.'

Indians are inevitably well aware that a high growth rate doesn't necessarily mean that the poor will benefit. There have been fierce debates amongst economists about the impact of the fast growth rate on poverty reduction and inequality. The economist Prime Minister is convinced that on neither count is India doing well enough. He has repeatedly called for 'inclusive growth' and for 'development that reaches all sections of society'. Ram believes that the slogan should be reversed, and that the Prime Minister should be speaking about 'inclusion *for* growth', making the fundamental point that if more Indians are included in development they will contribute to even higher rates of GDP. That takes me back to Nilekani's demographic dividend. If young Indians are not provided with health services and a good education as well as jobs they will become a burden on India, not an asset. The chapter 'The English Raj' discusses the impact of that colonial import on education. One reason the state is seen as flailing is the government's poor record of delivering all services, including education.

Social justice is essential if India is to have the opportunity to use the talents of every section of its population. The chapters 'Vote Banking' and 'Caste Overturned' indicate that significant changes have come about in the caste system and as a result India is becoming a more equitable country. But here again the weakness of governance proves to be a problem. Geography also hampers social justice. In a just society there should be reasonable equality of opportunity for everyone wherever they live. But India is developing in a very unbalanced way geographically. Economic growth is rapid in the west and the south and sluggish in most of the north and the east. I deliberately concentrated my travels in the north and the east to try to discover why they were not faring better. The remotest place Gilly and I went to was the state of Arunachal Pradesh in the far north-east, a region where the failures of both the central and state governments are particularly obvious.

Then of course there is the environment. It is now widely recognised, although not widely enough, that in the end any country that develops at the cost of its environment will have to pay a heavy price. That is bound to be particularly heavy in a country with a huge population like India. Gilly and I travelled to a forest in central India to discover why the government was having such problems in preserving tigers, the animal naturalists see as symbolising a healthy environment. In the chapter 'Saving the Tiger' the state government's Forest Department, which is charged with preserving the tiger, is part of the problem rather than the solution.

The problems of governance do come up time and again in these stories and, in spite of Ram's warning, that does seem something which is blocking the road to inclusion for growth. In the conclusion to this book I will pull together some of the threads in these stories and make a suggestion or two about improving governance. But I believe those problems can be resolved and that's one reason why I am optimistic. I even see hope in the current spate of corruption cases, allegations of corruption in the preparations for the Commonwealth Games, allegations of corruption in the allocation of spectrum for mobile phones, the allegations of corrupting MPs I mentioned, allegations of a corrupt land deal involving retired armed forces' officers, and that's not the end of it. The hope is expressed by a director of the multinational Tata in the chapter 'Entrepreneurship Unleashed' – and I share it.

There are other justifications for optimism in the chapters that lie ahead. The improved vigilance of the Election Commissioner, evident in 'Vote Banking', shows what can be done when corruption is tackled firmly. 'Caste Overturned' indicates that Dalits are now fighting for their rightful position in society. 'Building Communities' and 'Saving the Tiger' illustrate India's vibrant civil society. Development in the private sector is one of the reasons India is currently enjoying such a high growth rate. Indian companies have developed into global players, the governance of financial markets has improved and credit is more freely available. Some would argue that much still needs to be done, particularly to make government policies more transparent and less susceptible to the whims of ministers and bureaucrats. But the chapter 'Entrepreneurship Unleashed' shows what one Indian multinational has achieved in twenty years and what it may well be capable of achieving over the next two decades. When it comes to politics the chapter 'The Ramayana Revisited' suggests that at last politicians might be moving on from the sterile debate over the place of religion in society, and that development and performance when in power might be becoming the issues voters are interested in.

It's not just the performance of the government but also its role which will be major factors in the development of India. Nandan Nilekani is not alone in believing that the private sector should take over many of the roles the government currently performs, particularly in the provision of education and health services. But in the chapter 'Farming Futures' questions are raised about the private sector's potential.

Lastly I come back to *jugaar*. The chapter called 'Red India', about the Maoist insurgents known as Naxalites, demonstrates the dangers of not tackling a problem, just letting it drift on, because the country is managing to live with it. So perhaps the most important priority for India is to overcome its addiction to *jugaar* when it comes to the way its government functions.

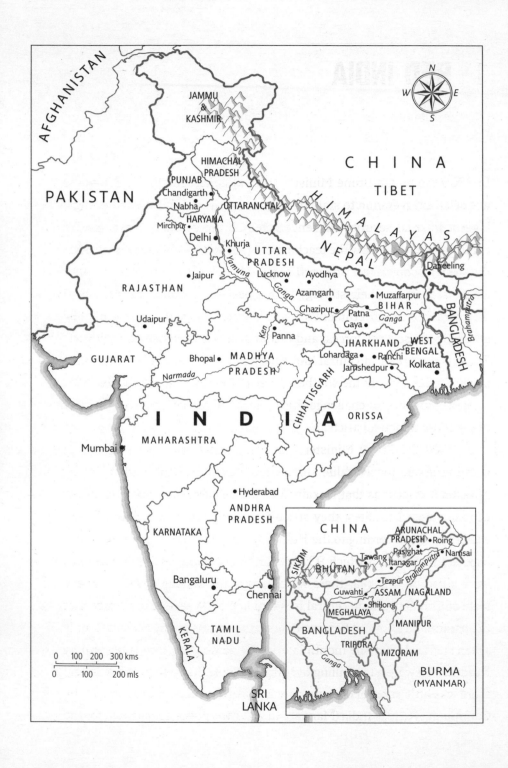

1 | RED INDIA

In 2006 the Indian Prime Minister Dr Manmohan Singh said: 'It would not be an exaggeration to state that the problem of Naxalism is the single biggest internal security challenge faced by the country.' Naxalites are communists who follow the teaching of Mao Zedong and are waging what they call 'a people's war' to overthrow the Indian state and replace it with a Maoist regime. Their strategy is to establish 'liberated zones' where their writ, not the government's, runs. They challenge the government by attacking the security forces, and essential services such as the railways. There is a corridor in central and eastern India running from the Nepal border in the north to the southern state of Andhra Pradesh in which the Naxalites are able to challenge the authority of the government in many of the more remote districts.

In 2008 the Prime Minister again felt it necessary to issue a stern warning about the Naxalite threat. But in spite of the bullish Home Minister's assertions that Naxalism would be curbed, and new plans for action against Naxalites, they still operate in large areas of central and eastern India. According to the Home Ministry, in 2010 there were 1,995 Naxalite incidents in which 937 civilians, 277 police and 161 Naxalites were killed. In that year there were particularly serious incidents in the state of Chhattisgarh, in central India. In one of these, eighty members of the paramilitary Central Reserve Police were ambushed by Naxalites; only seven survived. Just one month later in the same state a mine planted by Naxalites blew up a bus killing over thirty people. In 2010 in West Bengal there was little short of open warfare between Naxalites and cadres of the Communist Party of India (Marxist). In 2011 the police spokesman for the state of Jharkhand told me that there was 'a good presence of Naxalites in twenty per cent of the state'. Jharkhand and Chhattisgarh, with their dense forests, are the two worst 'LWE' or Left Wing Extremist-affected states, as the government puts it.

The Naxalite movement that holds sway over so many of the tribals or indigenous people who live in India's forests started from a remote village called Naxalbari, in a strategic corner of north-eastern India where the borders of India, Nepal and what was then East Pakistan and is now Bangladesh meet. There was considerable tension in the area because the landlords were evicting tenants called sharecroppers, who tilled the land for them in return for a share of the crop. There were also near-famine conditions and farmers were hoarding grain. The Communist Party of India (Marxist) had organised a peasants' resistance movement.

On 3 March 1967 three sharecroppers, accompanied by some hundred and fifty members of the Communist Party of India (Marxist), attacked and looted a landlord's granary. Encouraged by the success of the Naxalbari attack, other peasants rose against their landlords, capturing stocks of grain and harvesting crops on land they didn't own. When the landlords resisted them there were violent clashes. The authorities attempted to negotiate with the peasants but during the negotiations three arrows fired by tribal bowmen killed a police officer who had come to a village to arrest some of those involved in the movement. The next day a party headed by a magistrate on its way to the village was surrounded by an angry crowd. The police escorting the magistrate opened fire, killing ten people, six of whom were women. The uprising intensified and the local police effectively surrendered, making no effort to prevent groups armed with bows and arrows from roaming about the countryside, killing and sometimes beheading landlords.

The Communist Party of India (Marxist) was in a dilemma. It had supported the peasants' movement but now it was a member of the government of West Bengal, the state in which Naxalbari is situated, and so responsible for law and order. For some time the government took no coherent action against the uprising but on the fifth of July they ordered the police to mount a concerted campaign to restore order. The campaign started ten days later. By sheer force of numbers – fifteen hundred police were involved – and by keeping the leaders on the run all the time, the movement was rapidly crushed and seven hundred people, including some of the leaders, were arrested. In his book *The Naxalite Movement in India*, Prakash Singh, a retired senior police officer, said, 'The Naxalbari movement's importance was symbolic ... from Naxalbari the sparks flew all over the country and there was political upheaval.' The fires lit by those sparks are still burning.

The flames burnt brightly for a short time but then in the early seventies the Naxalites suffered severe setbacks, and they were eliminated in West Bengal, the state where the movement began. The former police officer Prakash Singh met Charu Mazumdar, one of the Bengali leaders of the original movement in Naxalbari, shortly before he died of a heart attack in a Calcutta jail. He found 'a lean frail man ... crestfallen and also perhaps disillusioned.' According to Prakash Singh, the one-time hero of the Naxalite movement '... could see that it was the end of the road for him. He knew that the revolution he wanted to bring about had failed.'

The Naxalites under Mazumdar's leadership certainly failed to 'liberate India', something he had told them they could achieve by 1975. He believed that the Naxalites should occupy urban as well as rural areas, and in his heyday his supporters, who included students as well as those his critics described as 'lumpen proletariat', created chaos in Calcutta. The Naxalites are no longer a presence in any city. This is not necessarily a sign of weakness but of a strategy different to Mazumdar's. Those opposed to him within the Naxalite movement always maintained that penetrating cities was contrary to Maoist strategy, which should concentrate on 'liberating' rural areas and surrounding the cities.

Mazumdar had no time for India's democracy. He maintained that 'no other path exists before the Indian people but the path of armed rebellion'. The CPI(M), whose members had escorted the three share-croppers who began the Naxalite movement, was elected to govern Mazumdar's own state of West Bengal in 1977 and remained in power continuously until they were routed in the 2011 elections. Subir Bhaumik, the former BBC Kolkata correspondent, once asked Jyoti Basu, who was Chief Minister of West Bengal for twenty-three years, whether he thought communist parties around the world would decide to participate in democracies or attempt to overthrow non-communist regimes violently. Jyoti Basu replied, 'Wherever we communists can do our politics freely and fairly and mobilise people to come into our fold without fear, parties will resort to parliamentary politics. But where such conditions do not exist they will be forced to take up arms.'

But in spite of all Mazumdar's disappointments Naxalism has survived and spread. Currently Naxalites have a presence in fifteen of India's twenty-eight states, giving them that corridor of territory.

Of course Naxalism has had its ups and downs. It's been weakened by internecine ideological and strategic conflicts, and opposed by the mainstream communist parties who regard it in Marxist terms as 'left sectarianism'. The Naxalites suffered a severe setback in the early nineties in the southern state of Andhra Pradesh, which was one of their strong-holds, when several important leaders along with nearly three thousand followers were arrested, and over eight thousand Naxalites were so demoralised that they surrendered. But the Naxalites recovered suffi-ciently to mount an attack on the chief minister of Andhra Pradesh, who narrowly escaped with his life. Recently, a police force called the Greyhounds, specially formed to fight the Naxalites in Andhra Pradesh, had considerable success, but in their book *Maoist and Other Armed Conflicts* Anuradha and Kamal Chenoy, who both teach at Delhi's Jawaharlal Nehru University, maintain that Naxalite cadres throughout India increased threefold between 2005 and 2008.

The Naxalite cadres are no match in numbers or equipment to the Indian security forces. Why then have the security forces not been able to deal with them more successfully? The answer most commonly given is because the Naxalites enjoy the support of the tribal people who live in the forests and have suffered most from India's malaise of bad governance. According to Anuradha and Kamal Chenoy, 'Marxist conflicts are fuelled by primarily economic and social justice issues related to land distribution, displacements, and evictions, illegal mining, access to forest products, and oppression due to the nexus between the police, local contractors and politicians that results in the perversion of politics and governance.'

In his book *Red Sun*, a remarkable account of travels in Naxalite dominated areas of India, Sudeep Chakravarti says, 'Maoism isn't our greatest internal security threat. Poverty, non-governance, bad justice, and corruption are. The Maoist presence in one-third of India merely mirrors our failings as a nation. The Maoist movement comprises people treated poorly, denied livelihood, justice and all the other ideals enshrined in India's constitution. Their leaders see in the country's present realities a certain futility of purpose and this fuels their belief in violent change.'

But the conversations I had on my visit to Jharkhand and the events which occurred when I entered a forest dominated by Naxalites suggested that the situation was more complicated. I came to doubt whether the Naxalite movement was popular because the tribals were alienated by the way the government treated them. In fact I doubted whether the movement was popular at all. The tribals who live in the forests do suffer from bad governance but it wasn't clear to me that they saw the Naxalites as the answer to this. It was clear that the Naxalites themselves were not always idealists inspired by Mao, and the police who are widely blamed for their failure to root out the Naxalites seemed to also be victims of bad governance.

Gilly and I chose to go to Jharkhand to learn more about the Naxalites for three reasons. First it was one of the two most Naxalite affected states. The second reason was that in spite of the Naxalites telling the tribals that Indian democracy was a sham, voters had turned out in large numbers for the recent elections to panchayats, or local councils, and the elections had been peaceful. The third reason was that I needed a local journalist to advise and guide me, and I knew one I could rely on in Jharkhand.

The journalist was Harivansh, the editor of *Prabhat Khabar* or *Morning News*, a Hindi language newspaper with its headquarters in Ranchi, the state capital of Jharkhand. Ranchi is 2,140 feet above sea level and at that height the climate is comparatively cool. Under British rule the town was the summer capital of the province of Bihar, to which the governor retreated from the hot weather in the Gangetic plain. I remember from my childhood that Ranchi also served as a more accessible place than the Himalayan town of Darjeeling for the citizens of Calcutta to escape from the heat. The Bengal Nagpur Railway would get passengers to Ranchi overnight, and for their convenience it had situated one of its two holiday hotels there. In addition to the cool weather, holiday-makers were attracted to Ranchi by the surrounding forests with their famous water-falls. When I visited Ranchi in 2011 I was told that people only went to a few of the waterfalls because most of them were now in areas dominated by the Naxalites.

When Jharkhand was separated from Bihar in 2000 and became a separate state, Ranchi developed rapidly, as all state capitals do. The occasional large bungalow with a sloping tiled roof, the Ranchi Club, which has seen better days, and the imposing Gossner Evangelical Lutheran Church are among the few remaining traces of the town's more elegant past. The British Raj administrative complex has been replaced by a huge black-glass, multi-storey monstrosity that accommodates the District Collector and his horde of subordinates. The central parts of the city are an unsightly jumble of shopping centres and high-rise condominiums unrelieved by green space between them. The main tourist attraction now is the house of the son Ranchi is most proud of, the charismatic captain of the Indian cricket team, Mahendra Singh Dhoni. Built just a few years ago, it's a multi-coloured, modern three-storey stand-alone house, built on land given by the government, and large enough for the captain's joint family.

When we landed at Ranchi airport, I saw the short and square Harivansh waiting to greet us with a bouquet of flowers. An eager, bustling man, he was almost too pleased that we had come to Jharkhand because of him. At one stage as we drove to the comparatively new Ranchi Gymkhana Club, where Harivansh had arranged for us to stay, I felt like saying, 'It's you who's doing me a favour, not the other way round,' but I thought that would be ungracious and found other ways of letting him know how much I appreciated all he was doing for me.

Harivansh could be described as a crusading journalist but he calls himself a Gandhian journalist. He said to me, 'There are two approaches to politics. There is the Gandhian approach and the Machiavellian approach. Gandhi insisted that the means mattered, not just the end.'

As a young man in the seventies Harivansh had been impressed by the Gandhian Jayaprakash Narayan, who was leading the nearest thing to a national movement against corruption and bad governance that India has seen since Independence. It was a movement that unnerved the iron lady, Indira Gandhi, and was one of the factors that led her to declare a state of emergency in 1975, suspending Indians' constitutional rights, including their freedom of speech, and postponing a general election. Harivansh's own remote village was near Jayaprakash's home. They both lay on a narrow stretch of land between two great rivers, the Ganges and the Saryu, on the border between Uttar Pradesh and Bihar. It used to take Harivansh twelve hours to reach the nearest railway station and a lot longer when, as often happened in the monsoon, the rivers flooded the village.

Harivansh had a successful career in national journalism in Mumbai and Kolkata but he gave that up when he was given the chance to edit the distinctly provincial *Prabhat Khabar*, when it was on its last legs. '*Prabhat Khabar* was virtually a corpse when I took over in 1989,' Harivansh told me. 'It was only selling four hundred copies but there were about two hundred and forty people working for it. Working would be the wrong word. We were not doing any of our own reporting. The paper was just printing news from other papers.'

'So why did you take on the editorship?' I asked.

'I joined the paper, giving up the offer of a job with the Reserve Bank of India, in order to see if I could use it as a means to lift social awareness, even though my decision distressed my father. He wanted me to join the bank because it was a government job and I would be secure. I wanted to move away from metropolitan journalism which didn't seem to serve a social purpose. I wanted to do the journalism of the forests and hills.'

Prabhat Khabar is now the largest-selling paper in Jharkhand. It has four editions within the state, and five more in the neighbouring states of Bihar and West Bengal. To achieve this success Harivansh has had to face competition from national Hindi papers with far greater resources that have tried to drive him out of the market by launching a price war, using marketing gimmicks like offering readers' gifts, and sensationalising news. *Prabhat Khabar* lost readership in 1990 when other newspapers exaggerated the numbers of those killed during Hindu extremists' first attempt to storm the controversial mosque at Ayodhya. This was the mosque that many Hindus believe stood on the birthplace of their god

Lord Rama, the divine hero of the great epic the Ramayana. *Prabhat Khabhar* published the correct figures and because of that it became known as a 'Muslim newspaper'.

I asked Harivansh how his paper had been so successful and he replied, 'Because we have been raising social awareness. We lend our ears to the voices of the people, and have developed ourselves as the forum for the suffering of tribal society, we've become their voice. To do this we hold listeners' courts with sittings in small as well as big towns. The readers are invited to tell us their plight and invited to suggest what we should put in the paper – and we listen. Now with all this economic liberalisation and the spread of commercialism newspapers have become products designed to make money. We have shown those who think only sensationalism and consumerism sells that issue-based and people-oriented journalism has its strengths. Journalism still need not be just a product, part of an infotainment industry.'

'One of the most common complaints I hear when I go into villages is about the corruption of government officials and how they don't listen to those who don't matter. Do you arouse social awareness about this?'

'Oh yes,' replied Harivansh, surprised that I should think he might not, 'we do and that gets us into trouble. There was the case when we insisted that people in one district had died of starvation due to the government's neglect. The government denied this and threatened to close us down. Then we broke the story about the famous fodder scandal, when tens of millions of rupees meant to be spent on feeding cattle were eaten by corrupt politicians and officials. You will remember that the Chief Minister of Bihar had to resign because of that. To punish us the government sent thugs under their patronage into our office and the police offered no protection. The government also cut their advertisements in our paper to the bare minimum.'

There are some senior officials who privately support Harivansh's campaign against corruption and his fight for better governance. One of them drew a chart depicting the journey of a government file from the proposal of a scheme to build a road and a bridge to the final sanction that allows work to start. The chart, which *Prabhat Khabar* published, is not unlike a snakes and ladders board. The file is a cube with elongated legs and arms and a large mouth that turns up and down according to his mood, not unlike the cartoon character SpongeBob SquarePants.

He starts his journey looking fit and bouncy. But when he arrives at the first square where he gets stuck, his mouth turns down as he rotates round the offices of the assistant engineer, his assistant, the chief engineer and his assistant. Next the file is sent off to the lekhpal, the official who keeps land records. He despatches the file to his chief writer, who sends him to another assistant engineer. The file is then returned to the lekhpal, who sends him back again to his chief writer. After taking the thirty-three steps involved in preparing the preliminary estimate the file jumps for joy. But the joy is short-lived as the file enters the state government's secretariat. There he comes across an official of undersecretary rank, an official of deputy secretary rank and eventually the secretary, by which time the poor file is exhausted. He sits down with his legs outstretched and his eyes glazed. But then he girds up his loins and carries on to the minister's office where he has to pass through the hands of an undersecretary, a deputy secretary, a personal secretary and a personal assistant.

That's not the end of the file's journey. From the minister's office he proceeds to the planning department, the chief minister's office and the finance department, which the file is told is the most difficult stage. Then he has to get through the Cabinet secretariat. The next square reveals that the upward journey of the file will take two hundred and fifty-three days if nothing is queried and each official clears him within one day, which of course won't happen. By now our file is stuck like a fly in a huge spider's web, looking thoroughly miserable with his legs dangling.

Our file still has to contend with the ninety-five steps of his downward journey, and it's not clear whether he ever reaches his destination and the projects are sanctioned, because in the last line of the chart the file is told that the most senior of the senior civil servants won't take any decision for fear of committing an irregularity or being involved in a scam. On hearing that, the file disappears but we, the readers, are told that in Jharkhand there are objections to most files because the minister 'wants his chicken kebab before the egg is hatched' – that is to say, a three to four per cent commission before anyone starts to implement the scheme. Commission is an English word which is now common in Hindi. Finally the civil servant who drew the chart makes some proposals for speeding up the process. They include 'the necessity of changing this difficult and rusty system. It was left by the British. They left such a system that will keep you slaves for the next five hundred years.'

It was because *Prabhat Khabar* was clearly on the side of the tribals rather than the government that Anuj Sinha, editor of the edition published in Jamshedpur, Jharkhand's second city, found himself taking custody of a local official in charge of the government's development programmes whom the Naxalites had kidnapped. Anuj was rung by one of his local correspondents to be told that the Naxalites were willing to release the kidnapped man, Prashant Kumar Layak, but they were only willing to hand him over to a senior journalist of *Prabhat Khabar*. Anuj was now working in the head office, where he explained to me, 'The Naxalites had faith in us because of our pro-people journalism. We take up similar issues to the Naxalites – both frequencies match.'

The Naxalites had said the *Prabhat Khabar* journalist must enter the forest by four in the afternoon or they would kill the official. It was one-thirty when Sinha got the phone call and the forest was a good two hours' drive away. 'I thought it might be my last day if I went into the jungle,' he told me, 'but I had a God-given chance to save a life. So I decided to go at once.' Realising that he was in as much danger from the police as the

Naxalites, he contacted the top levels of the government and was given an assurance that the police would not open fire while he was in the forest and would not 'hassle' him when he came out. In the forest Sinha was accompanied by the local journalist as well as two of his own staff he had brought with him.

'We received instructions on the local journalist's mobile,' Sinha told me. 'After driving to ten different places we came to a village hall where we were told to wait. Nothing happened, and nothing happened. Just as we were beginning to wonder whether the Naxalites were going back on their word a small boy appeared and said, "*Chalo* – let's go." We drove with him for another two and a half kilometres and then the boy said, "The car can't go any further." He led us down a narrow path for about half a kilometre until we came to a small hut. The boy went inside and spoke through a wireless set. When he came out he told us bombs would explode and sure enough there were two loud explosions.'

'Why was that?' I asked.

'I am not sure,' Sinha replied, 'but I was relieved because I knew we were then safely in their territory and there was no chance of the police intervening. But I was still worried about the Naxalites misunderstanding us.'

The boy then disappeared and Sinha heard the call of a crow-pheasant. This was answered by a similar call from the opposite side. Sinha then called out nervously, '*Johar, johar!*' – the tribal greeting. Back came the same greeting, '*Johar, johar!*' and a boy and two girls accompanying the Block Development Officer emerged from the thick jungle into the clearing where the hut stood. Shortly after that two more boys emerged. They were dressed in green uniforms with rubber sandals and their faces were not covered. Sinha asked whether they would allow a photograph to be taken and they agreed. It was he who insisted that they should cover their faces for the photo, so that they would think that he was sympathetic towards them and wouldn't back out or harm them. After posing for the camera, the young Naxalites said, 'We have done our job. We have kept our word,' and disappeared into the jungle.

I asked Sinha whether that was the end of the story and he replied, 'Oh no. Our troubles hadn't really started. After driving for some eight to ten kilometres in total darkness, the track was blocked by men carrying automatic weapons. We found ourselves surrounded. Thinking we had been caught by another Naxal group I opened the car door, stood up and shouted, "I am Anuj Sinha!" to let them know who we were. Back came the reply, "I am Superintendent of Police Navin. Give me the official. We won't let you be the heroes, we will hand him over. He's been released because we have surrounded this jungle and cut off all the Naxalites' supply routes. We have been here for six days." I was furious and shouted back, "What have you been doing? Cutting grass all this time?" They hauled the BDO out and I felt that if we hadn't informed the top levels of the government what we were doing, they would have encountered us.'

'Encounter' is the word for the police practice of shooting people they arrest rather than handing them over to the courts.

Sinha went on to say, 'News of the police action reached the Naxalites in no time. Their spokesman rang me and said, "I hear that the Superintendent of Police caused you trouble. I am sorry about that." What a network they have! The spokesman must have known what the police had done almost immediately.'

A network capable of gathering information about the police and disseminating it rapidly indicates a sophisticated and united organisational structure. But according to the police the Naxalite movement in Jharkhand is divided on caste lines.

The view of the Jharkhand police was put to us by Raj Kumar Mallik, the official spokesman who is also the Inspector General in charge of operations against the Naxalites. I was expecting the guards at the entrance of

Police Headquarters to search us and check our car as we arrived, but we were immediately let inside. As we approached Mallik's office a constable sprang to attention, saluted, and opened the door for me. There was a military air about the office itself, with its chairs set out in an orderly rank and clean, white, cotton coverings draped over them. The chairs were emblazoned with the badge of the Jharkhand police – a quiver with three arrows and, below, their motto in Hindi which translated means 'service alone is our aim'.

The spokesman sat at his large desk dressed in a khaki uniform with military-style badges of rank on his epaulets, black tabs on the collars of his shirt similar to those that indicate senior ranks in the British and Indian armies, a row of medal ribbons on his chest, a blue lanyard, and a navy blue and gold striped cravat, the colours of the Jharkhand police. But Inspector General Mallik himself did not have the appearance of a military man. He was short, with a round cheerful face, and although he was chubby his uniform seemed a size too big for him. His pepper and salt hair was untidily cut. Pink and yellow files were sprawled over the desk in front of him.

The spokesman started our conversation by describing what he saw as the split between the leaders of the Naxalites and their followers, saying, 'The Naxalites are a paradox. When we have interrogated central committee or politbureau members most of them seem to be convinced of what they are doing. They believe in Maoism and that means in destroying the state. When we interrogate the rank and file they barely know the outlines of the theory, but they do know that the government and the structures of government are against the poor. They have this fixed notion. But that's not as important as the split created by caste.'

The two major Naxalite groups, People's War and the MCC, the Maoist Communist Centre, joined hands in 2004 and this was thought to have made the movement more cohesive. This wasn't so, according to Inspector General Mallik. He explained that the MCC cadres who were dominant in Jharkhand had been mainly drawn from the Yadav caste.

Because they were traditionally hostile to the upper castes, who were the landlords, the Naxalites had found it easy to attract the Yadavs to their cause. Now, however, other castes were challenging the Yadav hegemony and this was causing splits.

'The glue was caste and now it's coming apart,' Mallik said and then went on, 'There is also a problem of deteriorating idealism. The Naxalites are into money and womanising now. But there is still some discipline in the ranks, if there is some order from the top usually it is carried out.'

Mallik then produced what he claimed was the transcript of a telephone conversation between a retired and a still active Naxalite, and read it to us. The retired Naxalite asked, 'How is it in the party?'

The active Naxalite replied, 'There is a different atmosphere now. In the party there are no rules or principles. Only looting, cutting, killing has any meaning now. Party leaders want only women and money. If you don't have these qualities they don't want you. Will they get the people freedom or lead them to destruction?'

The retired Naxalite's comment was, 'Here they are opposing capitalism and yet becoming capitalists themselves. They are behaving like a criminal gang.'

I couldn't tell whether the transcript was genuine so I came back to the question I started with. If the Naxalites were divided and degenerate why were they not easy targets for the police?

'We have hit them hard,' Inspector General Mallik said. 'Their influence has come down but it will take time to get rid of them because in the forest and hills there is a lack of communications. Their biggest asset is the IED, or Improvised Explosive Device. They can be exploded from a considerable distance, and they certainly impede our movement. But over the last two years there has been a clear policy that we should take them on and if things continue as they have recently, we will do well. But I can't say when it will be finished. We are operating in all areas now we are going after them.'

Gilly asked about the Saradana forest, one of the two areas of India the Naxalites describe as 'liberated', areas which provide them with a secure base from which they can fan out into the forests.

Mallik replied, 'With one thousand two hundred square kilometres of deep forest and seven hundred mountain peaks, Saradana is a most difficult area. During the last six months the police have mounted three operations. We don't generally get involved in long-running battles, just half an hour or so, but in Saradana we fought for two days in different places. They kept moving. Now we've started training in a big way. You'll see the effect in six months' time. We will be intensifying operations there.'

'What has been the impact so far?'

'We have killed them and then come out of the forest but we have also suffered casualties. Altogether we lost twenty-four boys last year.'

'Isn't that the problem? You go into areas, inflict casualties on the Naxalites, but you can't hold the territory. As you've said, you come out.'

'What are needed are development activities to follow on police operations. There is a development and credibility deficit. Development is done in fits and starts – it needs to be in a mission mode, to be done with zeal. But it's wrong to assume development will prevent Naxalism. Their aim is very clear – fighting to control the state, and it's difficult to find anyone who would argue against that by saying that present governance in India is good, so some will always be attracted by an alternative ideology. Development does shrink the ability to recruit, but this ideology will always attract some people because of the deficit of governance.'

But Mallik didn't believe it was the Naxalites' alternative to India's rickety democracy which gave them the support of the tribals living in the forest, support which is crucial for their survival. The police spokesman maintained the support came from 'fear of the gun'. He believed that no more than one or two per cent of the tribals liked the Naxalites. Nevertheless, it was he who told us that about twenty per cent of the state had what he called 'a good presence' of Naxalites. He put the number of their armed cadres at roughly one thousand five hundred and their local guerrillas at five hundred.

Through *Prabhat Khabar*'s contacts we were able to meet someone who described himself as 'linked ideologically and personally to the Maoists'. He wanted to call the Naxalites 'Maoist' and to be called a Maoist himself.

I asked him, 'How can you believe in Maoism when it has even been rejected by China?'

He replied, almost as if he had been tutored by Chairman Mao himself, 'I believe there should be equal rights over economic resources and I think the best mechanism for that is the Maoist one.'

Not surprisingly he would not give me his name and I had to commit myself to not identifying him in any way before he spoke to me.

When I told the Maoist that the police were not the only people in Ranchi who said the Naxalites were more interested in women and money than in spreading the ideology of Chairman Mao, he was distinctly displeased and snapped back, 'We are not greater or lesser humans than anyone. We don't say we have dropped from the sky. If we put wonderful sweets before our boys and say they are dishonestly got, still they may eat them. That can happen and the police take examples of this and defame us.'

'What about women?' I asked.

'That's the police again. They say we rape our women. We give rifles to women to fight for their rights so is it easy to rape them? It's logical that it's not so easy. The police also say the people are against us. If they were how could we survive? We are loved and therefore we are safe, and it's not surprising we are loved. If I started to tell you all the constructive work the Maoists do you would be exhausted. And what about the police atrocities? Many people come into the movement because of these but then they become politicised.'

The Maoist then listed a series of allegations against the police. They included five villagers shot in revenge for a landmine explosion that had killed two policemen, a woman and her two-year-old child killed when police ambushed Naxalites resting in a village, a man accused of being a Naxalite killed in the quarters of a senior police officer, and three school girls arrested on their way to watch a hockey match. That case was only dropped when the People's Union for Civil Liberties intervened. When I asked about the Naxalite violence he justified it as countering the violence of the police. Denying allegations that the Naxalites mistreated villagers the Maoist said, 'Occasionally an elderly person might be slapped, or a driver shot dead. Only bad people are afraid of the Maoists, if you are a good person you are not afraid.'

Because Jharkhand is so rich in mineral resources the fate of tribals who lose their homes and their lands to make way for companies to mine the minerals has become a major issue, an issue which the Naxalites are only too happy to exploit. The Maoist I met said, 'Companies mining bauxite and other big mining companies are obliged under the law to look after the people they displace, the people whose homes and livelihoods they snatch away. They are meant to do community development for the displaced villagers but they don't obey the law. The villagers should be given the right to control the land. Give them the right of ownership then they will protect the land and still get money.'

I had heard that the Naxalites themselves had financial interest in the mining. So I decided to go to an area where bauxite was being mined and which was 'heavily Naxalite affected'. We drove with Anand Mohan, a senior colleague of Harivansh, across undulating countryside interspersed with strange, rounded hillocks, each one a single gigantic rock. Gilly said they looked like the backside of an elephant. Anand pointed out a half-constructed brick building that was to have been a police post.

Apparently the man who had given the land had been murdered by the Naxalites. They were now demanding that the family pay them the two hundred thousand rupees life insurance they were getting and give them the dead man's two guns.

About an hour out of Ranchi we passed a crowd that had gathered in an open field right by the road. We stopped to investigate. There were about a hundred grim-faced onlookers. Two government vehicles were parked there. One belonged to the heavily armed police who had arrived and the other to the local Block Development Officer, Surender Kumar. He was a young man, clearly nervous speaking to journalists, who told us there had been a murder, and reeled off the bare facts: 'It must have happened early in the morning; it's a man called Sanya Oraon, he used to work in a brick kiln. According to his wife he is mentally disturbed, simple.' Then, in an attempt to ensure that we didn't get a bad impression of his block, he added, 'This is a most unusual crime, it's usually peaceful here, nothing like this normally happens. He was simple you know, he was simple, simple.'

We then asked how he had been killed and the Block Development Officer called over a policeman. He told us the victim had been beheaded and his arm had been cut off. As if to add weight to his statement the policeman struck his own neck and then his shoulder with the edge of his hand. Anand Mohan pointed out that beheading was a common way for Naxalites to punish people they believed were police informers. But the BDO said, 'I don't know anything about that. We don't know what has happened. It could be any sort of dispute.' The policeman eagerly concurred. The villagers who had gathered claimed to know nothing about the cause of the murder, so we continued on our way.

When we reached the town of Lohardaga we made for the Hotel Novelty. There in a dark room with bare concrete walls, tucked away under the first-floor reception area, we found Gopi Krishan Kumar, the local bureau chief of *Prabhat Khabar*. I at once told him about the murder. He made a call on his mobile, and then informed us in a matter-of-fact way: 'Not only was his head cut off and his arm wrenched off, the head and arm were taken away.' Then he dismissed this gruesome event, casually saying, 'Such murders are not big news here.'

Gopi then passed me a handwritten press release and said, 'We get a lot of these because the Naxalites are so split and each group wants to make us think they are important. That press release is from a new outfit, just formed by Manjeet, an ex-Maoist. He is alleged to have killed a bauxite mine owner recently because he had demanded a levy and the mineowner had not paid up.' The levy is the money the Naxalites raise from mining companies in return for allowing them to stay in business.

Every year on 15 November, the anniversary of Jharkhand's formation, *Prabhat Khabar* brings out a special edition. In one such edition the paper published a list of the prevailing rates of Naxalite levy for public works and private businesses. For road construction the rate was 5 to 10 per cent of the project cost, for canals and bridges 7 per cent and for railway works 5 per cent. Stone crushers were expected to pay 5 per cent of their earnings. For every truck of coal passing through territory they controlled, the Naxalites collected a thousand rupees, and brick kiln owners were expected to part with 15,000 rupees for every 'chimney'. No one contested the paper's figures.

The current day's paper, which Gopi handed us to read, was dominated by a story that seemed clear evidence of the Naxalites' access to big money. Three Naxalites from one group had escaped from a district jail, but the case had taken an unexpected turn when police recovered twenty million rupees in cash from the jailer's house – apparently the bribe the Naxalites paid for his help.

According to Gopi, another Maoist splinter group was strong in the area where a senior police officer had been murdered by Naxalites. This splinter group had been led by a Sanjay Yadav who had been killed by one of his own group or gang, as Gopi put it probably more accurately. The killer was then killed and the gang was now run by Sanjay Yadav's nephew. A reward for information about the leader of yet another group was announced in the day's papers. 'A police officer has just told me they know where he is,' Gopi told us, 'But they are not informing because it is a case for another district. All the police want is peace in their own station areas. "You keep quiet and I'll keep quiet" is the understanding between the police and the Naxalites, but this means the levy continues very strongly. The bauxite mines start only twenty kilometres away and there the levy is in force.'

We set out for the mines and just outside the town of Lohardaga we passed a sign with 'Hindalco Welcomes You' written on it. Hindalco is the largest aluminium rolling company in the world and it mines bauxite, or aluminium ore, in the hills we could see on the horizon ahead of us. A few miles further on we came to lumps of reddish-brown bauxite piled up ready for the aluminium manufacturers to pick them up. The bauxite had been transported from the mines but it could not be dumped close to town because of pollution concerns. The land was bare and dry, only in patches where there was some source of irrigation could we see fields of wheat, the last flowering of mustard, and yellow-orange flowers on leafy arhar bushes, a kind of lentil. We crossed a new railway line with no trains in sight. Gopi told us that it hadn't been completed because Naxalites had smashed the contractor's machinery.

As we approached the foot of the hills, we followed a narrow road through a tribal village. On its outskirts we saw a lone tree of a species I couldn't recognise, whose deeply fissured trunk showed its great age. A red and white striped flag hanging limply in its dense foliage indicated that this was a sacred tree, and a plaque on the new wall surrounding it confirmed that this was a *sarna sthal*, a place where tribal animists worshipped. Outside the village houses themselves were small pennants carrying images of the Hindu monkey god Hanuman. Tribals have been the targets of both Christian and Hindu proselytising so I wondered whether the pennants were evidence that Hinduism was ousting animism in this region or, as I have seen elsewhere, that tribals had assimilated Hinduism into their own religion. Beyond their houses the road narrowed even further and thorny bushes pressed in on either side. Our driver slowed down to a snail's pace to avoid scratching the car's paintwork.

Eventually we entered the forest. The tarmac road gave way to a track and we started to climb. Lurching in and out of potholes and round steep curves we came to a waterfall. The crew of a truck heavily laden with lumps of bauxite were sitting there eating their lunch. Then we started to climb up a straight narrow stretch. There was the mountainside to the left and a steep drop to the right. Round the bend at the top of the stretch came another overloaded bauxite truck lumbering slowly towards us. On and on it came. Its lights were glimmering, which is usually a sign that a driver is indulging in the Indian practice of exerting his right to the road and threatening us to give way. But there was nowhere for us to go, so we stopped.

As the truck crawled nearer and nearer, I thought the driver would stop, nose to nose, and there would be a massive argument about who was to reverse to the nearest passing place. It was all happening in such slow motion that it wasn't until the truck was upon us that I realised the driver wasn't going to stop. There was a bang and then the scrunching of metal crushing metal. Our car was pushed round and down the track. We would have been shoved over the edge of the road and gone careering down the mountainside if the right front wheel of the truck hadn't hit a rock protruding from the mountainside and shuddered to a halt.

Those of us in the front and middle seats clambered out, and stood staring at the truck. Our driver ran his hands over the mangled bonnet of the car, almost in tears. None of us noticed that Gopi Krishan Kumar and his colleague, only inches away from disaster in the rear, were struggling frantically to lift up the seat in front and get out of the door. Finally they scrambled out without jolting the car and sending it over the edge.

Three young men with scarves tied loosely round their heads and covered in red bauxite dust got out of the truck. Without any apology, but also without any of the aggression which usually goes with an accident, the driver said, 'My brakes don't work. Didn't you notice my lights were on to warn you?' It wasn't that the brakes had failed en route, the driver had loaded his truck and set out on a journey of at least twenty kilometres on a mountain track in the certain knowledge that he had no brakes. I don't quite know how, but I managed to control my temper. When Gopi remonstrated with the driver he appeared rather hurt and said, 'Don't you see, I did drive into that rock at the side of the road and that stopped my truck.'

What were we to do now? We were stranded in the middle of a forest, said to be a Naxalite stronghold, on a track that seemed only to be used by trucks coming down the hill carrying bauxite and a few cyclists, their bicycles loaded with firewood. Our car was blocking the road and so trucks couldn't get by and there was no chance of hitching a lift on one of them. A representative of the truck owner arrived on a motorcycle. He glanced at the scene, said to us, 'It's not that the brakes don't work, they are just soft,' and disappeared before we could argue with him or ask for help.

Gopi had an answer. 'I'll ring the Boss,' he said. When Gilly asked him who that was he drew her aside and whispered, 'The Superintendent of Police.'

When I learnt that the Superintendent had said he would send a vehicle for us, I set off with Anand and Gilly to walk to a nearby village, or hamlet might be a better word. A handful of small houses built from the red earth, and roofed with hand-made tiles, were scattered around a clearing in the forest. Within the hamlet there were cultivated plots, not big enough to be called fields, covered with purple pea flowers, and a few massive, mature mango and jackfruit trees.

There was hardly anyone about the place but we did get talking to one woman called Jhalo. She told us the hamlet was part of the village called Keknan Amba Kona, which had a population of one hundred families. When we asked whether the village was allowed to live in peace she said neither the police nor the Naxalites, whom she called the 'party-walas', bothered the village, and she clearly didn't want to say any more about them. But later we learnt that two policemen on a motorcycle had been blown up in the village during the recent panchayat elections.

Jhalo's father-in-law was sitting on the ground leaning against the wall of a house. He was even less communicative. Black hens, small enough to be bantams, followed by their chicks, clucked as they pecked the hard, unyielding ground. A boy, ten to twelve years old, naked except for a tattered shirt, lay on a cloth on the ground. He was suffering from what Jhalo called 'the itch' and had a tongue so swollen he could hardly move it. Jhalo said there were no government medical facilities, and anyhow she didn't want him to have an operation because 'a lot of blood would flow', so she had taken him to a local doctor who was obviously a quack.

Anand told her he would arrange for a vehicle to come to take her and the boy to the town and for him to have proper medical treatment. She agreed to the plan. 'He needs to be treated,' Anand said to us. 'If he's left like this, his life will be ruined.'

By now the sun was well down the sky and Anand was getting nervous. 'It's not good to be here much longer,' he said. 'We don't want to be in the forest after dark.' He went off to see if there was any news of the police rescue party. We walked on down the track until I saw what looked like a school. It was a pukka construction, a pink concrete building. There I found the schoolmaster, Ramesh Prajapati, talking to the ladies who had cooked the children's midday meal. The children themselves had already gone home.

Reports in Delhi suggested that schools didn't function in Naxalite areas but Gopi had told us that in the Lohardaga hills they had threatened to punish any teacher who didn't turn up for work. This school was clearly in regular use. Ramesh Prajapati told me he and one other colleague taught sixty-four children. Attendance was good but ten children had dropped out this year because their families had migrated. It was the teacher who told me about the two policemen who had been blown up, but he too insisted that everything was peaceful now and there was no trouble from the police or the Naxalites.

Back at the car there was still no sign of the police. We had some desultory conversations with women carrying loads of wood on their heads, but, not surprisingly, they had nothing to suggest beyond walking back to the town. A young man with a crowbar approached and started trying to dig out the rock that was holding the truck back. We looked down onto the open plain far below us. There was no sign of a vehicle approaching the mountains, although Gopi was again assured by police headquarters that help was on the way. When a group of four motor-cyclists appeared round the corner we all agreed that it would be better to ask them for a lift rather than wait for the police. We were beginning to lose faith in them.

It transpired that the motorcyclists were all teachers returning from schools further into the hills. They wore woolly hats instead of helmets and mock-leather jackets to protect themselves from the cold. I scrambled onto the back of the first motorcycle and we set off down the mountainside. The golden light of the setting sun softened the green of the forest foliage. My teacher avoided the potholes skilfully. There was no traffic to worry about until suddenly round the corner came a monstrous vehicle travelling at quite a speed. High off the ground, with huge tyres, square lines and a snub nose, it looked like a khaki box on wheels. Policemen were peering out of its cramped windows. I realised this was our rescue party and waved frantically, as did the others on their motorcycles, but the vehicle ignored us and sped on its way. A minute or two later a motorcyclist wearing camouflage uniform, with his face covered and an automatic rifle balanced across his lap, shot past in the opposite direction. Then came another, and another. Altogether I counted twenty motorbikes. They were our escort but they too ignored us. Somehow that didn't matter; we were happy sitting behind the teachers, who assured us we would be out of the forest before dark. The breeze was cool and fresh about our ears and the sky clear.

We left the forest, overtaking woodcutters weighed down with headloads of wood. On the plateau below we passed the occasional Jeep taxi, and groups of young girls with tightly bound plaits and neat school uniforms cycling home. Other children walked by the roadside, carrying satchels improvised from fertiliser sacks. The tiny goats of this part of India suckled their young in empty fields while women winnowed paddy on threshing floors. The first fleshy red flowers were open on the silk cotton trees and parakeets shrieked as they flew overhead. Roller birds perched on telephone wires seemed to watch us go past. Above them a near full moon had risen even before the sun had fully set.

When we eventually reached the town of Lohardaga, the motorcyclists posed for a photograph with us. My teacher, Jay Sarna, said he was returning from his remote school because there was a holiday coming up and he wanted to be with his family. Indian teachers in government schools are renowned for not turning up in the classroom. I didn't have the heart to ask Jay Sarna whether he was so diligent because the Naxalites had threatened teachers who didn't teach. It did seem clear to me that he wouldn't be teaching if his safety was not guaranteed by the Naxalites.

We were greeted with considerable relief by several officials and Gopi insisted that we head at once for his home, an old house in the centre of town with a sitting room decorated with the antlers of deer hunted by his forefathers. Forty-five members of his joint family lived in this house and in another just across the street. The ladies of the family immediately set about serving us a massive vegetarian meal, and when another local official dropped in to make sure we were safe, Gopi invited him to join us. I asked the official why such dangerous trucks were allowed to ply in the forest. He replied, 'All the worst trucks in the state get sent to the bauxite mines. If we stopped them the whole economy of the area would come to a halt.' That didn't say much for the government or for the owners of the bauxite mines.

It would be dangerous to draw too firm conclusions from one day in the forest but it did seem clear to me that the Naxalites controlled them and that the police didn't have a permanent presence there, otherwise they wouldn't have come to our rescue in such force. It also seemed likely that the teachers were teaching because the Naxalites had made it clear they wanted them to. This would support the belief that the Naxalites here had come to realise that preventing all the government services functioning was not the way to win the support of the villagers they had to live among. They were being forced to compromise with the present administration rather than fight to impose a Maoist system of government. It also seemed a reasonable guess to assume that the bauxite mine owners had to do a deal with the Naxalites to be allowed to continue their operations. This was contradictory because the Naxalites claim to be fighting against the mining companies who take over forest land, and so they should have stopped the mines functioning.

The suspicion that the bauxite miners were paying protection money, or a levy as it was known in Ranchi, was strengthened when on our return from Lohardaga, I met the dapper Bisheshwar Mishra, a retired general manager of the nationalised mining company Coal India. His last job had been in Jharkhand, in an area were there were eighty mines, some opencast and some underground. Mishra reckoned that 50 to 60 per cent of the areas where coal was mined were in what he called the Naxalite belt.

'So how did you work in those areas?' I asked.

'We had to pay money to them. The Naxalites used to tell us, "You are making money, so give us money."'

'What did they mean by you are making money?'

'When we asked our seniors how to deal with the Naxalites they would say, "You have to be tactful." But they wouldn't sanction any money, so when we asked where the money was to come from to be tactful they just told us, "You will have to manage." Once you manage for the Naxalites you can manage for yourself, and that's where the corruption came in. The Naxalites knew that many of our managers were making money in this way, that's what they meant when they said "You are making money."'

'Supposing you refused to pay?'

'The workers would not be allowed to work. Because the managers do work tactfully there is peace.'

The bauxite mines were in the private sector so I asked how private coal mines managed. Mishra explained that there 'the top' paid the Naxalites, they didn't leave it to their managers. As for the police he dismissed them as 'demoralised' and went on to say, 'They are helpless because they are the main target of the Naxalites, whoever you go to to complain, they are all scared.'

The police are everybody's whipping boy. No one seems to have a good word for them. But it's the police who bear the brunt of the battle against the Naxalites. To find out what life was like for the lower ranks of the police, I invited Dinesh Narayan Singh, an assistant sub-inspector who is joint secretary of the Jharkhand Police Association, to join me for a cup of tea on the terrace on the Ranchi Gymkhana Club. We sat in the comparatively mild spring sunshine, looking across to a magnificent tulip tree covered in bright orange flowers. He reminded me of an army sergeant-major. He had that air of authority. His civilian clothes were immaculately clean and pressed and he had a grim grin that made him look as though he took a delight in putting the fear of God into his juniors.

The Assistant Sub-Inspector complained to me, 'Our javans, or policemen, have to cope with the jungle, the hills, the lakes and the water-falls when they go on Naxalite operations. They are on duty for twenty-four hours. There are no living arrangements so many javans get malaria and other diseases from insects and lack of clean drinking water. There are also food problems; they don't get food on time. Many are left in the jungle or in the hills for six months at a time. Some bulletproof cars came which could be pierced by the bullet of a Lee-Enfield rifle, and some wireless equipment was bought which was useless. It had to be thrown away. It couldn't be repaired.'

A senior police officer, whom I met later the same evening and who talked to me confidentially, thought the whole strategy of the government was misconceived. He believed the police were being asked to fight the wrong war.

'This is not a war of bullets, as we are being told, it's a war of intelligence,' the police officer said. 'We are going to start a jungle warfare school here so I went for training with the National Security Guards and they told us, "We can perform surgical extraction of Naxalites." I asked them, "If I know where they are what do I need you for? It's not a question of how to extract a tooth but of which tooth to extract."'

It came as no surprise that the police officer blamed the government for the lack of intelligence. He considered the Intelligence Bureau to be 'bureaucratic and full of officers who behaved as though they had a nine to five job'. Then he went on to say, 'I am afraid that Pakistan's Inter Services Intelligence, the notorious ISI, is much better. They can go beyond the rules; we are tied down by rules and procedures that have to be followed. Intelligence should be result- not rules-oriented and it has to be bought so you must have the freedom to pay for it like the ISI has. In India the press often knows much more than the Intelligence Bureau.'

*

However, it was also a retired police officer who provided the only ray of hope in all the conversations I had in Jharkhand. Rajeev Ranjan Prasad was now living some miles out of Ranchi in the countryside on a dairy farm run by his wife. He sat me down on the verandah of his white bungalow overlooking a substantial vegetable garden. A serious, soft-spoken man, dressed informally in slightly crumpled trousers and a sleeveless sweater, he sat remarkably still with his hands clasped in his lap. He had a reputation for thoughtfulness, perhaps gentleness would be too strong a word, but the Maoist I met did describe him as 'a sensitive officer'.

The former Director of Police was also critical of the way the government treated the police. 'We have no voice in the government, we are nobody's constituency,' he said. 'If we were relevant to the legislative assembly, if legislators thought they could get votes by attending to our problems, things might be different. As it is we are used, deployed, and forgotten – reforms, they are for commissions to report and produce fat books which are then ignored. We need to reform our recruitment, education and structure. Because the police are not properly educated they don't deal with the public properly.'

The politics of Jharkhand had been unstable ever since Jharkhand became a separate state. Recently the government had collapsed and the state had been ruled by the Governor, who was appointed by the central government. It was during this period that the process for holding Jharkhand's first village council elections was started. The state's legislators hadn't wanted those elections because they would have meant that the money allocated for rural development would not pass through their hands but go directly to the village councils. However, when a new government was formed after Governor's rule, the legislators felt obliged to go ahead with the elections.

During the Governor's rule, Prasad had been his Security Advisor. He believed these local elections 'could be a game changer', and went on to say, 'They should mean that power is decentralised, and the villagers themselves will decide how the money should be spent, not the legislators. Now a large training back-up is the need of the hour. Villagers must be taught how to run panchayats, how to take decisions. That must happen now. We must not waste this opportunity.'

Prasad then confirmed the impression I had gained from the Naxalite dominated forest, the impression that the Maoists were not able to carry the people with them in their campaign to overthrow India's democratic system of government and install a Maoist system. When I asked him why the panchayat elections had been so peaceful when the Naxalites should have disrupted them if they had been true to their Maoist ideology, Prasad replied:

'People saw power coming to them, financial power coming to rural areas. That was why there was no trouble. Whenever the people's will begins to surface we find the Naxalites take a back seat.'

So perhaps that's the war India should be fighting to overcome the Naxalites: the war against the corruption, inefficiency, bureaucracy, and sloth, which prevents democracy functioning effectively at the grass roots and indeed at all levels of government – the war that *Prabhat Khabar* is fighting. That's the war that would allow the government to fulfil the people's will.

On its own the military operation, crushing the Naxalites, doesn't seem likely to succeed if the past thirty-three years are anything to go by. Talks are unlikely to get anywhere because the Naxalites' declared ambition is to overthrow the state by 2025, and no government can agree to obliteration. So far the Indian Naxalites have shown no sign that they would settle for a compromise with traditional democratic parties as they have done in Nepal, and how long that compromise is going to last is far from clear. The only option would seem to be winning over the forest-dwellers by providing them with good governance and protection so that the Naxalites have nowhere to hide.

2 | CASTE OVERTURNED

India is classified as a medium human development country in the 2010 United Nations Development Programme's human development index, but it comes pretty low in that index, 119 out of 158. That would not seem to say much for the achievements of sixty-three years of democracy. But there are other ways of measuring achievements, and one is to consider whether India is a more just country socially. Here there have been important efforts at social engineering to protect and advance two vulnerable communities, the tribals who live in the forests of India, including Jharkhand, and the Dalits or former Untouchables. After Independence the law provided for the reservation of special places in government service and educational institutions for Dalits and tribals. In Parliament and in state assemblies, seats were to be set aside which only they could contest. Now there are also what are known as reserved seats in village councils. Under the constitution the practice of untouchability was also outlawed, and Hindu temples that had previously barred Dalits were opened to them. These privileges have resulted in the creation of a Dalit middle class and it seems that changes are taking place in the circumstances and, perhaps more importantly, the aspirations of Dalits who have yet to achieve that status.

Mahatma Gandhi often warned that India would not be genuinely independent until discrimination against the castes lowest in the hierarchy, the Untouchables, was ended. He called them Harijans or children of God, but Dalit, the name they have chosen for themselves, more accurately reflects their position. It means broken or oppressed, and in many of the villages of India the Dalits were so oppressed that they were regarded literally as untouchable. In some villages even their shadow was considered polluting. The most menial tasks in the village such as disposing of excrement and removing dead cattle were assigned to Dalits. Almost all of them were uneducated and poverty-stricken.

Before independence a brilliant Dalit legal scholar, Dr Bhimrao Ambedkar, had led a movement to rouse his community and make them aware of the rights that had been denied to them by the caste system. Very few Dalits received any education but Ambedkar did come from a comparatively well educated family and he had the great good fortune to be given a scholarship by the ruler of the princely state of Baroda to study at Columbia University, New York. From there he went to the LSE and also qualified as a barrister at Gray's Inn in London.

Ambedkar insisted that Dalits could only find their rightful place in society if they became a separate electorate. Mahatma Gandhi was opposed to this, saying that it would isolate Dalits from the rest of the Hindu community, and do nothing to prevent the humiliation of untouchability. Gandhi eventually took up his own particular weapon, fasting. Ambedkar dismissed this as a political stunt but, to save Gandhi from taking his fast to the ultimate extreme, he did agree to a compromise that fell short of his separate electorate. After Independence, Ambedkar was appointed Law Minister, although he was not a member of the ruling Congress Party. It has been suggested that Gandhi might have used his influence on Nehru to make this appointment. As Law Minister Ambedkar played a crucial role in drawing up the constitution, which, in spite of many amendments, remains fundamentally as it was written.

But how far has India got towards becoming what Gandhi would have considered genuinely independent? To what extent has untouchability and all that went with it been abolished? Has the process of freeing Dalits from oppression been accelerated during the years of rapid economic growth? At the end of the debates on the constitution Ambedkar asked, 'How long shall we continue to deny equality in our social and economic life?' and he went on to warn, 'If we continue to deny it for long we do so only by putting our political democracy in peril.' Political democracy has survived, but what about equality?

One Dalit who has shown she is the equal of any politician is Mayawati, the former school teacher who is currently the Chief Minister of India's most populous state, Uttar Pradesh. She has overcome the double disadvantage of being a Dalit and a woman, and we will hear more of her in the next chapter.

Politics is not the only profession where Dalits are now to be found. There are many Dalits in medicine and engineering, which are the two professions most Indian parents want their children to join. There are Dalits in the prestigious elite cadres of the civil service and the police. There are outstanding Dalit academics, and well known writers. In fact there is no profession in which it would now be surprising to find a Dalit. Before Independence and quotas in education and government service, it was rare to find a Dalit in any profession. That was no reflection on their potential but on their position in society, which meant it was very difficult for them to get education. But the Dalit middle class remains a very small component of the whole Dalit community. Most Dalits still live in villages. Is their lot improving or are they still oppressed by upper caste communities? Once it was rare for Dalits to resist oppression. Are they standing up for their right to be treated as equally as any other Indian? Has rapid economic growth made any difference to the lives of the rural Dalits?

The village of Sherpur in the east of Uttar Pradesh was the scene of an incident in 1975 that showed how little the life of Dalits in rural India had changed during the first twenty-eight years of independence, despite the positive discrimination provided for under the constitution, and the promises of political parties. The story was described in a journal kept by a group of academics who worked in Sherpur, attempting to strengthen the Dalits' resistance to the high caste domination over them. The journal makes clear that the Dalits of the village were in effect bonded labourers, bound to serve one specific farmer. The farmers who dominated the village were Bhumihars, a caste that claims Brahmin status although agriculture is not a traditional occupation of the priestly caste. The journal said the attack on the Dalits was not an isolated incident. The conflict had been building up over a long period of time.

The specific incidents leading to the attack started with a Dalit leaving his Bhumihar landlord to work on another's land. His enraged master beat him. When his sister tried to intervene the Bhumihar beat her too. Then two Bhumihars were murdered as they slept by their tube well and their caste panchayat, an unofficial council, sentenced to death the man who had left his master, and one other Dalit. Although there was a police post in the village the Dalits were executed in public. As if this was not enough the Bhumihars collected all the kerosene they could find, and thousands of them surrounded the locality where the Dalits lived. Pouring the kerosene on the huts they set them on fire after looting them. They stole any cattle of value and thrashed the Dalits indiscriminately.

This brutal assault broke the traditional relationship between the Dalits and the Bhumihars, and the village economy collapsed. The only way the Dalits had survived was by working for their 'masters'. But the Dalits were no longer prepared to do that and many of the Bhumihars said they wouldn't employ them anyhow.

Perhaps because the case was particularly shocking, the lower courts tried the incident in three years, remarkably quickly by Indian standards. Eight Dalits were charged with the murder of the two Bhumihars, while thirty-six Bhumihars were changed with the attack on the Dalits. The Dalits were all found guilty and sentenced to life imprisonment. They remained in jail until in 1994 an appeal court overturned the verdict, and they were all freed. The Bhumihars were also convicted, but unlike the Dalits were let out on bail pending appeal, a status the Dalits knew might last their natural lifetimes, and for several of them that was indeed the case.

The freed Dalits' troubles did not end with their release from jail. After they returned to their village seven of them were killed in separate incidents. One, Shivlochan Ram, was abducted and his headless corpse recovered from a village well days later. No one was named responsible for the attack in the police report and no one was ever arrested. Another, Shivbali Ram, was beaten to death by hundreds of villagers. His family did not dare to write a police complaint, and the police accepted the version that 'a crowd' killed him in self-defence, protecting their village. No one was punished for his death, or for any of the others.

Eighteen years after the attack Gilly and I visited Sherpur because we had heard that the government had failed to fulfil its promises to rehabilitate the Dalits, and the press had forgotten all about them. We found that the government had built two lines of huts to house them. They were the cheapest sort of housing the government provides, little more than shacks. On that day the sun beat down on their tin roofs that were unprotected by any shade.

Outside one of the huts we found a group of young men far too busy playing cards to bother with us. When we asked whether the government had helped them, they said, 'You can see the government hasn't given us any jobs,' and went on with their game. As we walked on we came across Sita Ram Pal, an elderly man from a shepherd caste, wearing a kurta that had seen better days and a not very neatly tied dhoti. He told us that the press had forgotten Sherpur, the government had done nothing beyond erecting the huts and making small grants of land to some of the affected, and the Bhumihars were still bullying them. Two Dalit teachers had been appointed to the school but they were not being allowed to teach. Dalit women were beaten if they defecated in the farmers' fields. But what hurt the shepherd most was that the attackers were still out on bail with no sign of the courts finally convicting them. He said, 'We know who did it, so to see them free in our village is a constant reminder of our pain.'

We got a taste of the continuing bad feeling between the two communities. Stones were thrown at us as we walked out through the Bhumihar area of the village. Obviously the landlords objected to our talking to those they still liked to regard as their serfs.

The Bhumihars' appeal was finally decided in the Supreme Court in 1999, nearly twenty-five years after the incident. The judgement sentenced only ten people to five years' imprisonment for nothing more than arson.

Twenty years after our visit to Sherpur, I read of an incident in the northern Indian state of Haryana that indicated little had changed for Dalits living in rural India. According to the first stories in the newspapers, a group of Jats, a sturdy farming caste, had attacked Dalit villagers living next to them in the village of Mirchpur, burnt their houses and looted their property. A seventy-year-old man and his teenage daughter who had been crippled by polio died because they couldn't escape from their house.

One thing which certainly has changed since the Sherpur incident is the press. It has become much more vocal and visible. The extensive television coverage of the plight of the terrified Dalits who had fled the village, and their allegations against the government in a state ruled by his Congress Party, prompted Rahul Gandhi to visit Mirchpur. He promised the Dalits that his mother, the Congress Party president Sonia Gandhi, would keep a watchful eye on the situation. After his visit the officer who had been in charge of the nearest police station and a local official were arrested. But four months later a panel of MPs who visited Mirchpur reported to Parliament that many of the accused Jats had not been arrested, and cases had been prepared against just twenty-eight of them. The MPs also reported that the Dalits were under pressure from the Jats to compromise. In such circumstances compromising normally means withdrawing cases.

When we read the MPs' report Gilly and I decided to go to Mirchpur to see whether the Dalits there were being treated any better by their government than the ones of Sherpur had been thirty-five years ago. We drove about one hundred and fifty kilometres west of Delhi to reach Mirchpur. I hadn't travelled on this route for some years and so it was the first time I'd seen the new highway, and the proliferation of new schools, colleges and hospitals run as businesses on the outskirts of the district headquarters.

Situated on a main road, Mirchpur was one of those Indian villages that is growing into a small town. On one side of the road was a large pond in which sleek, black buffaloes wallowed contentedly. Horses grazed on its bank. The village stretched for a kilometre or more beyond the pond. With its five schools, two government and three private, Mirchpur was an educational centre for the other villages within a radius of ten kilometres. Villagers told us with pride that even in the British times there had been a school here. We got the Jat side of the story of the burning of Dalit homes from the co-director of one of the private schools. Not surprisingly, Shamsher Singh was out to minimise the whole affair and assure us that all was well now.

He maintained, 'It was all just the sort of mischief young people get up to. Then the press exaggerated it. They made it seem as though this was not a peaceful village. It was peaceful before the incident and now it is again. The tension in the village only started with this fight and now everyone is peaceful.'

Shamsher Singh confirmed the media reports that the incident had been sparked off by a Jat boy throwing a brick at a dog that barked at him. The dog belonged to a Dalit who had given the Jat 'a tight slap'. Then the relatives of the boy who had been slapped came to protest and, in Shamsher Singh's words, 'The matter took off, the mischief started.

People beat each other. Afterwards the media came and just listened to one side all the time, and then it became a caste conflict. Why have the media never said it was the Dalit who started it by slapping?'

'If it was just mischief how did so many houses get set on fire?' I asked.

'The hot weather was the cause. It was fifty degrees.'

'No – forty-five,' interrupted one of Shamsher Singh's colleagues, realising the improbability of the temperature reaching fifty degrees was not lending veracity to his version of events.

Shamsher Singh settled for forty-seven and went on, 'In their mischief the boys set alight a store and because of the hot weather the fire spread. You know what the houses of the poor are like – they just catch alight.'

The school was on the outskirts of the village. As we turned into the village proper to find the Dalits we noticed a freshly painted signboard pointing to the police post that had only been established after the attack on the Dalits' houses. We drove down a track slippery from the monsoon rains and squeezed between houses on both sides. Threading our way through traffic jams created by tractors, bullock carts, and herds of buffaloes, we passed the police in their usual posture lounging on charpoys, and eventually saw a sow with her piglets trotting behind her. That indicated that we had reached the Dalit area, which was as usual on the edge of the village. The Jats, who dominated the village, would never keep or indeed eat pigs.

I had thought that the Dalits might have had enough of journalists. They had, as usual, descended on Mirchpur in droves, and once the story dropped out of the headlines most had rushed off to the next 'breaking news'. However, four months on, the Dalits were still in dire straits because the Jats had imposed a social boycott on them. So they were anxious to tell their story. A charpoy and plastic chairs were produced and some policemen, aroused from their torpor, joined us. When their inspector arrived, an elderly Dalit called Gulab Singh hurriedly slid off the charpoy and squatted on the ground at his feet. The officer insisted that he sit with us saying, 'He is a good man. He is the watchman.' But instead of sliding back on to the charpoy alongside the inspector, Gulab Singh sat on a plastic chair.

After the inspector had noted down our names and other details he agreed to go so that the Dalits would feel free to talk.

They were members of the Valmiki caste, formerly considered among the lowest of the low, whose traditional occupation was sweeping. Their spokesman, Ramesh Kumar, was a small, lean, middle-aged man, with a perpetually angry look on his thin, angular face. He was wearing a vest and trousers. When I told him the version of the burning of their houses we had heard he said, 'That's untrue. The attack was planned. They came at us from four sides carrying kerosene and diesel to set the houses on fire.'

'When did it start?' I asked.

'It all started at ten-thirty in the morning. They came and attacked us, setting houses on fire with the diesel and kerosene. Some women and children were trapped in their houses, but we managed to get them out. But we couldn't get the elderly man and his disabled daughter out in time. At first we challenged them but they were too many. Then we ran and tried to save ourselves and they smashed our belongings, our TVs, our fans, our beds and burnt our houses.'

'Where did you run to?'

'We escaped into the inner part of our basti. They knew they would have been killed if they had come there.'

Ramesh Kumar agreed that the trouble had started with Jat boys throwing a brick at a dog. According to him, boys and young men from both sides gathered and there was a row. Two Dalits who tried to mediate were beaten and had to be taken to hospital. The next day the officer in charge of the nearest police station came to try to calm things down, but, according to Ramesh Kumar, no one listened to him.

Apparently there had been tension between the two castes ever since

1998 when the Jats had dug up the lane running through the Dalit section of the village. The Jats maintained that it was too high and was preventing water running off their lane.

The current social boycott started with the arrest of young Jat men accused of the recent attack.

'They are trying to get us to compromise, to withdraw the cases,' Ramesh Kumar explained. 'They are not calling us for work in their fields, and they are seeing that we don't get work under the government's employment guarantee scheme. We can't keep our animals here because they won't let us cut fodder. They won't let us take wood either. They don't let our ladies go to the latrine in their fields and we are too terrified to send our children to the school.'

An elderly man with a red cotton towel tied untidily round his head said, peering through the thick lenses of the spectacles askew on his nose, 'They won't sell us their milk or lassi either. There have been social boycotts before but never as bad as this one.'

'Yes, there were,' shot back Rajesh Kumar.

We were joined by a young man holding a small child. Ashwini Kumar spoke English and wore modern clothes and gold-rimmed spectacles, and so it was clear he was more educated and better-off than the other Dalits we were talking to. His father ran a shop in the village and he soon told us that he had an MPhil degree in education. I asked him whether the position of the Dalits had changed over the last twenty years. 'That's where the trouble comes from,' he said. 'There are reservations in all fields and now we are progressing everywhere. We are progressing in culture, in our economy, and education. Twenty years ago we could not have faced up to the Jats. Now we are competing with them in every field. They don't like it.'

Ramesh Kumar intervened: 'As long as they can put pressure on us everything is fine. But when people won't put up with the pressure then the trouble starts. We are not putting up with pressure now. We are educated now. We know the law and we are in service, in government jobs. They are jealous. Before they were happy because we worked in their fields, we were forced to, and in their homes, and were never paid the proper amount, they kept us dependent on them.'

But Ramesh Kumar was brought down to earth by another middle-aged Dalit, with hair dyed bright orange by henna, who said, 'Maybe we are stronger and they can't behave like they used to, but what is the use of that when we now don't have any employment? We have to go all the way to Punjab to work in the fields and that only lasts for three to four months. We used to work in the landlords' fields here.'

According to the Dalits some of the families who fled after the attack had returned but there were still some forty to fifty families living in Hisar, the District Headquarters, and other towns and cities. As for the question of arrests, the Dalits maintained that now only three of the Jats accused of the attack had still not been arrested. But they said it had taken 'great effort' to get the police to act.

'What of the future?' I asked.

'We'll go to Pakistan,' said one of the Dalits. The rest laughed. No one thought Dalit politicians would help them. They were written off as *dugdugis* – that is small toy drums – something that makes a lot of noise but achieves nothing. Someone said, 'We can only trust in Rama to bring improvement, there is no point in trusting in anyone but God.'

When I pointed out to Ashwini Kumar that he'd said things had improved he replied, 'We are neither slaves, nor are we free.'

The government had at least started to rebuild the Dalits' houses, but they took us to one that was still untouched. The roof had fallen in, the walls were charred by the fire. There was a burnt pair of trousers on the floor and a pile of blackened rafters. Outside, two trees had been badly burnt. All the houses were made of brick and they were not cheek by jowl so it seemed to me inherently unlikely that the fire would have spread on its own from one to the other, as the Jats were claiming.

After we got into the car Ramesh Kumar came up to the window and pleaded, 'Please make sure this is published in Haryana. Our only hope is if it keeps in the news.'

In the last few years there had been similar outbreaks of violence resulting from tension between Dalits and Jats in other Haryana villages. Shortly after the Mirchpur incident there was a report from the opposite end of India, the southern state of Tamil Nadu, where the dominant caste in a village had built a wall to separate them from the Dalits. The wall in the village of Uthapuram prevented the Dalits reaching the public roads. It stood for twenty years before a civil rights group created a furore about it. Then the government pulled it down with remarkable alacrity. But two years after the fall of the wall the civil rights group was quoted in the report as saying, 'The ground situation at Uthapuram has not improved at all. The reopening of the road was a mere token gesture. The police thrash the Dalits whenever there is an altercation between communities. Only a month ago fourteen of them were arrested. After they were released on bail they were re-arrested.'

Indian social scientists, human rights activists and journalists tend to see incidents like Mirchpur as evidence that oppression of Dalits and discrimination against them are still routine in Indian villages, and that sometimes the cauldron of hatred between the castes boils over. Kancha Ilaiah, a professor in the social science department of the prestigious Osmania University in Hyderabad, has written a book called *Post-Hindu India*, with the sub-title 'A discourse on Dalit-Bahujan socio-spiritual and scientific revolution'. *Bahujan* is a term that covers all backward castes, as well as Dalits, tribals and religious minorities, in other words all those that Kancha Iliah regards as oppressed by the high castes. To call it an angry book would be an understatement. Kancha Ilaiah says the birth of his book was 'a gut-feeling that the Indian nation is on course for a civil war that has been simmering as an undercurrent of the caste-based cultural system that Hinduism has constructed and nurtured for centuries.' At another stage in the book the social scientist issues an even more dire warning. 'A civil war is inevitable. The twenty-first century is moving towards that direction,' he says, and quotes several incidents which occurred comparatively recently to justify that view.

The basic problem, according to Kancha Ilaiah, is what he calls 'spiritual fascism', a fascism that used religion rather than racism to create and justify the concept of superior and inferior castes. This fascism, he maintains, is what Brahminism has instituted and perpetuated, and he warns that 'political democracy operating upon a spiritual-fascist social base may collapse at any moment'. But Kancha Ilaiah does end his book on a more optimistic note. He says India must move into a 'post-Hindu phase'. What's more he believes in 'the new consciousness of the Bahujan social forces, that points towards that direction', and hopes 'that this century is a century of their dreams and a century of the realisation of their dreams'.

There is, however, a school of thought among Dalits which differs from the widely held pessimistic view that they are still the victims of oppression and discrimination, and that India's economic progress has done little or nothing to diminish this. Dr Narendra Jadhav is a Dalit with a remarkable track record as an economist, a university administrator, and a bestselling writer. He spent many years in the Reserve Bank of India, becoming the central bank's chief economic advisor, worked for the IMF, and was Vice-Chancellor of Pune University, said to be the world's largest traditional university. When I met him he was sitting in his office in the impressive building on Parliament Street in Delhi that houses the Planning Commission, the institution that draws up the central government's five-year plan for allocating financial and other resources. He was by then a member of the Commission.

Suits are by no means obligatory in Delhi's government offices, but Dr Jadhav was wearing a suit and a bright red tie. I thought it would be rude to ask him whether he was dressed in this distinctly non-Indian style in honour of Dr Ambedkar. In his statues – there are plenty of them all over India, and more are being added all the time – Ambedkar almost always wears a dark blue suit. This is to demonstrate not just historical accuracy, but that the hero of the Dalits believed modern Western culture held the key to freeing his community from the caste system.

With his neatly trimmed grey beard, his immaculate English and his confident but not over-stated manner, it was difficult to imagine that Narendra Jadhav was just one generation away from a Dalit who fled his village and came to Bombay, as Mumbai was known then, to escape from the cruelty and humiliation of his life in a village. The economist was understandably proud of his father, describing him as 'a foot soldier in the Ambedkar movement', and 'a tough cookie who spoke little but spoke by his actions.'

Narendra Jadhav's book *Untouchables* is the story of his father Damu and his mother Sonu. It has sold more than one hundred and fifty thousand copies. Much of the book is based on a remarkable document, the story of Damu's life written by Damu himself, although he had no formal education. His last job was working on Bombay Port's railway line at the most junior level. He started writing after he retired, and stopped when he saw his son admitted into a government school. The headmaster had been reluctant to register the boy but when Damu threatened to follow Gandhi's example and demonstrate non-violently, he relented. Damu said, 'When I saw my child sitting in the classroom I knew that the progress of my family had begun.' Narendra was the youngest in the family and his father saw to it that they all got a good education.

Narendra Jadhav's book starts with the incident that led Damu and his wife Sonu to flee their village and start a new life in Bombay. It's an incident that illustrates the routine brutality inflicted on Dalits by junior officials in the last days of the British Raj. Damu had already spent some time in Bombay and taken part in Ambedkar's social movement, so when he returned to the village he was reluctant to accept the humiliating duties which custom allotted to Mahars, his Dalit caste. Nevertheless one day Damu did accept the duty of running alongside a revenue official's pony trap as he drove into the village, and singing his praises so that everyone would know an important man had come. As Damu was walking home after the official had left, he was accosted by a policeman who ordered him to go and guard a dead body floating in a well until an officer came to write a report.

Damu had to sit by the well throughout the night without any food, and without being able to tell his wife where he was. The next morning the Fauzdar, or police officer, entered the village sitting arrogantly astride his horse, whip in his hand. After inspecting the well he ordered Damu to remove the body. Damu protested that the dead woman was from a high caste and it would be regarded as sacrilege if, as a member of a Dalit caste, he touched her body. The story as Narendra Jadhav wrote it went on with the Fauzdar thundering, 'You motherfucking son of a bitch, do you see this whip. Do you want to see it lashing across your mouth and getting at your tongue? You have my orders. Do as you are told.'

Damu pleaded with the Fauzdar again and eventually said 'no' firmly. A cousin who had come to give Damu some food tried to persuade him to obey the Fauzdar, saying, 'You should respect the Fauzdar Saheb. We are dependent on them for all our needs. Even if they get angry with us and beat us, we have no choice but to obey them.'

The Fauzdar lashed Damu with his whip but he continued to resist. The Fauzdar bellowed, 'I know the reason why you lowly creatures are suddenly meeting our gaze and raising your voices, talking back to us. It is all due to that Mahar Ambedkar. He thinks that just because he has learned a book or two he will suddenly become a high caste Brahmin from a Mahar. And you listen to his talk and start thinking that by talking back to us you can get away with it.'

Enraged by this insult to Ambedkar, Damu grabbed the Fauzdar's whip, causing him to fall to the ground. The Fauzdar screamed at his constables, and they fell on Damu, beating him and lashing him with the whip. Damu cried out, 'I will die but I will not bow down before you. Come on, beat me all you can and kill me. Let the world know that a helpless Mahar was killed doing his duty. See the entire village is witnessing your atrocities.' At that the beating stopped, the village headman intervened, and Damu staggered home supported by his cousin.

Narendra Jadhav is now very optimistic about the present and the future for Dalits. But I suggested that the reports of incidents such as Mirchpur indicated that Dalits still suffered widespread oppression and discrimination in villages.

'It's a shame that there are still incidents of discrimination,' he replied, 'but when they happen Dalits don't take them lying down. One often gets the wrong impression from media reports. These incidents aren't as common as they used to be. Whenever such atrocities take place they normally get reported, releasing public anger and compelling societal and governmental intervention. There is no doubt that there is a sense of liberation. Dalits have now started asserting their caste in a democratic manner and are finding voices of support from places and people far outside their village boundaries. Now that their energy has been unleashed, it's only a question of time for the dreams of Ambedkar to be fully realised. Don't you see what a silent revolution is already taking place? In every sphere of economic activity and at every level of decision-making in the governance of our polity, you will find Dalit girls and boys coming up. The criticality is over and Dalits are now unstoppable.'

'What about Ambedkar, your father's hero?' I asked. 'Has his influence survived?'

'Oh yes,' he said vigorously. 'I give credit mainly to Ambedkar, who was not only a hero for my father but for millions of people including myself. He is the man who brought about the change. He made us ask a very simple question: "It may be in upper castes' interest to be our masters, but why should it be in your interest to be their slaves?" Only when my father asked himself that question did he decide to rebel.'

'As an economist how important do you think the economic developments over the last twenty years or so are?'

'As an economist I would say the graph is going up because people like me are getting education and contributing. There is a tremendous enthusiasm for education. In upper caste houses I find nine out of ten parents complain about the attitude of their children to education. I also go to the slums where my friends and relatives are. There I find little Dalit girls studying. They are motivated. They form groups and study under one bulb. Do you know that two million Dalits gather every year to mark the anniversary of Dr Ambedkar's death, and the bookstalls set up on that occasion have a turnover of ten million rupees?'

Chandrabhan Prasad, an effervescent Dalit independent researcher and activist, is an enthusiastic propagator of the optimistic view about the present position of castes like his. He believes it is very important for Dalits to put the past behind them and look to the future. He once said to me, 'The past will always drag us down. There has to be a fundamental rupture with it.'

When I asked him about Mirchpur he said, 'The atrocities which do happen are because the Dalits are now able to look the other people in the eye.'

To add substance to his view that Dalits were on the move, that their humiliation was now in the past, Chandrabhan got together a team of academics – two from the United States, one from India and himself – to undertake a study called 'Rethinking Inequality'. It involved a survey of two blocks – a block is an administrative unit – in Uttar Pradesh, one of the most backward states of India. One block was Azamgarh in eastern Uttar Pradesh, the other was Khurja in the west. The survey was designed and implemented by Dalits themselves.

Economists usually measure inequality in terms of how much people spend, how much they consume, and what their income is. This misses out the inequalities in social life. What is particularly important for the Dalits is that the usual economic surveys do not assess the inequality of the caste system, with the discrimination and indignity it inflicts on them. Chandrabhan's survey investigated whether there had been changes since 1990 in caste practices, both within households and within village society. This was the period in which India changed from a government-directed to a market economy. Although there is plenty of evidence to suggest that the rapid growth of India's GDP is not reducing economic inequality, according to the survey team that is not standing in the way of improving social equality. The survey showed that changes in society were far greater than the changes in Dalit assets would suggest. This challenges the common assumption that there is a direct link between the indignity Dalits living in rural India suffer and their poverty.

But how to measure social inequality? The survey asked questions about what Dalits ate, what they spent their money on, how they were treated by other castes, and what differences had come about in the ways they earned their livings. The aim was to discover whether the humiliating differences between them and the rest of society had decreased. For instance, certain foods and drinks had marked Dalits as different. When they worked for farmers they used to be given water mixed with sugar cane juice in the winter and molasses in the summer. This was often part of the meagre reward they got for their work. Those drinks have largely disappeared. Dalit meals used to consist of roti – unleavened bread – flavoured with chutney. Now they regularly ate tomatoes and flavoured their food with cardamom and packaged salt. As the survey says, 'foods serve as a metaphor for cultural hierarchies'.

At first it seemed strange to me that the survey should have asked Dalits whether they spent money on toothpaste, hair oil, and shampoo. But then I reflected on the humiliating dress and appearance that used to be forced on Dalits. They were certainly not intended to look smart. For instance the men were not allowed to wear clothes that covered their ankles and usually went barefoot. Women for the most part didn't wear petticoats. So the fact that the Dalits are smartening themselves up with toilet products, wearing shoes or slippers and petticoats, is an assertion that they are no longer prepared to put up with the old social markers which discriminated them from the rest of the village. The survey says changes in grooming and dress are 'an assertion of social aspirations'.

Dalits in villages used to be almost entirely dependent on working for upper caste farmers. It was very common for them to be effectively bonded to those farmers by a system known as *halwaha*. A *hal* is a plough and under this system a Dalit was responsible not just for ploughing an upper caste farmer's field but also for maintaining his bullocks, and was not allowed to change his employer. Jagjivan Ram, commonly known by the respectful title of Babuji, was the outstanding Dalit leader in the Congress Party, both before and after Independence. He is quoted in the survey as saying, 'Ninety per cent of our people are agricultural labourers – rather agricultural serfs. If you have to see remnants of slavery you go to a village and see a *halwaha*. For a few rupees he is forced to mortgage himself to a *kisan* [farmer] and serve him on a mere subsistence allowance. These *halwahas* are not free to go over to the other villages on higher wages.'

In the villages surveyed the *halwaha* system has virtually disappeared, and so has the humiliating practice of Dalits removing the dead cattle of upper caste farmers. Now some Dalits have become farmers themselves and they hire upper caste farmers to plough their fields with the tractors that have seen off the bullocks. Some have maximised their earnings by farming someone else's land in exchange for a share of the crop.

Much of the Dalits' humiliation was enforced on them by their dependence on working for upper caste farmers. They simply couldn't afford to challenge them. The survey shows that not only have the old bonds that shackled Dalits to their masters been broken but Dalits are also moving out of agriculture altogether in considerable numbers. They have now moved into professions that they were earlier debarred from, becoming masons, tailors and small shopkeepers. Over the last twenty years there has also been a marked increase in Dalits migrating to the big cities to get work.

What about the crucial point, relations between the Dalits and the other castes? Upper castes used to refuse food served by Dalits. Now the survey shows that they will drink tea and eats snacks in Dalit homes. The very fact that Dalits now drink tea themselves is described in the survey as 'a clear social marker'.

Dalits used to be humiliated at upper caste weddings by being seated separately. That happens much more rarely, but interestingly Dalits are less interested in attending those weddings than they used to be. The survey speculates about two possible reasons. One might be that Dalits want to demonstrate their independence. Another might be that with the improvement in the food they eat, feasting at weddings is no longer the attraction it used to be. I do wonder about that one.

The Dalits' own weddings are an effort to show that anything the upper castes do they can do if not better at least as well. The most obvious change that has come about in Dalit weddings is that the bridegroom now arrives at the bride's house in a car or a Jeep. Previously the best he could expect was a bullock cart, and many Dalit grooms walked to their bride's house. The sweets served at a wedding have gone up a notch or two also. Some would undoubtedly criticise the expenditure on weddings in particular as not just wasteful but also dangerous because it can all too easily lead to the bride's father getting into debt. The survey counters that criticism, saying, 'We feel this would be missing the deeper point of the positive change that Dalits feel that they are entitled to as much as anyone else – that it is socially appropriate for them to engage in social practices that have long been the province of the upper castes.'

The conclusion of the survey report starts by saying it reveals, 'very substantial shifts in Dalits' lives, consistent with a growing sense of empowerment and opportunity and declining ability of others to impose social inequalities'. But the conclusion goes on to warn, 'Caste has not disappeared as a social construct. It is very much alive,' and admits that there are still 'tensions and atrocities'. However, it suggests these might be 'the result of the very rapid improvements for Dalits which unsettle existing relationships'. While stressing that the survey was limited to the state of Uttar Pradesh, and certainly did not 'speak to anything like all of India', the conclusion also points out that there are a very large number of Dalits in that state. Although the report does not attempt to define the cause of the improvements revealed by the survey, it does say that in the market reform era 'prosperity raised the standard of living and the social fabric of the village has changed much for the better'.

Reading a survey is one thing, meeting the respondents in their villages is another. So Gilly and I set out to visit some villages in Khurja block. Travelling along the six-lane highway out of Delhi took far longer than it should because most of the traffic lights were not working. Traffic of every sort, from overloaded trucks to cycle rickshaws, coming from four different directions, competed to cross each junction. On the outskirts of Khurja we passed *dhobis*, or washermen, traditionally a Dalit occupation, standing up to their thighs in water beating clothes to get the dirt and stains out of them. The water was filthy, so it was a wonder that the clothes got clean, but we could see they did because there were shining white sheets laid out to dry in the sunlight.

Khurja is a typical North Indian town, expanding higgledy-piggledy, without any planning. It is about sixty miles east of Delhi. But Khurja does have its unique identity. It is renowned for its crockery, and, something neither of us knew before, it is a centre of the meat trade. Meat in large quantities is exported from Khurja to the Arab countries. Khurja also has its own college where we were to meet Dr Rajesh Paswan, who was to accompany us to the villages.

The college had clearly seen better days. Part of it was built in the Indo-Saracenic style with delicate domes and thin, spindly towers. Its cloisters were built in what I call 'British Raj Decorated' because of its pointed arches, which were a feature of English architecture in the early Gothic period. Modern classrooms built in the unimaginative, standard, Indian Public Works Department style detracted from the grandeur of the original construction. The college cannot be said to be preserving its British heritage well. There is an air of dilapidation about the place, but it is preserving its Indo-British name. It is called the Nathimal Ram Sahay Edward Coronation College. Nathimal and Ram Sahay were two Indian businessmen. Edward was of course Queen Victoria's son, King Edward VII. The hostel where we found Dr Rajesh Paswan still bears the name of John Hewitt, a British Governor of the United Provinces, as UP was then known.

Dr Paswan was warden of the hostel. When he was appointed he had been the first Dalit to join the college teaching staff. He had been selected on the Dalit quota, but was well qualified for the job with a PhD from Delhi's Jawaharlal Nehru University. His parents, themselves teachers, had obviously inculcated their belief in the value of education in their sons. Rajesh's brother, Atul, had become a software engineer. Remarkably he had established himself in Japan where he was CEO of Indo-Sakura Software, a company he founded in 2005 and which provided 'innovative business solutions' to the Japanese across the Osaka, Nagoya and Tokyo region. The turnover of the company was more than 2.6 million dollars a year.

Rajesh's subject was Hindi but on the wall of his room at the top of the hostel was a poster announcing the deification of English – as I was to learn later, another of Chandrabhan's projects. I suggested that there was something of a conflict of interests here. Surely he should be encouraging the study of his subject, Hindi, in the college but here he was promoting English. Rajesh laughed and just said, 'Rozi roti ka savaal hai – it's a question of earning my bread. English is the language that will get us Dalits ahead.'

Rajesh had sent one of his sons and his daughter to an English medium boarding school in NOIDA, the city that has sprung up opposite Delhi, on the eastern side of the river Yamuna. He intended to send his second son there too, when he was old enough. The local schools, Rajesh maintained, were English medium only in name.

The main picture in Rajesh's living room was a portrait of the fourteenth-century Dalit poet-saint Ravi Das, seated in the lotus position, with his hand raised in blessing. He had been the subject of Rajesh's PhD thesis. In the bedroom hung a huge portrait of another of Rajesh's heroes, Dr Ambedkar. Usually shown clean shaven, this time Ambedkar was sporting a moustache, pencilled in by Rajesh's son.

Rajesh told us that Dalit students who had come to the college on the reserved quota had often done well. Some had gone into the elite cadres of the civil service and the police, much sought-after careers. Some had become officers in the paramilitary forces, and one Dalit former student was general sales manager of a firm in Bangalore. But Rajesh did suggest it wasn't that easy for Dalits to do well in college, saying, 'Dalits can be a little unsure of themselves. I help individual students, I do morale boosting, because they do feel hesitant, they do feel a little under pressure.'

Twenty-one per cent of the seats in the college are allocated to Dalits. When they graduate they can compete for the government jobs that are reserved for their community. Rajesh felt reservations gave Dalits space. There has been a move to get India's private sector to have quotas for Dalit and tribal employees. So far this has been resisted by the captains of industry, but there are signs that they are becoming aware of the need to recruit more Dalits to prevent the government forcing reservation on them. Rajesh pointed out to us that India's largest business house, Tata, had recently issued a recruitment advertisement for one of its companies that read, 'We specially invite members of the Scheduled Castes and Scheduled Tribes community, who meet the requirements, to join Tata BP Solar.'

I asked Rajesh whether he had faced any discrimination in the college.

He smiled and replied, 'No, but you see my caste name is Paswan and so people might have thought I was a relative of the politicial leader Ram Vilas Paswan and so had influence. But to be fair I actually think I was respected because I was well educated and because I was a social activist.'

Rajesh had coordinated the survey in Khurja. For six months continuously he had worked on it after his teaching duties were over, only taking three days off to celebrate the festival of Holi. The surveyors had all been local Dalits, and they had greeted people with '*Jai* Bhim!' – Victory to Bhim, a shortening of Ambedkar's first name.

'It was important to do this,' Rajesh explained. 'It established that the surveyors were one of them. I also told the boys that they must take tea or water whenever they were offered, otherwise the villagers might think they were refusing them because they were Dalit tea and Dalit water. Our people are very suspicious of government surveyors and wouldn't have spoken openly if they hadn't known that we were Dalits too.'

'What was the reaction to the results?'

'They amazed Dalit intellectuals and left-wingers, but not ordinary people because they knew what was going on. The intellectuals are not aware of all sorts of things which are happening. Even I was surprised to learn that upper caste people are now prepared to do our work, work they once thought would pollute them.'

'What work?'

'Other castes regarded brooms as things you shouldn't touch. Sweeping as work only Dalits should do. But when our Chief Minister announced that village sweepers would become permanent government employees, with all the benefits that go with that, rather than just casual labourers, people from every caste came forward to get the jobs.'

After being introduced to the College Principal, and waiting an inordinately long time to drink the obligatory cup of tea with him, we eventually set off for the hamlet of Harinagar. As we were entering the hamlet we passed a modern life-sized statue of a paramilitary policeman in khaki uniform. We pulled up outside a substantial house. Gardens are very rare features in villages, but a skilled and keen gardener had clearly been at work here. As this was the best house in the village the villagers thought it was the most appropriate place for our meeting. But it was stiflingly hot inside, and there was no electricity for the fans, so we suggested that we should sit outside in the shade. Charpoys were placed under a large mulberry tree, just by a tube well, and villagers gathered around us.

We learnt that only Dalits lived in this hamlet, and for the most part they were comparatively prosperous. Eight families had tractors. Most of the villagers were certainly not exercising their right to dress smartly. But then Roshan Singh, a middle-aged farmer wearing an under-vest, said what they wore had not been a problem for them: 'We were never put under pressure by higher castes because we were far away,' he told me. 'The main village is one to one and a half kilometres away, and we had land. My grandfather had bought three hundred bighas of land. Those Dalits who didn't have land, they were under pressure.'

'Are they still under pressure?' I asked.

'Those who worked as labourers were always troubled,' Roshan Singh replied. 'They didn't get proper wages, but those who had jobs were fine. Now some of our community are running shops, working privately. Now there is more work, we can find work in factories, and there is lots of construction work going on. Before it was just the landlords our community could work for.'

Then the one man who was smartly attired in a neatly pressed, stylishly patterned shirt took over the meeting. It transpired that he was the owner of the house and had planned the garden. Stocky, but not stout, with a full head of neatly cut black hair, Devi Saran Singh looked every inch the military man he was. He told us he had taken a commission in the paramilitary Border Security Force, or BSF as it is known, 'to improve his financial position and serve the nation'. Two other brothers had joined the force. One of them, Mohan Lal, had been killed in the operation against Pakistani soldiers who in 2002 infiltrated across the line of control in the Kargil sector of Kashmir. The statue we had passed was a representation of Mohan Lal, and the village school was named after him.

Devi Saran Singh had peculiarly narrow eyes that gave him a severe, almost cruel appearance. Clearly thinking he was a cut above the rest of the villagers, he told us, 'Maybe their living standards have improved, but there is not much improvement in poverty. Then they had no money, now they have no money for irrigation and fertilisers and they can't go to the bank again and again since they can't repay their loans.'

'How do you think your community is treated by the upper castes?' I asked.

The self-satisfied paramilitary police officer replied, 'I am treated well by upper castes because they think in my position I may well be of use to them, help them. But the situation remains that even a poor Brahmin will be respected by our community and theirs, while they certainly will not respect a poor Dalit.'

The BSF does not reserve a quota of posts for Dalits and so Devi Saran Singh had got in on his own merit. But he did feel that there was some discrimination against him.

'My promotions are delayed,' he told me. 'I am not getting them on time. The same thing is happening right now. I should already have been promoted to my next rank. But they never say "you are not doing well", or give an explanation. They just delay the promotion. In the same way the other officers don't talk, but they do have ill-feeling in their hearts. Now transparency is coming so it will be difficult for them to discriminate.'

I asked the paramilitary police officer about his family. He had a son he wasn't very pleased with because he spent his time watching cartoons and the Discovery channel on television. His daughter was an altogether different case.

'She's trying for IIT,' he said. IITs are the prestigious Indian Institutes of Technology that export so many of their graduates to Silicon Valley and other destinations in America, Europe, and Australia. Devi Saran Singh went on to boast, 'Because I am in the BSF I can afford to give her tutors and coaches. She got ninety-three per cent in her tenth standard exams. If I'd had the same facilities I would have got a much better job. When I was doing my MSc I spent most of my time travelling from town to village and in the village there was no electricity.'

A girl called Jyoti, sitting among the villagers, was already at university studying zoology. She wanted to be a doctor. Devi Saran Singh told her she was wasting her time doing this degree, she should have gone straight to medical college. Jyoti, surprisingly defiant for a woman and one so much his junior, looked Devi Saran Singh in the eye and said, 'You have got this all wrong. I didn't join medicine because I got into a private college but we didn't have the fees. I hope by getting this degree to qualify for a government medical college which we can afford.'

Another girl, Kumari Brijesh Gautam, was less fortunate. She said, 'My family's condition is down so my education is of a simple type. I have studied but can't speak English. There isn't the atmosphere in the village for it. We don't have money for me to study further and get a professional qualification so that I can get a good job. I really feel hatred for the force but I have no choice but to apply to the police. I hate them, but what can I do?'

The villagers protested because her father, who was a non-commissioned officer in the railway police, was sitting opposite. But the young girl continued in a barely audible voice, 'The police are the most good-for-nothing people. Whoever commits a crime gets away with it and someone else gets punished.'

Rajesh Paswan, who had brought us to the village, said, 'Whatever your career, it is particularly good that Dalit girls are now getting educated and getting proper jobs.'

Nangla Sherpur was also a Dalit village. There we were introduced to Rajpal Singh, who was described by his fellow villagers as 'an international man'. He was a bandmaster, in charge of one of those bands that accompany wedding processions, and so an expert on weddings, which the survey had seen as such important markers of Dalit status. Rajpal Singh told us that twenty-five years ago the band was always fed separately at a wedding because they were all Dalits. 'They made us eat where they put their shoes,' he said. That was particularly insulting. Now apparently the band eats with everyone else although the bandmaster did say ruefully, 'Sometimes they don't feed us.'

'What about the guests? Do Dalits go to upper caste weddings?' I asked.

'The real problem before was that those people didn't come to our weddings. That was what hurt. Now they do. Now we sit with upper castes and they offer us tea. There is no hostility, no untouchability because we are more educated and prosperous.'

There were some thirty villagers sitting with us. I asked them whether having a Dalit woman as Chief Minister had helped them. There was a chorus of agreement, and a man called Rajesh Singh, who seemed to have taken it upon himself to be our guide, said, 'Chief Minister Mayawati has brought our community together. Before, the landlord would tell us to sit at the back. Now we know we have a political contact. This is true of officials too. They have to behave properly with us. They used to behave badly.'

A mobile phone rang and I asked how many there were in the village. Back came the reply, two in each family. That seemed to me a bit of an exaggeration but I didn't challenge it.

I noticed that two of the oldest men were wearing Sikh turbans and had long straggling beards. When I asked about this I was told that Nangla Sherpur had once been a village of Dalit Sikhs but almost all of them had cut their hair and shaved their beards during the anti-Sikh riots which followed the assassination of Indira Gandhi.

On our way out we passed a statue of Dr Ambedkar wearing particularly large black horn-rimmed glasses. When I pointed him out to Rajesh Singh, who was still acting as our guide, he said with pride, 'The government puts up statues of Gandhi, Nehru, Indira, and Rajiv but we put up statues of Dr Ambedkar. To us he is a God.'

The third village we visited was Isanpur. It was shared by Dalits and upper caste Thakurs or Rajputs, traditionally landlords. We found the Dalits as usual living in a separate part of the village. They were less upbeat and more angry than the Dalits living in their own villages. One of the older villagers, Harkesh, did say that there had been changes. 'We now sit on the same level. They respect me,' he explained and went on, 'Before, if they were sitting down to eat they would tell us to eat separately. If we went to meet them we had to sit on the earth, not on the carpet.'

But Battan, an angry, elderly villager with a long, lugubrious face, contested this view hotly, 'These are all small matters. There's been no change in their hearts. We still cannot offer water in their Shiva temple. I am sixty-two years old, and what I saw in my father's day I see today.'

Some of the villagers tried to interrupt but Battan wasn't going to be stopped: 'They still hate everything I touch. I cannot sit with them on a charpoy. When everyone has eaten then they feed us. I haven't been to any function for twenty-five years but my family tells me what happens. Yes, some things have changed. Before, we lived in huts, now we have a house but that has made them angry. They are jealous that we wear decent clothes but they can't say it out loud.'

Battan paused for a moment and then added, 'Before, if we were talking to a Thakur we had to stand downwind of him. They can't insist on that now.'

This group of Dalits didn't think their economic circumstances had improved. There was less work on the land because there were no bullocks, and so no ploughing. They did get work at harvest times and got paid in grain. None of them had land of their own.

As there was no ploughing and there were no bullocks I assumed that the *halwaha* system had died out. But when I asked whether that was so, the villagers shouted, 'Bhura – he is a *halwaha*.'

But Bhura, an elderly man wearing a vest, which seemed to be the standard dress for the Dalits of this village, said, 'That's not exactly so. Yes, I work every day for a farmer but I am not bonded. I have worked for the same farmer from the beginning to now and, see, I'm in my old age, but that doesn't mean I am bonded. He pays me one hundred rupees every day.'

'What do you mean beginning?' someone asked.

Bhura pointed to a young teenager and said, 'A little smaller than him. About twelve, I suppose.'

When I asked what changes he'd seen in his long working life he replied:

'There have been improvements in the last twenty years. They don't swear at us and curse us any longer. My employers' family is not rude to me. But I can't sit on a charpoy with them, or eat from their dishes. I keep my own dishes there because they give me one meal a day.'

The topic then moved on to what Dalits clearly regard as crucially important: employment. As they are all labourers I asked whether they got enough work. But Battan cut that discussion short by asking me scornfully, 'If there was enough labouring would we all be sitting around here in the middle of the day?'

When I asked about education I was told there were no graduates in the Dalit community of Isanpur. But then someone pointed to a young woman and said, 'She's a graduate.' The woman muttered, 'I'm high-school failed.'

The government had built houses and improved their roads and paths but it didn't seem to be doing much to help their economy. No one was in government service and the Dalits maintained that none of them had been given Below the Poverty Line cards that would entitle them to cheap grain and other facilities. There were two young men sitting on the edge of the group. One said, 'That's not right, we have got BPL cards and we have been given work.'

Battan shouted back, 'Yes and you are the special men of the Pradhan.' The Pradhan is the village headman.

As we drove back to Khurja I thought of that statue of Ambedkar with his thick glasses and the villager who said to me, 'He is a god.' Gandhi has always been little short of God to me, although he would be appalled to hear that as he always resisted any attempt to sanctify him, let alone treat him as divine. I have seen countless similar statues of Ambedkar in different parts of India but for the first time a statue made me wonder whether in my admiration for Gandhi I had paid insufficient attention to Ambedkar. I had often written of Gandhi's movement to eradicate untouchability and ensure the Dalits were honoured, of his calling them Harijans, or Children of God. But that was perhaps romantic or at least unrealistic, whereas Ambedkar had been thoroughly realistic in calling those who belonged to his and other untouchable castes Dalits, or the oppressed.

In the late thirties the Mahatma devoted himself to dealing with the problems of villages and villagers. The problems he addressed were lack of sanitation, deficient diet and inertia. Ambedkar on the other hand saw the problem as cultural. He once asked, 'What is a village but a sink of localism, a den of ignorance, narrow-mindedness and communalism?'

Although Ambedkar's words are very harsh I can now understand why he passed that judgement on village India.

Ambedkar was speaking in the constituent assembly debates in 1948, just one year after Independence. If he were alive now how would he judge village India after nearly sixty-five years of Independence? I think he would be pleased by the evidence in the survey, and in all the villages we visited, that Dalits are refusing to accept their birthright is a life of humiliating service to the dominant caste in their village. He would not be surprised that the dominant castes are unwilling to accept this change and resent Dalits' demonstrations of their equality. Therefore Ambedkar might well have seen incidents like the attack on Dalit houses in Mirchpur as Chandrabhan Prasad does – caused because the Dalits are now able to look the other people in the eye.

Although Ambedkar would surely wish that the economic growth of the last twenty years had been more equally distributed he would have welcomed the disappearance of the *halwaha* system, and any evidence that Dalits were no longer morbidly dependent on dominant castes for their livelihood. But in Mirchpur it's clear that the Dalits are heavily dependent on the dominant Jats for work, and that they are suffering because denying them that work is part of the social boycott.

Ambedkar, like Narendra Jadhav's father, was a great believer in education, so he would have welcomed the attitude of the paramilitary police officer Devi Saran Singh who, while well educated himself, was determined his children should be even better educated. Then there was the young girl in that hamlet who was making such an effort to become a doctor. On the other hand there was the other young girl in Harinagar who feared her education would only lead to a job in the police, a force she hated. If Dalit enthusiasm for education is to bear fruit there have to be worthwhile jobs for them to go to. They won't be able to qualify for those jobs unless the standard of education in rural India is improved.

All in all, I believe that Ambedkar would have agreed with Narendra Jadhav that there is a silent revolution taking place. But he would have realised that in many places, such as the Dalit quarters of the village of Isanpur, the last village we visited, that revolution has hardly started. If it is to gather pace rapidly then India needs to become less dependent on agriculture for employment. At present the figures for the number of people reliant on agriculture for their livelihood vary between 60 and 70 per cent.

India's random urbanisation, with job-seekers pouring into the big cities, must be replaced by the planned creation of towns all over the country that generate employment, provide affordable housing, and transport for those who want to travel to work. In its recent report on Indian urbanisation, The McKinsey Global Institute has warned, 'If India continues with its present unplanned urbanisation path it will result in a sharp deterioration in the quality of life in its cities, putting even today's rates of economic growth at risk.' The report, not surprisingly, highlights governance and planning as two of the major problems.

Employment, education, protection from the jealousy of dominant castes, such as the Jats of Mirchpur, should all be the concern of the politicians Dalits elect. Sadly, as the Dalits of Mirchpur said, they do all too often behave like *dugdugis*, makers of loud noises.

3 | VOTE BANKING

Although there is widespread cynicism about politicians at all levels of Indian society, and the Dalits of Mirchpur are not alone in regarding them as just *dugdugis*, makers of loud noises, Indians still love their politics. It's the only national sport that can be compared to cricket, and like cricket it attracts large crowds. One of the most colourful politicians was the stalwart Chaudhary Devi Lal, who strode majestically across the political scene in the northern state of Haryana, adjoining Delhi. After fighting for freedom he entered politics and remained a dominant figure until he died in 2001, rising to be deputy prime minister for a short time. Chaudhary is a title given to important farmers and Devi Lal prided himself on his rural background. He also prided himself on the size of crowds he could draw.

When I was the BBC correspondent in Delhi I was forever getting phone calls from Devi Lal saying that he was going to have a massive rally and I must attend. The crowd was always going to be the biggest ever and there was going to be a helicopter to get me there. Taking up Devi Lal's offers would have been very partisan, but once there was a rally that did mark an important turning point in Indian politics, and so I drove there rather than accepting the helicopter ride. I had to walk the last half mile or so because the road was jammed with hundreds of tractors with trailers. There were even some bullock carts which had brought Devi Lal's supporters to the rally. The rally was in a comparatively remote part of Haryana but the crowd was massive. There was no spare space so many men had climbed up trees. I managed to squeeze in behind the platform on which Devi Lal and the other speakers, including the former Prime Minister Charan Singh, a Chaudhary too, were sitting.

Devi Lal was a tall, broad-shouldered man with a crumpled face who still looked like the wrestler he had once trained to be. His voice was deep and gravelly. His height was exaggerated by the green turban piled loosely on top of his head. When he stood up to speak he bellowed, 'This meeting is so important that Mark Tully from the BBC has come.' I was intensely embarrassed but worse was to follow. Charan Singh turned round, grabbed my hand and tried to drag me onto the platform. There was an unseemly tussle between me and the former prime minister before I could free myself. Meanwhile I also had to fight off Devi Lal, who was trying to honour me by putting his turban on my head.

Indian politics are not much about ideology. Left and right only seem to matter when it comes to the communists. Even there, as the long reign of Jyoti Basu, the communist who was Chief Minister of West Bengal for twenty-three years, shows, personalities play a major role. The politics of Chaudary Devi Lal's home state were dominated by personality clashes. His party was a one man band. He himself didn't bother to conceal his contempt for issues that were not directly linked to the welfare of farmers, such as free electricity for tube-well pumps, and subsidised fertiliser. I once found him in a foul mood. When I asked him what was wrong he said, 'I can't stand all this table work.'

I pointed out that the table work that day had been rather important, a discussion about the manifesto for an election which was coming up. 'Idiot,' he growled back. 'I can't count how many elections I have fought, but I can tell you I have never read a single manifesto.'

Caste matters as much if not more than personalities in Indian elections, particularly in North India. The farmers of his own Jat caste were Devi Lal's constituency and he always needed additional support from other castes with their own leaders, which was why he was forever cobbling together unstable alliances that involved sacrificing the leadership to someone else. Although he was chief minister of his own state twice, as well as attaining the rank of deputy prime minister, it was once said of him that he was like a shunting engine: he put the carriages together and then another engine came and took the train away.

Attending rallies like Devi Lal's, and meeting politicians, meeting voters too, trying to assess trends, and travelling in rural India were what gave me such great pleasure when covering elections. In the 2009 General Election I had the good fortune to be commissioned by the Delhi paper the *Mail Today* to travel where I liked and report on the elections. The constituencies I visited gave me a chance to assess whether in North India caste, community – in the case of Muslims – and personalities were still all important, and whether there was any indication that left and right were becoming issues.

The first place I chose to visit was Azamgarh, a town in eastern Uttar Pradesh. Uttar Pradesh, or UP as it is always known, has the largest population of any state, and a diversity that makes it a mini-India. A sizeable number of Azamgarh's voters were Muslims and an experimental Muslim party was in the field.

In Indian elections people are classified by their caste or their religion. Politicians, journalists and psephologists, all talk of 'vote banks' of Dalits, or former untouchables, OBC or Other Backward Castes, and the upper castes. But these groups are not solid blocks that will all vote one way. They are heterogeneous collections of castes and sub-castes, each with their special concerns that can be reflected in the ballot box.

Muslims are regarded as a very valuable vote bank too. But Muslims are also divided into what are in effect castes, although they would not put it that way. They are sometimes called *qaum*, that is to say communities, or *biradari*, meaning brotherhoods, and are often defined by professions or occupations. So, for example, you have *nai* or barbers, *qasai* or butchers, and *julaha* or weavers. Indian Muslims are also divided by their social status. There are groups of Indian Muslims whose family trees go back to Afghan, Turkish or Arab ancestors, and even to the tribe, friends and family of the Prophet himself. These communities are known as *ashraf*, or the noble ones. The historic split between Shi'a and Sunni divides Indian Muslims too. Among the Sunnis there are two major sects, the Barelvis and the Deobandis, and many minor ones. Then there is the Sufi tradition. So it would seem that if there is such a thing as a Muslim vote bank then it must have many different accounts in it. Nevertheless the government, politicians and Muslim leaders do believe in that bank.

In 2005 the government set up a commission to study the 'social, economic, and educational status of the Muslim community of India'. The findings of the Sachar Commission, as it was known, made dismal reading. According to the report, 31 per cent of Muslims are below the poverty line, their literacy rate is lower than the national average, and they are under-represented among university students, both graduates and undergraduates. Those Muslims who do graduate are more likely to find themselves without a job than any other group of Indians. Government jobs are still the ambition of most Indians because of the security and the prestige they offer. Even messengers in government offices command respect among their own communities. According to the Commission, Muslims have a considerably lower representation in jobs in the government, including nationalised industries, than any other group. Nationalised banks have declared many of the areas where Muslims are concentrated as Red Zones, which means managers there are advised not to give loans. So the dismal litany goes on, understandably giving Muslims a common sense of grievance.

Many Muslims also feel, with justification, that they suffer as a community at the hands of the police. The weekly magazine *Tehelka* published a series of reports telling the individual stories of Muslims who it would appear had been wrongly arrested and imprisoned because in none of the cases were the police able to secure a conviction. The accused

Muslims had been associated with a Muslim student organisation, SIMI, which was banned in 2002. It was alleged to be an anti-national, terrorist organisation, bent on destabilising the nation. Because the ban was open to widespread misuse by the police it had to be reviewed by a tribunal every two years. So the police, according to *Tehelka*, framed charges of plotting terrorist acts and preaching sedition against innocent young Muslims in an attempt to justify keeping the ban in force. *Tehelka* maintained that hundreds of Muslims were arrested in cases alleged by the police to involve SIMI.

Figures originally contained in the Sachar report seem to confirm that the police targets Muslims. The report revealed that the percentage of Muslims in India's prisons was higher than their percentage of the population. In the state of Maharashtra, which includes Mumbai, Muslims formed 10.6 per cent of the population but 17.5 per cent of the prisoners. In Mahatma Gandhi's home state of Gujarat 25 per cent of the prisoners were Muslims while they only formed 9.06 per cent of the population. These figures were removed from the report before it was tabled in Parliament. The report also quoted someone as saying, 'Every bearded man is considered an ISI agent.' The ISI is the rogue intelligence agency of the Pakistan army.

Muslims who are arrested suffer from the Indian police's all too common practice of using torture to extract evidence. Two years before the election, the *Indian Express* published a report about Muslims who had been arrested in connection with two bomb attacks in Hyderabad, one of India's most modern cities and a rival to Bangalore, India's IT capital. An investigation by the state government found that while under arrest the young Muslim men had been stripped and beaten, hair had been pulled from their beards, and they had been given electric shocks.

In the year before the election two young Muslim men were shot dead and one injured when police went to a house in Delhi to arrest them on suspicion of being terrorists. A police officer was also killed in what came to be known as the Batla House incident. What actually happened was hotly disputed, with the police claiming that they came under attack and many Muslims maintaining that the young men had been shot without any justification. The press argued over the two different versions of this event, an unofficial public hearing was held, but the government refused Muslim leaders' demands for an inquiry conducted by a judge. This inevitably inflamed Muslim anger and heightened their suspicions. Azamgarh was the home of the young men who were shot, so some two thousand Muslims from the UP town hired a special train and travelled to Delhi to demonstrate against the government.

Because of the Batla House incident, and its aftermath, some leading Muslims in Azamgarh decided to set up their own party called the Ulema Council to fight this election. I wanted to find out whether Muslims had become so disillusioned with all the composite parties which had claimed to represent their interests that they would now vote for a party of their own, even though it had no chance of winning.

In honour of Kaifi Azmi, one of India's greatest modern poets, who spent much of the latter part of his life in his ancestral village near Azamgarh, the railways have provided the town itself with its own overnight connection to the capital. It is appropriately named the Kaifiat Express, but unfortunately the railways have not given it a very honourable status.

The train starts from Old Delhi, the capital's original station. Built like a fortress it has a much more impressive frontage than New Delhi but is less prestigious. It tells a seasoned traveller something about the train he is going to travel on if he finds it is departing from Old Delhi. So Gilly and I were not surprised to find a rather grimy Kaifiat Express awaiting us in the gloom of the ill-lit station. Our carriage had seen better days. An air-conditioning vent was broken, as was a lavatory seat. A window was patched up with brown sticky paper, and the bottom was falling out of the lower bunk. But that didn't really matter.

What did worry us was the loud banging we heard as the train got up speed. It seemed to be the sound of wheels clanging against the side of the tracks. But when we alerted the ticket inspector he was not unduly concerned. 'If you are worried,' he said, 'fill in the complaint book.' That book never materialised. We did arrive in Azamgarh the next morning almost on time, with the wheels still clanging but the carriage upright, so perhaps we were being a little alarmist.

I'd expected to find a dusty and down-at-heel eastern UP town but Azamgarh was a cut above the average. It was more open, less crowded, and the river Tons flowing through it was pleasantly full of water for the time of year. The election was being fought in May, at the height of the hot weather in North India when many rivers are reduced to a trickle, or have dried up completely.

Maulana Amir Rashadi, Chairman of the Ulema Council, clad in immaculate white clothes and cap, with his trouser legs stopping several inches above his ankle, was just about to set out from his madrassa to campaign in the villages. I joined him in his air-conditioned car to listen to a lecture on the reasons why he had decided the Muslims needed a party of their own. He maintained that 'dishonesty with Muslims started at partition'. Nehru, the Maulana claimed, had partitioned India because he was afraid that if the Muslim League leader Mohammad Ali Jinnah had stayed in India he would be 'an alternative possible Prime Minister'.

The Maulana went on to accuse Sardar Patel, India's formidable first Home Minister, of regarding Muslims' loyalty as 'not secure', and so keeping them out of key posts. Then suddenly the cleric-turned-politician changed tack, poked his finger at me and barked, 'Tell me, does the constitution say a Muslim can't be Prime Minister? If not, why has no so-called secular party chosen one as Prime Minister?' When I reminded him that the previous President was a Muslim, and two other Muslims had held what was officially the highest office in the land before him, the Maulana scoffed, 'The President. He is just a rubber-stamp! It's the political leaders who have the power and they are all corrupt and liars.'

I suggested this was a rather harsh judgement but the Maulana wasn't having any of it. Looking at me as though I was solely responsible for the sins of the British Raj, he said, 'You came here with your East India Company to loot the country and rule over us. Now there are East India Companies on every corner with every politician looting.'

All the parties who have ruled UP, except for the right-wing Hindu Bharatiya Janata Party, or BJP, have claimed that they are the protectors of the Muslim community, but the Maulana maintained no party had fulfilled the commitments it made during elections. 'All we got is lollipops,' he said contemptuously. 'We have been sidelined. These parties come to us and tell us - you must vote for us because we are secular and we will protect you from the communal BJP. Now we are going to tell them if you want our support you should come to our party. We are not going to you.'

Forming a party of Muslims, which was unlikely to win a majority on its own in any seat in Uttar Pradesh, seemed more like a gesture born out of frustration than a strategy for redressing Muslim grievances. But when I met the Ulema Council's candidate I thought again.

Dr Javed Akhtar is a tall grey-haired orthopaedic surgeon, very popular locally because he treats poor people for free. He had no intention of becoming a politician, but police raids on Muslim homes and arrests of young men following the Batla House incident had convinced him his community needed to form a party. 'Look what happened to my own son,' he said. 'The police came looking for him. They raided my house, they had no warrant. It was an illegal attack on my home. Then after a few days the anti-terrorist squad came here. They told me, "We've heard that your son is innocent but we have doubts about others. If you can locate the others we will free your son."'

There is widespread anger among Muslims in Azamgarh fuelled by reports of random arrests, not all of which can be confirmed. The Muslims also resent the reputation Azamgarh has gained. The BJP Member of Parliament from another eastern UP town described it as 'a nursery of terrorists'. Dr Javed said, 'Our name has been blackened. Azamgarh has been called a nest of terrorists whereas in fact this is a peaceful prosperous town and we are a prosperous community. We feel the police are out to destroy our economy and our education by targeting our students.'

Although the Ulema is a term usually used in India to describe the body of Muslim clergy, Dr Javed insists that the Ulema Council is not a clerical party. He intended to see that the name was changed to make that clear. Explaining the party's strategy he said he was aiming to make it sufficiently large to become a potential force in UP politics. Then, he believed, the Ulema Council would attract others who were not Muslims but shared their ideals and wanted 'to fight for justice'. He explained that the model was based on the success of the Chief Minister of Uttar Pradesh, Mayawati, a Dalit woman. She had first built up a Dalit vote so solid that it seems to be set in stone, as one local journalist assured me. She had then added to her vote bank by choosing candidates from among high castes in the hope that they would bring votes from their banks with them. This was such a success that in 2007 she won an absolute majority in the UP State Assembly elections, the first absolute majority any party had won since 1991.

The Ulema Council had already set out on Mayawati's course by choosing non-Muslim candidates in three out of the five constituencies it was contesting. Dr Javed was under no illusions about the chances of the Council's candidates. 'I know we won't win,' he told me, 'but we want to gain enough votes to show that the idea of a Muslim party has potential. Then we can build on that.'

When I pointed out that in his own Azamgarh constituency the danger was that the Ulema Council would split the Muslim vote and let the right-wing Hindu BJP in, he replied, 'We have had enough of that logic. In the past we did vote in a block to keep the BJP out but what happened? The Muslims who were in the party we voted for were frightened. They didn't dare raise their own voices because they were afraid they would be thrown out of the party.'

The man most likely to suffer from the Ulema Council's intervention in Azamgarh was the candidate of Mayawati's Bahujan Samaj Party or BSP, Akbar Ahmed, a Muslim himself. On our way to meet him our car, with its large press sticker, was flagged down by a group of Muslims walking to one of Dr Javed's meetings. When we got out of the car we were surrounded by men all wearing white kurtas and Muslim prayer caps. 'We will die or go to jail but we won't vote for anyone else,' one insisted. Another complained, 'Daily there are cases against us.' The litany of grievances went on, 'The cruelty has started in excess since the Batla House incident', 'The government is threatening us, they want to force us to vote for them', 'We won't put up with the tricks played on us any longer', 'This is the first time in India anything like this has happened, next time we will win the election.' The supporters of the Ulema Council were particularly anxious to introduce us to one Muslim, Rashid, who had come all the way from Dubai just to vote for Dr Javed. 'Five hundred have come from Dubai,' he told us. 'We are going to show Mayawati and Congress that neither can have our vote.'

When we eventually managed to persuade the ecstatic supporters of Dr Javed to let us go, we drove on to the small town where we were expecting to find Dumpy, as Akbar Ahmed is always known. Inevitably his schedule proved to be worth little more than the paper it was written on and there was considerable confusion about when he had left and where he had gone. But we were told which road he had taken so we set off, hoping that we were on his route.

Eventually we did come across a meeting of the BSP. The audience, sitting on the ground, protected from the sun by colourful canvas tenting, was listening to a speech by the leader of their caste, the Rajbhars. He was stressing the need for all castes to come together to support Mayawati. She had appointed him speaker of the UP Assembly and he had to explain that this was a greater honour than being a minister. The Rajbhars had obviously hoped that when they sent him to the Assembly he would become a member of the cabinet and then be able to use his position to do them favours. The speaker didn't want his fellow Rajbhars to feel he'd failed them. Dumpy was not sitting beside him but on the edge of the dais, trying not to look bored, and glancing anxiously at his watch from time to time.

When the meeting was over Dumpy's entourage charged towards their convoy of vehicles. As I was trying to scramble into the back of Dumpy's open four-by-four the vehicle shot forward, nearly taking my foot with it. Fortunately much shouting brought it to an equally sudden halt and hands appeared from everywhere to deposit me unceremoniously on the floor beside Dumpy. We then set off for an hour and a half's drive along bumpy, potholed roads, with Dumpy standing on the seat greeting villagers we passed, joking with his colleagues, and from time to time talking to me.

He agreed that Muslims were very angry about the arrests of their young men but maintained central government police were responsible not Mayawati's UP police. 'What can Mayawati do about that?' he asked. 'The Congress is in power at the centre and they probably arrest the young Muslims to give her a bad name.'

Dumpy also admitted that Muslims did have genuine grievances about the number of jobs they got in the government and in public sector undertakings. He had been a politician ever since the seventies when he was a member of the group surrounding Indira Gandhi's impetuous younger son Sanjay, who considered laws and conventions as barriers in the way of his plans to revolutionise India, and so ignored them. After Sanjay died when the light aeroplane he was piloting crashed, Dumpy hitched his star to Sanjay's widow Maneka, who became a bitter opponent of her brother-in-law, Rajiv Gandhi. Maneka ended up in the BJP, which was anathema to Dumpy. On his journey to the BSP he had done more than his fair share of party-hopping, winning several hard-fought electoral battles, and earning a reputation for unparliamentary language and unparliamentary behaviour.

In the last Parliament Dumpy had entered the chamber with his head wrapped in a red and white checked scarf like those Yasser Arafat used to wear, and some Indian Muslims still do. Dumpy was protesting against the police practice of producing young men from Azamgarh in court with the same headwear to emphasise, according to Dumpy, that they were Muslims when they were seen on television. When the BJP members of the house objected vociferously to Dumpy's attire he shouted at them, 'If every Muslim in Azamgarh is a criminal, please arrest me also.' The Speaker couldn't control the uproar that followed and adjourned the House.

The four-by-four charged recklessly along the bumpy byways of Eastern Uttar Pradesh. To make myself heard above the rattle of the battered bodywork and the roar of the engine, I had to shout at Dumpy: 'In all your years in politics what have you achieved for the Muslim community?'

'Bugger all!' he yelled back, then hurriedly added, 'Well, at least not much. The trouble is that political parties have just used Muslims as vote banks. But at least Mayawati's number two is a Muslim, and he holds eleven important portfolios.'

Dumpy's main opponent was an old rival, Ramakant Yadav. He had been a party-hopper too and was now standing for the BJP. When I suggested that he shouldn't be a threat to Dumpy's Muslim constituency, which was most unlikely to vote for the right-wing Hindu party, he fumed in his staccato style, 'What do you mean? I believe the bastard has financed the Maulana and his Ulema Council, so that they will take away my vote and he'll scrape home. But I hope to fix him. Every time I speak I remind people of the murder charge against him.' Like many candidates in these elections Ramakant had been charged with a serious offence but due to India's convoluted legal system he was still on bail.

'Do you concede that the Ulema Council is highlighting genuine Muslim grievances?' I asked.

'Of course I do. The mainstream political parties have been bloody fools as well as liars. I know better than most that they have pissed off Muslims and so there is obviously a danger that many of them will vote for the Council. That will split my vote and let Ramakant in. If that doesn't happen I know I'll beat the bastard.'

Dumpy also had some harsh words for the local press. That morning Hindi papers were full of campaign news of the various candidates. This, a local journalist told me, was something of a new development in the current campaign. It was part of what is known as 'paid news'. Candidates reached a deal with local newspapers for a certain substantial sum of money, and their campaign was covered. As one journalist said to me, 'Why should we have to trail them around the place, and spend our money to do so, this makes much more sense. And we don't have to chase all those worthless independents who can't pay.' I asked Dumpy if he had a 'package' with any of the local press.

'Bah!' he exploded. 'One paper asked me for lakhs of rupees if I wanted coverage. I told them to take a running jump, I'm not paying. So I don't get coverage, I am relying on the fact people know me.'

It was dark by the time we reached Dumpy's next meeting, where this time he was to address upper caste Rajputs. He hoped that he could persuade them to bank their vote with him. His line on this occasion was to be: 'Mayawati is no longer just an advocate of the Dalit cause, and doesn't just give tickets to Dalits in elections but also to high caste candidates.' But as I had a story to write I didn't stay on to hear that speech.

It was very difficult to assess what would happen to Dumpy. There was clearly considerable enthusiasm among Muslims for the Ulema Council. On the other hand Muslim fear of the BJP was widespread too. In Azamgarh there was the possibility that Muslims voting for the Ulema Council would bring about the downfall of the only Muslim candidate in the field with a chance of winning, Akbar Ahmed – Dumpy – and so hand the constituency to the BJP.

A Muslim shopkeeper in Azamgarh reminded me of another problem posed by the concept of a Muslim party. He said, 'I fear that the formation of a Muslim party will divide us from other communities and give ammunition to parties who anyhow say we are anti-national.' He suggested a better alternative would be for all Muslim MPs of whatever party to stand together on Muslim issues. But then he added, 'That will not happen so long as MPs are afraid of their party leaders – people like Sonia Gandhi of the Congress and Mayawati – and so are unwilling to go against party policy.'

After talking to the shopkeeper, I saw that Muslims in Azamgarh and elsewhere in India are in a double bind. They have been let down by politicians from mainstream parties who have taken their votes but failed to offer them any more than 'lollipops'. But if they form their own party they become easy targets for those who make political capital out of demonising them as being anti-national.

The Sachar Report on the status of Muslims suggests they would have fared better if, like the Dalits, they had special places in educational institutions and quotas of government jobs reserved for them. But that would be opening a Pandora's Box. It would breach the secular principles of

India's constitution by officially identifying a community by religion, rather than by their social status. This would put a torch in the hands of Hindu fundamentalists who would try to set the country alight. However, in the southern state of Tamil Nadu there are already reservations for certain Muslim communities who are poor. But the Islamic clergy don't like this because they fear it amounts to admitting that the Hindu institution of caste exists among Indian Muslims.

As I mentioned in the previous chapter, Dalits have certainly benefited from reservations. They represent about 16 per cent of the population but now occupy about 17.5 per cent of the posts in the Central Government. The articulate Dalit middle class formed the backbone of Mayawati's BSP, which was founded as a party of all the oppressed people of India but was fundamentally a Dalit party. The exploitation, oppression, and particularly the stigmatisation of Dalits accounts for the party's success in Uttar Pradesh, and the election of a Dalit woman as Chief Minister of the State – a very remarkable achievement.

Mayawati had proved to be a controversial Chief Minister. In the statement of her assets she filed before the election that brought her to power in 2007 she admitted to being worth 520 million rupees. That is a vast sum of money to acquire for the daughter of a government clerk who started her career as a schoolteacher. But Mayawati claimed much of her wealth came from contributions made by her followers who, she maintained, 'want to see a Dalit's daughter rich as well as powerful'.

Mayawati is a symbol of hope for Dalits – one of them and yet someone who didn't just accept her fate but had aspirations and fulfilled them. It's because Dalits have tended to be the poorest of the poor that Mayawati believes they take pride in her wealth as well as her political power. That's why she feels she can be blatantly extravagant, buying for instance a large property in the most expensive residential area of the national capital Delhi, and spending lavishly on her property in the state capital, Lucknow.

As Chief Minister she has demonstrated her power by treating her cabinet colleagues as peons, or messengers. She hasn't even bothered to call cabinet meetings on a regular basis. She has challenged the mighty Indian Administrative Service, or IAS, the replacement for the British Raj elite civil service cadre that was known as the country's steel frame. The IAS likes to think it should have a monopoly of all top government jobs and that no politician can afford to ignore it. But Mayawati did not choose an IAS officer for the key post of Cabinet Secretary. She appointed a pilot with no administrative experience.

To demonstrate her power throughout Uttar Pradesh and to arouse Dalits' pride in her, she peppered the state with statues of herself and her mentor Kanshi Ram. He was the former government employee who had founded the Bahujan Samaj Party. Kanshi Ram and Mayawati had a close association lasting twenty-five years, during which the party that had started from scratch was built into a powerful political force.

The Dalits, like the Muslims, had good reason to think that they had been taken for a ride by the mainstream parties, and so needed a party of their own. For many years they had accepted the Congress Party as their protector and champion. But the Congress remained a predominantly upper caste party and took the Dalit vote for granted.

Since Independence there has been only one Dalit member of the top leadership of the Congress Party recognised as a leader in his own right, the redoubtable Babu Jagjivan Ram. He was a senior minister in every Congress government until 1977 when he fell out with Indira Gandhi at the end of the Emergency she had declared. As we saw in the last chapter, he wrote in the strongest terms against the slavery of Dalits in Indian villages. However, unlike Mayawati, Babuji did not put himself forward as a champion of Dalits. Once when I was interviewing him and I described him as a Harijan leader, Mahatma Gandhi's name for Dalits, he replied angrily, 'I am not a Harijan leader, I am a national leader.' After Indira Gandhi was defeated in the 1977 general election, Jagjivan Ram made a bid to become Prime Minister of the opposition alliance that came to power but he was out-manoeuvred by another veteran former Congressman, Morarji Desai. So Jagjivan Ram became for Dalits, or Harijans, the best Prime Minister they never had.

In this general election Mayawati was hoping that she would make up for the loss Dalits suffered when Jagjivan Ram failed to make it to the top job. She was campaigning as a candidate to be the next Prime Minister, and the press were rating her a serious contender. There appeared to be a possibility that neither of the two national parties, the Congress and the BJP, would win enough seats to enable them to form a coalition. Then several smaller parties might get together to form a minority government. Mayawati knew that the leaders of the different parties would slit each other's throats in the battle for the top job, but thought she might win enough seats to emerge victorious from the bloodshed. Her government would be unstable and almost certainly short-lived, but that didn't matter to her or her supporters. The important thing was that a Dalit should have become Prime Minister, no matter for how short a time.

After leaving Azamgarh I drove to the town of Ghazipur only some thirty miles away for a Mayawati rally. Ghazipur, situated on the banks of the Ganges, downstream from Varanasi, is the town where Lord Cornwallis died. He was the British Governor General who, towards the end of the eighteenth century, introduced major reforms in India which curbed the powers of the East India Company merchants and laid the foundations of orderly governance. He established a civil service, reformed the legal code, and introduced what he believed would be a fairer and more effective way of taxing land. Known as the Permanent Settlement, the system for collecting land revenue gave rise to feudal, often absentee, landlords and is usually held responsible for the backwardness of agriculture in the areas where it was imposed, which included Eastern UP.

Lord Cornwallis, flanked by a sorrowing Hindu and a grieving Muslim, still sits in the centre of a domed monument erected by the British inhabitants of Calcutta in his honour. His monument is one of Ghazipur's surviving links with its British past. The other is the opium factory that the government still runs. It goes back to the days when farmers of Eastern Uttar Pradesh were obliged to grow poppies to provide opium for the East India Company's trade with China, days brilliantly recalled in Amitav Ghosh's novel *Sea of Poppies*.

We found Mayawati's candidate, Afzal Ansari, who had been the sitting MP for Ghazipur, in his election office in a spacious half-built house in the centre of town, attending to an endless procession of workers who were making arrangements for the biggest event of his campaign – his leader's rally at the Lanka ground in Ghazipur the next morning. A lanky six foot four inches tall, with a curly mop of black hair and, like most men who want to be considered men in northern India, a moustache, he was resplendent in a startlingly white homespun cotton kurta and pyjama, a politician's standard uniform.

We were old friends, and the moment he saw us he rose to welcome us, a broad smile lighting his face.

'My goodness,' Gilly greeted him, 'you look like an advertisement for Surf.'

'The pyjamas stand up on their own,' he replied, 'they've so much starch in them. And what do you think of these?' he asked, putting on a pair of once fashionable droop-eyed glasses.

'Very good if you want to look like a Mafia boss from Dubai, but otherwise don't touch them.'

'I lost my glasses in a meeting yesterday, and these are the only ones I can find I can read with,' he explained, taking them off apologetically.

Tea served in small plastic cups had arrived and we sat down. He was looking a little tired. This had not been an easy campaign. Afzal had been able to achieve little for his constituency during his term as he had spent most of it in jail. Just as he was finding his feet as an MP a politician from a rival party, the BJP, had been shot dead, and he had been named in the case as a conspirator. Absolutely convinced of his own innocence, and the ability of the courts to recognise it, he had lost no time in surrendering to the authorities, and had been remanded to judicial custody. The complexities of the Indian legal system, and delaying tactics that could be deployed by lawyers – part of what has been termed 'adjournment culture' – then began to dawn on him. He remained in jail for over three years while his bail applications were considered and the case was gradually put together. Finally bail was granted and Mayawati, in search of winning candidates, had offered him the BSP ticket for Ghazipur. As he had formerly been in the Socialist Party, this meant he was having to get to know a new party and new party workers.

In his favour was the reputation he had gained over the twenty years he had been in public life as a state legislator, and what his supporters saw as the grave injustice he had suffered by being falsely accused in the murder case. But then there was the reputation of his younger brother Mukhtar. Mukhtar, in looks almost a carbon copy of his brother, couldn't have been more different. He cultivated the image of a Mafia don, and was proud of it, never happier than when he had been featured in *Time* magazine. While Afzal maintained a separate political identity and played by, and made others play by, the rules, Mukhtar believed in standing by his friends right or wrong, and rules were never his strong suit. As a result he had spent many years of his life in jail facing trial for serious crimes, but continued to win his elections as a state legislator by large majorities from behind bars. He was now Mayawati's candidate for the holy Hindu city of Varanasi, and his supporters were mounting a strong campaign. However, Mukhtar had also made implacable enemies and was accused in the same conspiracy case as Afzal.

'I realise,' Afzal admitted sadly, 'that, though no one will say it to my face, the image of a Mafia don that is now attached to me because of this case is a minus point for many voters. But many people know me personally and I don't believe that is enough to defeat me. My information is that the BJP knows their candidate hasn't a hope of winning and so they are planning to transfer their votes to the Socialist Party candidate. The big challenge I face is to get out enough voters to beat both of them put together. The meeting tomorrow will help to enthuse the workers, raise the tempo, but, between you and me, if they gang up on me, this is going to be tough.'

Another group of workers came in to discuss the next morning's arrangements. Before he turned his attention to them, Afzal asked, 'You will be there tomorrow?'

'Oh, yes,' I said, 'we'll be there.'

As a BBC correspondent I always had difficulty in assessing the size of India's vast political rallies. The police would give one figure, the organisers another, and the opposition a third. Nobody would accept the police figure, so I had to make my own assessment, which inevitably came between the opposition's and the organisers' claims and satisfied neither. As we joined the crowds heading for the Lanka ground it was impossible to say how many people were there. With considerable pushing and shoving we managed to get through to a seating area near the dais that was bedecked in blue, the colour of the BSP.

Afzal was standing at the back of the dais. Suddenly he spotted us and strode over. 'There must be a hundred thousand people here,' he shouted over the din around us. 'There's such a big crowd even outside the ground that people can't get in.' I thought his estimate might have been a bit over the top, but in the end the figure didn't really matter to Afzal because Mayawati congratulated him for organising the biggest rally she had attended so far.

It's a tradition of Indian political rallies that warm-up men and sometimes women keep the crowd occupied with speeches until the star speaker arrives. Mayawati was so determined to demonstrate her power and prestige that no one, not even the candidate for the constituency, was allowed to speak at this or any other of her rallies during the election campaign. Instead a succession of singers attempted to keep the crowd happy. They evidently thought they would be judged by their volume rather than their accuracy in hitting notes. Sometimes the singing deteriorated into nothing much more than a rant. Inevitably the songs were paeans of praise for Behenji, or sister, as Mayawati is always known, and anyone who assured the crowd that she would become Prime Minister got a roar of approval. As Behenji's arrival grew later and later, occasional announcements were made about her location. They had little relation to reality. At one stage we were told: 'Behenji's helicopter has left Varanasi, and she will be with us in ten minutes.' Half an hour later we were told she had just left Lucknow, some two hundred miles from Varanasi in the opposite direction to Ghazipur.

When the helicopter eventually landed the crowd went mad, cheering, singing, shouting slogans, struggling to break through the barricades erected to keep them in their place. But Mayawati was unmoved. Climbing out of the helicopter she didn't even wave at the crowd but climbed straight into a white Ambassador and drove for two hundred yards to the dais. As she got out of the car she was hidden by a giant hoarding depicting her with hands raised in triumph against the background of the Parliament building in Delhi. When she emerged on the dais, high above the crowd, an acolyte announced, 'Our Messiah has arrived!' using a word that does literally mean Messiah.

Mayawati was wearing her trademark freshly laundered and crisply pressed cream kameez with long sleeves and cuffs. The crowd's clothes were stained with sweat. But she made no excuse for keeping her supporters waiting in the dry summer heat of North India. Mayawati read her speech rather as though she had returned to her days as a teacher. It was a strangely flat performance, with none of the theatrical emotion of Indian political oratory.

The change of direction she had made to broaden the appeal of her Bahujan Samaj Party so that she wouldn't just be dependent on her Dalit vote bank was obvious. Embracing all the deprived of India, of whatever caste or creed, she said, 'The Congress and the BJP are in the hands of capitalists, so they don't care for the poor, just for capitalists. They want to come to power with money earned through our blood. When Congress and BJP were in power in the centre they passed no law for the eradication of poverty.' She appealed to the crucial Muslim vote by saying that she wanted to provide reservations, quotas in government jobs and educational opportunities for them.

But when I mixed with the crowd pouring out of the ground after Mayawati left it became clear that most of those who had come to hear her were Dalits and they regarded her as their property, the guarantor of their self-respect. One middle-aged man remarked, 'Behenji may not have been able to do much about our economic problems, but at least now we can drink tea in teashops on equal terms with everyone else.' When I suggested to him that if Mayawati had not spent so much money and time on erecting statues she might have been able to do something about his economic problems, he replied, 'There are so many statues of Mahatma Gandhi, Nehru and others who have no meaning for us. So why shouldn't we have our heroes' statues?'

Several Dalits said that the criticism of Mayawati came from the higher castes, who couldn't tolerate being ruled by a Dalit. A young woman walking beside her husband was amongst the most vocal of Mayawati's supporters. Stopping and turning towards me, she said, 'They hate us, they can't tolerate us unless we are slaves. Now that our time has come with Behenji what do you think they are going to say? That it's absolutely fine? No, they will talk all sorts of rubbish about Behenji to give her a bad name.' As she walked off the woman looked back and shouted, 'We won't lie down again, we won't be trodden on again.'

Another Mayawati in the making, I thought.

It's reckoned that 80 per cent of the Dalits voted for Mayawati in the election to the Uttar Pradesh State Assembly, two years earlier. That was a remarkable achievement because Dalits are divided by castes – they are not a united community. Her aim was to bring different Dalit castes together under her umbrella in other states too, but that was proving very difficult. Even in Punjab, which has the highest percentage of Dalits, and was the home of Kanshi Ram, the founder of the BSP, Mayawati had not become a major player in the state's politics.

Bihar is the state where governance has been so ineffective that it's been said that Karl Marx's prophecy has been fulfilled and the state has withered away. Buddhism and Jainism were born in Bihar. It was the centre of the Mauryan Empire, the first Empire that stretched over most of India, and the heart of the Empire ruled by the Guptas, regarded as the golden age of Hindu rule. During the British Raj members of the prestigious Indian Civil Service belonging to the Bihar cadre were considered the elite of the elite. However, since Independence Bihar has come to epitomise all that is wrong with the administration of India. One of the reasons often given for this is the role that caste plays in its politics. The politics of Bihar have come to be dominated by the Other Backward Castes, and the parties they have formed.

The constitution says India will be a casteless society. The Congress and the BJP's official position is to deplore what they call 'casteist politics'. But they are both fundamentally upper caste parties, and so feel threatened by the rise of OBC and Dalit parties. Furthermore they are not averse to appealing to caste loyalties when it suits them. Journalists almost invariably report the influence of caste in politics disapprovingly, and so do many but by no means all academics. But, like it or not, the reality of India is that caste has become what the distinguished anthropologist M.N. Srinivas called 'the unit of social action'. The high castes have only themselves to blame. They didn't find much space for lower castes in the Indian independence movement, and after Independence they continued to dominate every field. So it was inevitable that those who were deprived would use the institution that had made them unequal to fight for equality.

We set out for Bihar. There I was particularly keen to find how voters viewed their Chief Minister, Nitish Kumar. He'd had a very good run in the press because journalists believed he had at last provided a government that did govern Bihar in spite of heading a rickety coalition. His own party was the Janata Dal (United), which was anything but united, and although Nitish was a socialist and an avowed secularist, he was in alliance with the right-wing BJP. Fifty-eight at the time of this election, Nitish had a good head of grey hair but a face that was still boyish and often broke into a gentle, warm smile. He was an undemonstrative politician who didn't believe in rabble-rousing.

We drove from Eastern Uttar Pradesh to Buxar in Bihar, crossing the Ganges in the hope of catching a train to the state capital Patna.

I say 'hope' because the Bihar government's inability to maintain law and order had made train-running in the region somewhat erratic. Sure enough when we got to Buxar station we were told the train on which we had a reservation in the un-air-conditioned section hadn't even left Mughalsarai, about one hundred kilometres away. But a very helpful Assistant Station Master, or ASM, told me not to worry as he could get us on another train which was expected shortly. Displaying considerable knowledge of the arcane railway rules, which make changing a ticket well nigh impossible, the ASM was able to persuade the official in charge of reservations to stamp our tickets so that we could board the alternative train. But I would never have got onto the train had it not been for a burly coolie, as porters are still known in India. He pushed me through passengers who were blocking the door of the compartment to prevent anyone else squeezing into the vestibule, making life even more uncomfortable for the passengers packed into it.

Eventually I established a place for myself crammed up against the washbasin outside the loo. This caused much grumbling from passengers who wanted to wash, but I held my ground until a group of six men sitting on a berth meant for three squashed up even further to make room for me. They were trade unionists returning from a conference in Lucknow. One of them complained, 'This train wouldn't be so crowded if a ticket inspector ever bothered to come and check who has tickets and who doesn't.' Because the trade unionists were only passing through Bihar on their way home to the eastern state of Assam, there wasn't much point in asking them about Nitish and his claim that at last Bihar had a government that worked.

Hawkers selling tea, cold drinks, bottled water, sweets, roasted *channa* or chickpeas, peanuts in their shells, *pakoras* and other cooked snacks, somehow managed to make their way down the train. I asked one of them, a young man selling slices of cucumber, what he thought about the general election, but was brushed aside with a curt, 'I can't think anything about elections. I don't have time.'

When it became known that I was a journalist a few people gathered round my seat, making the trade unionists' space even more congested. They were, on the whole, enthusiastic about Nitish. A pharmaceutical company salesman said, 'Roads are being built, hospitals are at last functioning, you can now go out on the streets of Patna at night.' An IT teacher rated Nitish 'positive'. A retired government servant was more grudging. He would only go as far as to say, 'At least the feeling under Lalu isn't there. The people were not happy with him.'

Lalu Prasad Yadav was the Chief Minister of Bihar until he resigned after being accused of involvement in a scam. He then told his one-man-band party to choose his wife, Rabri Devi, to succeed him. Her political experience was limited to being a silent observer of all that went on in an Indian politician's house. So Lalu ruled Bihar for fifteen years, first as Chief Minister then as the man behind his wife's throne. A charismatic politician much admired for his rustic humour, Lalu was not however highly regarded for his administrative skills.

In Patna I found one of my favourite old-style politicians in, his house so near and yet so far from the Chief Minister's bungalow he had once occupied. So far because Jagannath Mishra had been in the political wilderness for the last twelve years, and the Bihar Congress, which he once headed, had been in the wilderness even longer. Sitting in his by no means palatial house, wearing a white waistcoat, a white kurta, and a flowing white dhoti, he too could have been an advertisement for the washing powder that washes whiter than white. On his forehead was a red tilak. The picture of an old-fashioned Bihari gentleman, the former Chief Minister greeted me with folded hands and said, 'Sit down, sit down. I'm so glad to see you. It reminds me of those days when you used to criticise my government.' Cackling with laughter he went on, 'Now I am nowhere but I still have my supporters.'

When I asked Jagannath about Nitish's campaign to sell himself as the Chief Minister of a government that works, he replied, 'That's all very well, but it depends what people think. Who knows whether people will think the government is working. But anyhow the point is caste, that is what counts in Bihar, and the Congress Party managed to lose the support of every caste that traditionally supported it.'

A Brahmin himself, Jagannath Mishra believed 1990 was the turning point for his party in Bihar. In that year the non-Congress government at the centre implemented the report of a commission, known as the Mandal Commission. That had advocated extending reservations in government jobs and educational institutions to castes known as OBCs or Other Backward Castes. Previously reservations had been limited to tribals and Dalits. Mandal gave a boost to the OBC parties that were the first substantial threat to the Congress monopoly of power.

The Mandal Commission report had been shelved for twelve years because it was a political hot potato. No one wanted to antagonise the influential upper castes, who obviously did not welcome the prospect of having the number of government jobs and places in educational institutions open to them reduced still further by the addition of quotas for the OBCs. When Mandal's recommendations were implemented the upper castes did object violently. Almost two hundred students attempted to burn themselves to death and sixty-two succeeded. More than fifty people were killed in clashes between the police and protesters.

The Congress found itself in a bind. It didn't want to antagonise its high caste supporters but it knew it also needed the support of at least some of the OBCs. Jagannath Mishra believed the Congress had come down too firmly on the side of the upper castes in Bihar and so lost the OBCs. To compensate for their loss of OBC support, Congress had then formed an alliance with Lalu and his OBC party. Jagannath opposed that alliance and was thrown out of the Congress. He explained, 'I warned them people would think there was no difference between us and Lalu and so our support base would go and it did. The upper castes went to the BJP and it grew. We were left with no legs to stand on. Congress is nowhere in this state.'

In this election Congress had thrown away the Lalu crutch and was standing on its own. Jagannath didn't rate their chances very highly: 'Congress should be able to win back OBCs from Lalu because people are fed up with him and they should be able to win some Muslim votes but they have no leader. They don't trust a local leader with real support. The man they have appointed as Congress president has only fought one election and in that he was very badly beaten.'

Did Jagannath believe he might be the leader the Congress was looking for? His reply was guarded: 'I have no ambition any longer but my last desire is to bring Congress back in Bihar.'

*

To get a balanced view of the caste equations in this election I went to see Saibal Gupta of the Asian Development Research Institute, an expert on Bihar's convoluted politics. He explained that Lalu was in trouble because, while he had succeeded in raising the status of his own caste, Yadavs, and other OBCs so that the administration had to show them respect, their empowerment had been 'symbolic rather than substantive'.

Saibal went on, 'The OBCs could at last speak to, even challenge, officers in charge of police stations who used to lord it over them, but with Lalu there were no land reforms, no taking over of economic power, no change in the economic power structure.' Nitish, whose backward caste was Kurmi, had tried to ensure that OBCs were put in influential positions in the administration and he was pushing power down to the village level, allowing *mukhiyas* or village headmen to sign cheques.

Nitish was also trying to exploit the divisions within communities. Lalu had concentrated on pleasing the castes known as Upper OBCs so Nitish was concentrating on the lower category. Taking advantage of the divisions within the Dalits, Nitish had provided special schools for the poorest Scheduled Castes, as Dalits are officially known, and they had become known as Maha Dalits – extremely oppressed. Nitish was also exploiting divisions among Muslims. He was targeting the poorer Muslim communities. Lalu had tried to form Muslims into a vote bank but Saibal said he'd only appealed to the leadership, who were mainly from the more prosperous Muslim communities.

It's easier to follow a bad act than a good act, and the received wisdom was that in terms of governance and economic development, which Nitish hoped would matter even more than caste in this election, Lalu's fifteen years had been a bad act. Nitish was claiming that his act was much better. But Saibal didn't think Lalu was entirely to blame for the poor performances of his governments. 'Bihar has never been well governed,' he said. 'There is no proper state structure, no system in the functioning of the government. What's more, sixty per cent of Bihar's revenue went when it lost its only industries to Jharkhand. Bihar doesn't have any industry worth the name now.' The state of Jharkhand was carved out of Bihar in 2000 and it covers an area rich in minerals with steel mills, coal mines, and ancillary industries.

'So is Nitish really doing any better?' I asked Saibal.

'The state finances are better managed. Health services have improved. Nitish has appointed two hundred thousand teachers so education should improve too. Crimes haven't decreased but convictions have.'

'How has this been achieved?'

'Because Nitish is attempting to build up a state structure and introduce systems in the functioning of the government. Lalu didn't cooperate with the bureaucracy. Nitish does, so bribes are higher but the work gets done.'

I suggested that bribes getting higher and introducing systems seemed to be contradictory. Saibal replied, 'That is the way the system works in India.'

The achievements Saibal listed seemed remarkable considering that Nitish had been in power only four years, so we set out to see what the position on the ground was.

I had dreadful memories of the roads of Bihar, but the main highway south that I took was in excellent condition. When I commented on this the driver said, 'This road is always well maintained but wait till you see the other roads I have to drive down, although I have to say they are improving.'

On the outskirts of the town of Jehanabad we stopped to talk to some potters working beside the main road. Kneading soft clay with his fingers, a youngish man with a small boy sitting beside him pointed to some dilapidated shacks and said, 'This is where we still have to live. We have been promised houses but nothing has happened. Lalu, Nitish, Congress – what have they done for us? We are not going to vote for anyone, but the impression is that the vote is going Nitish's way and they say he has done a lot, but for us nothing.'

'Look at that boy,' the potter's wife said. 'They tell us to send our children to school. None of us send our children. Do you know how far the school is from here?' and without waiting for an answer she went on, 'Two and a half miles. They would get killed walking along this road.'

She pointed to the pink pottery piled up by the roadside. 'They also tell us they will help us to sell our pots but this is the only way we can do it. They don't give us shops or anything like that. It's all talk, talk, talk – and nothing happens.'

I was reminded of the first time I covered an election campaign, and the labourer clearing a ditch who asked me, 'What does it matter who I vote for? He will only put my vote in his stomach.' Time and time again during election campaigns the poor have said to me, a plague on all their houses. Yet the figures show that, contrary to most democracies, in India it is the poor who come out to vote while the prosperous stay at home. I have always believed this is at least partly because, in spite of all they have learnt from experience, poor people still hope that if their candidate wins he or she might be able to get some benefit for them from the government. They see members of Parliament and of State Assemblies as facilitators not legislators, people who 'get work done' when the bureau-cracy is refusing to do it, which is often.

That was confirmed by one of the customers of a teashop in Jehanabad who said, 'First of all we have to fill our bellies. Only then will we think about issues. So those who say we will vote on caste basis are wrong: we will vote for who we think will work for us.' Another voter, a member of Lalu's Yadav caste said, 'We will vote because it is our right, and we will vote for him, but we won't do it from our hearts.'

Turning off the main highway, we did come across evidence that Nitish's government was working. The road was in bad shape but a modern road was being constructed to replace it. We drove through dead-flat countryside. The rice crop had been harvested and because of Biharis' brutality to trees, there was little or no greenery to relieve the monotony of the brown fields. Eventually we came across a school in the middle of nowhere. Boys in light blue shirts and dark blue shorts were lining up for their mid-day meal. The buildings were brand new and the headteacher Rishikesh Kumar told me the school had only been opened a month ago. It was a boarding school for Maha Dalits and all the staff were Dalits.

Finally, we reached the small town of Goshi. There in the government health centre we found Dr V.S. Kashyap treating an itinerant sadhu for high blood pressure. Many other patients were waiting to see him. The doctor showed me his register in which details of the one hundred and twenty-four patients seen by him or his staff the day before had been logged. When I said the press gave the impression that doctors didn't bother to attend government health centres in Bihar he replied, 'That perhaps used to be true, but what can you expect if doctors don't get their salary on time and they don't have any medical supplies? I have been here one year now and I get my pay and I have what I need, including anti-rabies vaccine and emergency supplies. You see, if an honest man sits on the chair then things will go ahead. If a dishonest man, then everyone else will be dishonest.'

In the town of Gaya, which is less than an hour's drive away from Bodhgaya, where the Buddha gained enlightenment, we came across a group of Muslims standing outside a mosque. I didn't expect to find any supporters of Nitish amongst them because of Nitish's alliance with the right-wing Hindu BJP, which is anathema to most Muslims. But the improvement in health services under Nitish's government had impressed the Muslims. They told me that under Lalu no one even bothered to go to the hospital but now patients were thronging there. They agreed that they would have voted for Nitish had it not been for his alliance with the BJP, but one summoned up the courage to shout excitedly, 'I am one hundred per cent for Nitish, one hundred per cent.'

We found Mayawati's caste politics working in the small town of Khizr Sarai. Her enthusiastic supporter described himself as a Chamar, a Dalit caste, and he was pursuing his traditional occupation, sitting by the roadside mending shoes. But Mayawati was not a factor in Bihar yet, and so the cobbler indicated that he might vote for Nitish because he felt 'things were better under him'. And that was the general view of the inevitable gathering that assembled as I was talking to him. One phrase from my conversation there stuck in my mind. When I asked what the Congress prospects were I was told, 'Congress is nothing but a vote-cutting party,' and in Bihar that is what the results were to show.

The next day we drove across the bridge over the Ganges into north Bihar and headed for Muzaffarpur, the state's second largest city. I wanted to visit the Lalit Narayan Mishra College of Business to discover how backward Bihar really was and discuss Nitish's prospects of moving Bihar forward. Lalit Narayan had been Jagannath Mishra's brother, Railway Minister under Indira Gandhi, and renowned as a fundraiser for her party. He was killed in Samastipur, a town not far from Muzaffarpur, when a bomb exploded while he was addressing a meeting. It is still not known whether his fundraising activities had anything to do with his assassination.

When I asked the staff of the College how Muzaffarpur was progressing, they laughed and replied, 'It isn't. It's going backwards.' A pharmaceutical factory had just closed and moved to Hyderabad. A factory manufacturing chewing tobacco had closed too. There was union trouble in the freight wagon factory, and its future was insecure. Although the town is surrounded by lychee and mango orchards, the lone fruit-processing plant wasn't working. The thermal power station, run by the state, had been closed until Nitish did a deal with the National Thermal Power Corporation to restart it. Even then Muzaffarpur was only getting electricity for seven hours a day. This meant that Muzaffarpur was left with nothing much more than a wholesale cloth market and a handful of small industries.

'So why is Muzaffarpur in such bad shape?' I asked.

Salamat Ali, who taught IT, replied, 'All the concentration has been on caste so we don't have state-of-the-art infrastructure.'

'We don't have any infrastructure,' another teacher chimed in.

'Yes, that's true,' Salamat Ali said. 'Just look at the railways, for example. We have had five railway ministers from here and our line is still not electrified. It takes twenty hours to get to Delhi one thousand kilometres away, that is fifty kilometres an hour. Is that any speed for a modern train?'

'What about an airport?'

'You must be joking. There is a small one but it's only used by politicians.'

If Muzaffarpur had an airport and a faster railway service it might attract tourists. It could well be a jumping-off point for travelling overland into Nepal, and it could attract pilgrims in large numbers. The Buddha is said to have preached his last sermon at nearby Vaishali, and Hindus believe that Sitamarhi, also nearby, is the birthplace of Sita the wife of the God-king Rama. But Muzaffarpur only boasts one hotel worth the name, described by one of the Business College staff as 'three-star, just'.

So, with no opportunities in business, commerce or tourism, I asked what happened to the students after graduating in business management.

'That is the sadness,' Salamat Ali said. 'Like a girl who knows she is going to have to leave her family when she marries, a Bihari boy knows he will have to leave the state after studying if he is to get a good job. Even then the tragedy is that Bihar has such a bad name our students have difficulty in getting jobs outside because they are Biharis. I'm proud to be a Bihari, and everyone should be proud of the place they belong to, but the fact is that life here is a struggle and we have to move out.'

As seen from Muzaffarpur, Bihar needs much more than Nitish kick-starting the government machinery. There must be massive and effective investment in its infrastructure so that industry is attracted and bright Bihari students don't have to leave home. But it still seemed likely to me that in this election many voters would be happy with the fact that the government was at least working, and would not worry that so far there didn't seem to be much progress on longer-term issues such as infra-structure.

So how did the results turn out? Did they show that Muslims were fed up with all political parties in Uttar Pradesh? Were Dalits in Uttar Pradesh disillusioned by their arbitrary, authoritarian heroine? Did the voters of Bihar have as high an opinion of Nitish's government as I had reported?

When at last the month-long election came to an end and the votes were counted, the results came in remarkably rapidly because electronic voting machines had replaced the old-fashioned ballot boxes. The victory of the Congress and its allies soon became clear, and by mid-afternoon I was watching an excited – I might almost say overwrought – television presenter declare, 'It's a sweep, it's a sweep!' This wasn't too good news from my point of view because throughout my coverage of the campaign I had been sticking to the line that the results would vary from state to state. But after carefully examining the figures I felt confident to write in next day's *Mail Today*, 'I would still be reluctant to see a national trend in this election.'

Shortly after the election I was delighted to read an article by Yogendra

Yadav, one of India's most highly regarded psephologists, in which he said, 'The weak and hesitant voice of the mandate doesn't lend itself to simple headlines.'

The Booker Prize-winning novelist, and acerbic social critic, Arundhati Roy has suggested that the Indian electorate would never deliver a mandate that lent itself to simple headlines. She has said, 'Interpreting an Indian election is about as accurate a science as sorcery. Voting patterns are intricately connected with local issues and caste and community equations that vary, quite literally, from polling booth to polling booth.'

Scholars from all over India who believed that it was possible to do better than sorcery got together to produce the National Election Study 2009. They sent 1,847 trained investigators out to interview voters randomly selected in what they called 'the largest and most comprehensive study of an Indian general election, perhaps of any election in the world'. How did they view the mandates for Dr Javed, Mayawati and Nitish?

As he had feared, Dumpy did go down to the Ulema Council in Azamgarh. Seventy thousand Muslims voted for Dr Javed, and they did enough damage to Dumpy to hand victory to the BJP. This was the first time Azamgarh chose to be represented by a member of parliament from the BJP. When I rang Dr Javed after the election and asked him how he felt about the BJP's victory he was unrepentant: 'We have supported the Mayawati party in the past and got nothing so why should we feel sorry if her candidate, Akbar Ahmed Dumpy is defeated? Actually her party has only made things worse for us.'

Dr Javed was very satisfied with the Ulema Council's performance in Azamgarh and three other constituencies where they had put up a candidate. He described the results in the other three constituencies they had fought as moderate. He made it clear that the attempt to do a Mayawati themselves, to attract non-Muslims to their party just as she had attracted non-Dalits to hers, would continue. But it has to be said that the survey described the Ulema Council's performance as a failure to mobilise Muslim support.

As for Mayawati, she failed to deliver on her promise to become the first Dalit Prime Minister of India. She couldn't win seats in states other than UP, and she didn't do that well in her own state. Her score was a disappointing twenty out of the eighty seats contested. Among the losers were Afzal Ansari and his brother Mukhtar. The BJP supporters did indeed ensure Afzal's defeat by throwing their weight behind the Socialist candidate. Mukhtar, in jail throughout the campaign, put up a good fight but was pushed into second place by one of the BJP's most senior and respected leaders.

The Congress Party's success throughout the country meant that the leaders of the smaller parties never had the opportunity to fight the battle to be Prime Minister that Mayawati had hoped for and some pundits had predicted. But the survey of results showed that Mayawati's BSP was still by far the largest party in UP. Her share of the votes in that state only fell marginally below the share she won in the 2007 election that swept her to power in UP. So there must have been many more Dalits who felt, like those I interviewed coming out of the meeting in Ghazipur, that criticism of Mayawati was a high caste plot to discredit her.

What about Nitish? His campaign paid off handsomely, giving him and his ally the BJP thirty-two out of the forty seats in Bihar. According to the post-poll survey, 87 per cent of those who were questioned said they were satisfied with the performance of Nitish's government. So perhaps performance counted for more than caste in this election. But it would certainly be premature to write off caste or indeed community as a factor in Bihar. After all, Nitish had done his caste calculations with his creation of the Maha Dalits. His wooing of poorer Muslims also seemed to have worked. It appears that many of them voted for him, overcoming their aversion to his coalition partner the BJP.

So it seems that Jagannath Mishra was at last proved wrong and the issue of governance trumped caste in this election. If this trend continues, democracy should play its role in ensuring that Biharis are not born to emigrate from their home state, and because politicians will realise that they won't get elected on the basis of their caste, they will have to deliver. Nitish Kumar describes himself as a socialist, but that doesn't seem to count. What the majority of voters want delivered is the education, the health services, the jobs and the infrastructure which are necessary to narrow the gap between the prosperous and the poor. The Bihar result is a wake-up call to politicians. They received another wake-up call in 2010 when Nitish's coalition swept the polls in the State Assembly election. If the politicians don't hear those calls from Bihar the voters could lose faith in democracy.

4 | THE RAMAYANA REVISITED

During our election coverage we hardly heard of the ideological issue that dominated Indian politics for many years, the battle between secularists and those who argue for a Hindu nation. This was in sharp contrast to twenty years ago when that battle was raging.

Developments in Indian television provide a possible explanation for this. In 1987 a televised version of the Hindu epic the Ramayana outraged Indian secularists. The 78-episode serial was relayed across the country. In the epic the God-king Rama, an incarnation of the God Vishnu, battled to rescue his wife Sita from her abductor, the ten-headed demon-king Ravana. The series ran on what at that time was the country's sole broadcaster, the government financed and controlled Doordarshan.

The journalist Pankaj Pachauri, writing in the respected news magazine *India Today*, fulminated against a television service paid for by all Indians 'broadcasting a Hindu religious sermon'. Aruna Vasudev, one of India's leading film critics, raised a more fundamental point. When I tried to defend the serial she replied angrily, 'You can no longer call India a secular country after the Ramayana has dinned home its Hindu message week after week.'

These secularists represented the view still held by many Indians that there can be no role for religion, particularly for Hinduism because it is the majority religion, in the public life of a secular republic such as India. Many Hindus feel this view of secularism leaves them with no room to take pride in their religion and its role in the long history of Indian culture. To them the secularists seem to be saying that to be avowedly Hindu is to be communal, that is to say to be aggressively Hindu and antagonistic towards other religions. On the other side of the shouting match, which has drowned the voices of those who would like to debate the role of religion rationally, are the supporters of Hindutva. They maintain that India should be a Hindu nation. Although their interpretations of what that should involve vary, they all argue that India should acknowledge that its culture is rooted in Hinduism.

Politically, the Congress Party, dominated by the Nehru-Gandhi family, champions the secular cause, and the Bharatiya Janata Party campaigns for what it calls Hindutva. Allowing people to express their religious faith in public ways and yet preventing religion becoming a political issue requires a very delicate balancing act anywhere in the world. This is particularly true of India with its large Hindu majority, its significant Muslim minority and its variety of other religions. Unfortunately, this balance has not been maintained in India. By making Hindutva a political issue, the BJP and the Hindu organisations to which it is affiliated have created religious tension from time to time which has led to riots. By their narrow view of secularism the Congress has given the BJP and other Hindutva advocates ammunition.

At first it appeared that the secularists were being unnecessarily alarmist about the Ramayana. The serial seemed deliberately designed to flop. Writing at the time, I pointed out that there was no suspense because the Ramayana was such a well-known story. There was no hint of sex, and the violence was reduced to electronic gimmicks acceptable for children's viewing. Describing the great battle between the armies of Rama and Ravana, I wrote: 'The protagonists never came near each other – they shot electronic arrows sparking like fireworks and sending out highly coloured rays. After protracted flights the arrows would collide in mid-air, spit at each other and then return to their quivers. When the time eventually came for someone to die, his enemy's arrows would slowly dismember him. An arm might be sliced off first – the viewer would see the whole limb flying away. Then perhaps another arm would soar into the sky, then the head, then the torso.'

The story of the Ramayana proceeded at a snail's pace and the language was archaic. There were no big stars, then considered an essential element in an Indian hit. Apart from Dara Singh, one of India's most renowned wrestlers, who played the role of Hanuman the monkey god, the actors were previously unknown. But in spite of these apparent weaknesses, the serial was a huge success. Its popularity became legendary. Trains made unscheduled halts at stations where television was installed. Newly appointed government ministers put off their swearing-in ceremonies so as not to miss an episode even though their astrologers had told them the date and time originally chosen was highly auspicious. A bride delayed her appearance at her wedding to watch the Ramayana. No taxis were available at our local stand on Sunday mornings because all the drivers were inside our office, watching the programme.

Discussing the Ramayana twenty years later with Moti Sagar, one of its co-directors, he admitted that the production had lacked a certain reality. 'For example,' he said, 'nowadays when you see someone flying in one of our serials you do think they are flying. In the original serial Hanuman just went across the screen against a blue background lying flat on his stomach with one leg lifted.'

'What about the language?' I asked.

'The language has been adapted to some extent as well. For today's viewership it needs to be simpler. But it still has to have a classical flavour.'

So what was the key to the huge success of the Ramayana? Some years ago Moti's father, the late Ramanand Sagar, chief producer and scriptwriter of the Ramayana serial, told me he believed that he had been chosen by the monkey god Hanuman himself to tell the story of his exploits in the rescue of Rama's wife Sita. Therefore he attributed the success of the serial entirely to Hanuman, Rama's lieutenant.

Moti Sagar believed the key to success was the power of myth. 'I think myth has a tremendous power in India,' he told me. 'The god Krishna has said, "Believe that I am God and don't worry." That belief – it's OK, God is there – has gained so much support, and of course people believe Rama is God, so the Ramayana assures them all is OK. There perhaps in some ways is the reason for the success of the Ramayana and the continuing success of religious epics on television.'

I had argued that protesting against the televising of a great national epic was taking secularism too far. I certainly didn't find Hindu nationalism spreading amongst our taxi drivers. But I began to have my doubts when the right-wing Hindu nationalist Bharatiya Janata Party, the BJP, launched a nationwide movement in the name of Rama. The movement's aim was to destroy a mosque in Ayodhya, and replace it with a temple. Many Hindus believed the mosque stood on the site of Rama's birth. The BJP and the Hindu organisations affiliated with it also maintained that a Hindu temple had stood on that site but it had been destroyed by the Mughal Emperor Babur.

To whip up fervour for the Rama Temple, in 1990 Lal Krishan Advani, one of the two most important BJP leaders, set out on a *yatra*, a political pilgrimage, from the Somnath Temple on the west coast to Ayodhya in the northern state of Uttar Pradesh. Wherever Advani went, crowds flocked to see him standing in a vehicle got up to look like the chariot popular art portrays as Rama's. In his speeches Advani poured scorn on the pseudo-secularists, as he called them, who were opposing the Rama Temple. The whole country was in turmoil, with riots breaking out in several places, although Advani always maintains there was no violence in the places he visited.

The 'chariot' was eventually stopped by Lalu Prasad Yadav, then the Chief Minister of the state of Bihar. But the arrest of Advani only heightened the fervour that his *yatra* had created. Supporters of the temple movement from all over India poured into Ayodhya. The Chief

Minister of Uttar Pradesh ordered his police to arrest anyone entering the state from elsewhere in India but it was too late. Large numbers of *kar sevaks*, or volunteers to serve the temple, perhaps as many as 70,000, had already reached Ayodhya. One morning they formed a human battering ram and attempted to force their way through the police defences to attack the mosque. Some succeeded but were chased away before they could do much damage. But the *kar sevaks* continued to fight the police for three days. The violence spread to other towns in Uttar Pradesh.

In 1992 there was a second, and this time successful, attack on the mosque. Hindu extremists were allowed to gather in Ayodhya for what the BJP had assured the government would only be a ceremonial start to the construction of the temple. The government had not given permission for the actual construction of the temple to start nor, of course, for the mosque to be touched. But in spite of the BJP's commitment to maintain the mosque intact, the crowds broke through the police cordons surrounding it and tore the structure down. Riots broke out again in many different parts of India. There were widespread fears that secularism was in danger of being overwhelmed by a militant and nationalist Hinduism centred on the figure of Rama.

Throughout the temple movement Rama was presented as the epitome of a Hindu warrior. BJP leaders inflamed their supporters by describing the mosque as a symbol of Hindu slavery, and called on Hindus to imitate the valour of Rama, and avenge what they described as an insult to him. Many scholars linked the rise of this fervent Hinduism to the Ramayana serial and to the television version of the other great Indian epic, the Mahabharata, which followed it. In his book *The Hindu Nationalist Movement and Indian Politics*, the historian Christophe Jaffrelot says, 'These adaptations of the sacred epics tended to create a national Hinduism.' He also quotes the American scholar Lloyd Rudolph as suggesting that the serials were 'playing a leading role in creating a national Hindu identity, a form of group consciousness that has not hitherto existed'. Leaders of the Rama Temple movement agreed with the scholars on the role of the Ramayana serial. Ashok Singhal, the President of the Vishwa Hindu Parishad or World Hindu Council affiliated to the BJP, said, 'The Ramayana has done a great service to our movement.'

Perhaps, then, I was wrong to defend the televising of the Ramayana. But maybe those who warned that secularism was in danger were also being unduly alarmist. Secularism has survived and yet Hinduism is far more prominent on television nowadays. The monopoly of the government-controlled television broadcaster was one of the monopolies broken early in the era of reform. As a result private sector television channels have proliferated. Viewers now have a choice of over four hundred different channels, some international but mostly Indian. Entertainment channels broadcast the Hindu epics and stories from Hindu mythology, and there are several faith channels which teach non-stop Hinduism.

In this multitude of channels the Sagar family have found a sizeable market for their genre of television epics. When I spoke to Moti Sagar, his company was mass-producing material to fill as many as eighteen slots every week. Episodes were being edited up to the last moment and only reached their broadcasters on the day of transmission. Moti Sagar told me, 'There have been two hundred and seventy episodes of just one epic, the story of the God Krishna, and it is still running. Let's see how many more there are to come.'

Moti Sagar went on to explain that he had to be very careful with Krishna because of the stories about him as a very attractive young man. 'I cannot afford to offend Hindu society,' Moti Sagar said. 'If I show Krishna doing things a Hindu God would never do I will face a big problem. We couldn't show anything naughty, not any touching at all in the episode when all the gopis or milkmaids fell in love with Krishna and he stole their clothes while they were bathing. So what did we do? We put an image of the Lord Krishna inside each gopi.'

The Sagars have also made series about the lives of two of the most prominent recent Hindu gurus. But there has been no secular backlash against any of these serials.

What is even more surprising is that there has been so little criticism of the Hindu preachers who have flourished on television since the airwaves were opened up. Unlike Moti, they directly propagate Hinduism. On the eve of the Hindu festival of Dhanteras I watched a young woman soberly dressed in a blue and grey sari discussing with an elderly Acharya the significance of the festival and how it should be celebrated. Acharya is a title given usually to priests and pandits who are particularly renowned for their learning. They were appearing on a channel called Hamar TV that broadcasts in the North Indian regional language of Bhojpuri.

I never discovered the Acharya's name because the young woman only referred to him reverentially as Acharya-ji. Clad in a saffron kurta with a red and gold scarf draped over his shoulders and a long necklace of sacred beads round his neck, the Acharya spoke with the authority of someone who knows exactly how things should be done and the cadenced tones of a reciter of Sanskrit texts. He explained that Dhanteras was the Vaid or Doctor of the Gods, and so his festival was the proper time to start a course of medical treatment. At the same time he advised that Yamraj, the God of Death, should be worshipped. But because it was inadvisable to call Death into your house worshippers were told to go to the south side of a crossroads, light lamps there, and pray for a long life. Those who could afford to burn ghee or clarified butter in their lamps were encouraged to do so, but the Acharya said it was all right for the less well off to use cheaper oils. There was no end in sight to the Acharya's advice so, during the next burst of advertisements, I decided to channel-surf.

I found a more commercial side to 'Hindu' television on the Jagran channel of Zee TV, one of the original and most successful independent television companies. *Jagran* in Hindi means wakefulness, and in modern Hinduism *Jagrans* are held to arouse Hindu zeal. This evening a young man with a flowing black beard was selling amulets in the form of medallions embossed with the image of a five-faced Hanuman. The young man urged women to make sure they used the amulets to protect their husbands and children when they went out of the house. To remind them how powerful the monkey god was, he recited some verses from the Hanuman Chalisa, a very popular prayer consisting of forty verses praising the god and relating the miraculous acts he had performed.

Then, to bring listeners down to earth again, a woman appeared on screen standing at a table peeling potatoes, watched by visitors. She told them, 'Nowadays people don't believe in *nazar* – the evil eye – but when my child got ill I showed him to all manner of doctors and he didn't get better, I couldn't stand it any more. So I took refuge in Hindu *dharma* and this medallion. My son immediately recovered, and has never had another day of illness. Now the whole family takes refuge in Hanuman.' Finally came the tele-shopping hard sell including the toll-free telephone numbers to ring to buy the amulet.

Hindu television has made many of the preachers who appear on it regularly national figures with vast followings. One of the best known is Swami Ram Dev, a comparatively young yoga teacher originally from Haryana, the state next to Delhi. When Gilly and I visited him in the yoga centre he has built just outside the holy city of Haridwar, where the sacred river Ganges flows from the mountains into the plains, we found him sitting on a stage in a building resembling a vast aircraft hangar. We were told it occupied two hundred thousand square feet. The sides were open but as it was mid-winter they had been covered with plastic sheeting to keep out the cold. A long line of men and women were filing slowly past the Swami, having their *darshan* of him.

Darshan means seeing. Perhaps a better translation would be 'getting a sight of', because a *darshan* is a powerful experience, and one specially sought out. People will go to great lengths to have a *darshan* of a deity, or indeed of a person considered to be great. Hindus will stand awestruck in front of the image of a god or goddess. Overcome by devotion they submit to the deity. In return many Hindus believe the eyes they are looking into will confer not just benefits but power on them.

Having a *darshan* of a great person is more than just sightseeing, or celebrity-spotting. Time and again I have noticed at political rallies that the audience will sit for hours in the sun waiting for the star speaker to turn up and greet them. Then some will leave without waiting to hear what the speaker has to say. They've had what they came for, their *darshan*. They have been blessed.

More than five thousand people had already filed past Swami Ram Dev that day, and there was still a line of people waiting. He had a brief word with some as they came up to him and slapped others jovially on the back. All those having a *darshan* were potential yoga teachers who had come for a training course. A headmaster told me two thousand five hundred people had come from his state, Himachal Pradesh, in the western Himalayas. When I asked what the attraction of Swami Ram Dev was he replied, 'We were always interested in yoga but when we saw him on the television we were inspired because he was building the national character. Now we have seen to it that the government has promised yoga will become a compulsory subject in our state and it has already desig-nated land to build a yoga centre.'

We were back in the hangar at four-thirty the following morning to learn about Swami's nation building by taking part in his daily yoga class – to be broadcast live on the Aastha television channel. Aastha, meaning 'Faith', is controlled by his trust. The temperature was hovering around zero and there was no heating. Like many in the audience, we were swaddled in shawls and several layers of sweaters, with woollen hats and thermal underwear as additional protection against the cold. The Swami was just wearing his trademark saffron silk lungi, a cloth tied round his waist and extending to his ankles, and a thin saffron silk shawl wrapped round his body. A couple from the audience that filled the hangar presented him with an overcoat, cut in the Himachal Pradesh style, along with a hat not unlike the hats worn by another mountain people, the Swiss. They had woven the cloth themselves in their own village. Swamiji wrapped the coat round himself and donned the hat, explaining at the same time, 'It's one of the habits of a Swami not to feel the cold. We can control our bodies so that we don't need heating in the winter or air-conditioning in the summer. You see then that I don't need the coat and I wouldn't normally accept it but because these good people have woven it themselves I will.'

Swamiji began by leading the audience in uttering *Om*, the sound which represents the divine in Hinduism. High notes of a flute fluttered above the long-drawn-out, low monotone. A prayer which ended with shanti, shanti, shanti, peace, peace, peace, followed. Then Swamiji addressed his audience, both those with us in the hangar and those viewing on their television sets. He told us that Bhagwan, or God, had made him a medium to speak his word and do his work, explained that he worked eighteen hours a day, and called on everyone else to do their work properly. Bemoaning the present state of India, he asked why there was such a shortage of water, electricity and roads, attacked the corruption of the political leadership, and claimed the country had the potential to be a great nation within one year if only people would foreswear corruption. Swamiji spoke as demagogues do with plenty of crescendos. One crescendo ended on the exhortation, 'Before you go to sleep count what you have done for the nation.' The discourse finished with the vast audience roaring, '*Bharat Mata ki Jai!*' – Long live Mother India!

After calm had been restored Swami announced that he would now show us some yoga – starting, he said, with Yogic Jogging. The audience burst into laughter as they imitated the Swami leaping up and down, his arms flailing in all directions, his hat falling over his eyes. We did our best to join in, hampered by all the layers of clothing we were wearing. Then came a variety of what I call press-ups, lying tummy down on the floor and then pressing the body up with the hands. They seemed to leave even the Swami a bit breathless, but just in front of me a white-haired man who can't have been less than seventy continued bobbing up and down long after Swami had stopped. Eventually the exercises became more static.

To demonstrate the importance of breathing in yoga, Swami, who had by this time shed his coat, opened his shawl, and showed us his bare torso. First he extended his stomach into a bloated belly. Then he took a deep breath, withdrawing his tummy until it almost touched his backbone, and wiggled his belly button around in the cavity which formed. At the next stage in the long lesson the class became something like a Christian Charismatic Service, with members of the audience coming forward to relate the miraculous cures Swami Ram Dev's yoga had achieved for them.

After sitting cross-legged on the ground for more than two hours all my joints were aching, and the cold had got to my bladder. The television transmission was still continuing and as I was sitting right in the front there was no way I could sneak out unnoticed, so I had to accept the humiliation of walking out in front of that audience of thousands and, for all I knew, in front of the television audience too.

That afternoon we were taken to meet Swamiji in his flat at the top of the guesthouse where we were staying. The Swami entered, dressed still in his flimsy saffron garments, and sat on an ornate throne. There were one or two stray grey hairs in his black beard but other than that there was no sign of ageing. I estimated he must have been in his thirties.

Although I had come to interview the Swami it soon became apparent that he intended to interview me. A television crew was summoned and the Swami gave them directions about the 'two shots' and 'three shots' he wanted. He told us he had three crews permanently resident in his yoga centre. After scribbling some notes on my background and career he turned to the camera and introduced me with the spontaneity of a professional television presenter.

The Swami was fascinated by the fact that I had been born in Calcutta. 'You are the first person I have met who is white and who was born here – not just you but your forefathers too,' he said. Swamiji only speaks in Indian languages so we spoke in Hindi, which also surprised him apparently because he went on to say with wonder, 'Both of you speak Hindi and you are from the West. Very few people from there speak Hindi but very many Indians speak English.'

After going into the details of my career, the Swami eventually said, 'Now it's your turn.'

I first asked him about his life before he became a Swami. He told me tradition did not allow a Swami to discuss his early life but then went on to tell me about his childhood in a Haryana village as the son of illiterate parents. 'People know about this,' he said. 'Because there have been controversies about me they have gone to my village and found out.'

Apparently Swamiji had been a weak child until he learnt yoga by watching others. He left school at fifteen wanting to be 'a great man' and knowing that he would never marry. He was initiated in one of India's ascetic orders on the bank of the Ganges and taught in *gurukuls*, where students are instructed in the traditional Indian system of education. After spending time in the Himalayas living austerely in caves, he set up a trust to teach yoga.

'Was that easy?' I asked,

'At first five or ten people came, and then one hundred to two hundred, then I got my break.' Break is one of those English words that has gone into

Hindi but pronounced with a very heavy accent it confused me. Swami said impatiently, 'bar...ek, bar...ek, bar...ek', until I got the meaning.

The Swami's break was a twenty-minute slot to teach yoga on one of the 'god' channels. 'What a reaction I got!' he exclaimed. 'Within one to two months people started coming to me. Then I did a programme in Delhi and ten thousand people came. That was 2003. It started my relationship with Aastha channel and I got a daily slot. Now I appear for two and a half hours every morning on Aastha and in the evening too. I appear on other channels as well.'

'How on earth do you manage to spend so much time on television?' I asked.

Swamiji laughed, 'I have one thousand three hundred hours of recorded programming.'

'So you are the television Swami.'

'No, I am Swami Ram Dev,' he replied, laughing again.

Both Gilly and I had come to Haridwar influenced by the prejudice of the elite of Delhi against television godmen, and indeed against all manifestations of popular Hinduism. But we were won over by the Swami's childlike enthusiasm and his sense of humour. He never missed a chance to have a laugh.

I was particularly interested in Swamiji's views on those who would consider him communal. He said, 'It is a result of ignorance to say that religion is communal. I am connected with everyone who is a good person. I am connected to Muslims, to Christians, to Buddhists, to Sikhs, to Jains. I was invited to Deoband.' Deoband is the best-known Islamic seminary in India.

Swamiji maintained that no one accused him of being communal. When I suggested that twenty years ago people would certainly have done and there would have been very strong criticism of his appearing on television, he replied, 'There is much difference now. Hindus and Muslims have come closer to each other, otherwise why would they call me to Deoband? They called me because they know we are all one, that we all come from the same ancestors. I tell everyone that we must not think this is good, this is bad, this is ignorance, we mustn't speak wrong of anyone's religion, this is the meaning of secularism.'

It is impossible to confirm the Swami's claim that over two million people attend his yoga camps every year, or that he is seen by two hundred and fifty million television viewers. But he also claims that millions of people are 'offering their services and wealth' to his trust. There certainly is some evidence to support that. The Swami told us that he had no money, no land, no house, no wife. But during the few years that he has been appearing on television a trust he has set up has built two campuses at his yoga centre and they include an ayurvedic hospital and a university.

We were also taken to see a health village just opened where naturopathy and yoga healing are practised. Among the therapies available are colonic irrigation, mud bath treatments, bathing in a whirlpool, acupuncture and magnet therapy. Among the prescriptions for good health I saw were: 'Abdomen has no teeth, chew well, achieve mental performance and get fit' and 'Twice loudly laugh and seven hundred smiles a day keep doctors, diseases and drugs away'. We met Dr Nagendra Niraj, the chief medical officer, who certainly practised plentiful smiling and a lot of laughing too. 'A smile is a divine gift,' he told us.

Television has also made Swamiji a big businessman, or rather I should say has turned his trust into a big business enterprise. It has been manufacturing ayurvedic medicines for some time now, but only a week before we arrived a vast new factory was inaugurated in what the trust has called a 'Food and Herbal Park' of two hundred and fifty acres. Factory workers standing on both sides of a production line sifted stalks and leaves from tart green amla berries as they passed on their way to a giant crusher that was capable of producing twenty thousand kilograms of juice per hour.

The engineer in charge, Sukvinder Malhotra, who had worked in Germany and the Middle East, as well as India, told me that within weeks the factory was expected to begin extracting juice from other fruit and vegetables, including apples and mangoes, cucumber and bitter gourd. This was only the start of it. Candy, detergents, body oil, as well as soap were all to be manufactured. There was to be a flour mill, and extracts of herbs were to be prepared. As we tramped up and down the long sheds of the factory Malhotra told us proudly, 'All the machinery will be the latest design and we will work to the highest standards of hygiene. We plan to export, and have applied for the approval of the US's Food and Drug Administration. We are being very careful about the environment too, treating all the effluent and using bio waste as fuel.'

'How many people are going to work here?' I asked.

'That's one of the beauties of what we are doing,' he replied. 'We will employ some six thousand people and many will come from the immediate locality.'

When I asked what the Swami's role in all this was, Malhotra said, 'Our brand ambassador of course,' and he showed us some packaging with the familiar black-bearded face prominent on it.

Swami Ram Dev insists that he has no stake in the Food and Herbal Park, and maintains its profits will be spent on social service, including free accommodation and tuition, but it is a combination of the draw of Swami's message and the power of television which has attracted all investment in the project. The trust land alone, apparently financed by donations, must be worth a large fortune.

Sants or saints, Hindu holy men, were prominent in the Ayodhya movement. At its height they were seen almost daily on television, but in news bulletins not on their own programmes. They were political prelates, loyal to the BJP, and considered valuable assets because of their following. But the popularity of the Swamis, Acharyas, and other Hindu television stars, who do not preach politics, has eclipsed the BJP's sants, and that might be one reason why the Rama Temple issue is dormant and there has been no other Hindutva issue to follow it. Of course there is always the possibility that one of the television Swamis might enter politics, but then that would be on their terms, not the BJP's. Swami Ram Dev seems to be ambivalent on this. He told us that he had nothing to do with politics. But now he's considering forming a political party and he has taken a prominent role in a national anti-corruption campaign.

The BJP, and the World Hindu Council to which the political *sants* belong, were both spawned by the Rashtriya Swayamsevak Sangh, or National Volunteer Corps, normally known as the RSS. Its cadres are dedicated to promoting Hindutva, or a Hindu India, and its volunteers used to provide the workforce for the BJP. Many of the stormtroopers who pulled down the mosque in Ayodhya were from the RSS affiliated organisations too. When I suggested to the RSS spokesman Ram Madhav that the television *sants* were outshining his, he disagreed.

'There is no question of rivalry, or outshining, or anything like that,' he said firmly. 'We have different roles. We emphasise society, they emphasise the spiritual side of life. We don't have separate cultures. They teach, we train; we are the application part. We accept that these people like Ram Dev are gurus and have the right to interpret Hinduism. So there is no conflict with them.'

'So you are both on the same side, so to speak?'

'Well, I wouldn't exactly say that. Many of those who don't like our Hinduism do like "new-age" and they see the television Hinduism as new-age. So there are many followers of men like Ram Dev who are not in tune with the RSS, but of course there are many who are.'

The spokesman has devoted his whole life to the RSS. At the age of twenty-eight he became a *pracharak*, which literally means a preacher but is in fact more of an organiser. Pracharaks do not marry, they work full time but get no salary. Ram Madhav has no home either but lives in his office. A *pracharak*'s lifestyle commands respect in a country that reveres austerity and self-sacrifice. But unlike the *sants* and *sadhus*, *pracharaks* do not wear any distinctive clothes. Ram Madhav wore a striped kurta, cotton trousers, and sandals. He sported a neat moustache instead of the flowing beard which is one of the hallmarks of a traditional holy man.

There have been several reports suggesting that membership of the RSS is on the decline and that television with its 'god-men' is one reason for the decline. Ram Madhav didn't accept that either.

'We have been told since the nineties that we are on the decline, so we should have disappeared altogether by now but we haven't. This year we have collected signatures from thirty thousand villages for our Protect the Cow campaign. The *sants* have been roped in for this. I do admit in urban areas there is a change in lifestyle and that does affect all organisations, but,' he hurriedly added, 'we still have some fifty thousand *shakhas*, so there is no sign of the RSS fading away.' A *shakha* is a cadre of RSS volunteers directed by a *pracharak*.

'But if your influence is not on the decline and *sants* who are as popular as Baba Ram Dev are really on your side, why aren't the BJP's Hindu issues taking off?'

'Well, that may be because we stopped asking our RSS cadres to campaign for the BJP because we didn't want to be closely identified with one party, or thought of as a political organisation. People of different political persuasions come to our village meetings and we want them to be there and feel welcome. But I think the issues we raise, the issues which so anger us and the people we call the pseudo-secularists are still alive – issues like Hindutva.'

'The head of the RSS has recently been very publicly involved in the BJP's selection of a new leader so how can you say you are not a political organisation?'

'He was only advising, not actively choosing,' the spokesman retorted.

*

When I met Ram Madhav in 2009 the BJP had recently lost its second consecutive general election and was embroiled in a leadership crisis and a dispute over the way ahead. The ideological crisis was caused by the feeling amongst one section of the party that Hindutva had lost its sheen; that the party should now widen its appeal by promoting itself as a right-wing, but not particularly Hindu, alternative to the Congress.

Lal Krishan Advani, the politician whose journey across India had raised the temperature of the Rama Temple movement to boiling point, had been the BJP's candidate to be Prime Minister in the election they had just lost. He was now at the centre of the leadership crisis.

Advani is a sprightly octogenarian whose energetic campaigning in the last election would have exhausted men twenty years younger. I once asked him what was the secret of his good health and energy and he replied, 'I think it's perhaps because I don't eat very much.' When I asked whether he did yoga or other exercises he replied, 'No, nothing like that.'

For the last forty years he and the BJP's former Prime Minister, Atal Bihari Vajpayee, had formed a partnership at the top of the BJP. Vajpayee was the soft face of the party. He cultivated an image that would appeal to a much wider section of the electorate than those who were attracted by Hindutva. Advani played the role of the hardliner who kept the Hindutva vote intact.

Perhaps surprisingly he has never been a particularly observant Hindu. He was brought up in what is now the Pakistani province of Sindh and there most Hindus, including his parents, were followers of Guru Nanak, the founder of the Sikh religion. Many Hindus in Sindh were so broad-minded that they respected Sufism and paid homage to Sufi saints at their shrines. Advani himself was educated at a Christian school and in his autobiography he wrote: 'My school's reputation, the loving and nurturing by its teachers, its architectural beauty and its quiet environs – all these made me proud to belong to St Patrick's.'

When I went to see Advani in his official bungalow in Delhi he had still not made up his mind whether to step down from the leadership of the parliamentary party. I asked him first about the election – whether he felt it showed that the party's Hindutva agenda was too narrow, that it didn't appeal to a wide enough section of the electorate.

'It might be better for us to talk of Bharatiyata, which is a word more like Indian-ness,' he said. 'But the point is that Hindutva is not the name of a religion. It is more a way of life in India which can be regarded as Indian culture. Do you know that the Archbishop of Hyderabad told me he could support our cultural nationalism?'

'But wouldn't you agree that your party's support for Hindutva has created an allergy towards Hinduism?'

'I regard this allergy towards Hinduism as stemming from the concern for vote bank politics. That is pandering to the minorities, particularly the Muslims to create a vote bank, telling them they are in danger from the Hindu majority. This has created what I have called pseudo-secularism, which has nothing to do with traditional Indian secularism. You know that Hinduism is so varied that you can't actually appeal to Hindus in the name of religion, no matter what they say about my politics. But vote bank politicians do appeal to minorities like Muslims and Christians in the name of their religions because their religions are not varied.'

When I suggested to Advani that his Rama *yatra* and the whole Rama Temple movement was an attempt to build up a Hindu vote bank, using religion to appeal to Hindus, he made the rather strange claim that the support he received showed the Temple movement was secular, saying: 'The response to the *yatra* made an impact on many intellectuals who began to understand the deep feelings of Indians and realise that the Rama Temple movement was secular. I said to myself for the first time I have been able to communicate that when we talk of Hindutva, or project the party's viewpoint, we are not being communal. Those who criticise us for being communal are pseudo-secular. The proof is many intellectuals were converted to Hindutva by the *yatra*.'

I pointed out that leaders of the World Hindu Council and other organisations affiliated to the RSS and identified with the BJP certainly did insult Muslims and Christians in their speeches. Advani couldn't deny that, but he went on to say, 'It's not the RSS point of view nor the BJP's. I have told those leaders, "You talk a language which may only justify Islamic fundamentalism. Please don't."'

Eventually I came back to the word 'Bharatiyata' which Advani had suggested might replace Hindutva in the BJP's vocabulary, and suggested this meant he felt the party should have an agenda with a wider appeal than Hindutva.

He shot back angrily, which was rare for him, 'What agenda? Let me tell you that in China do they say that we have put aside the Marxist agenda? They can do what they want and still say they are Marxists although they are not. Nobody says they have a new agenda or they have given up their old agenda. One keeps on evolving. It is evolution. All I've said to you is evolution. It will continue to be. There has to be diversity and change in India.'

'So now is there to be further evolution?'

'Yes, always.'

One of those whose views of secularism were changed by Advani's *yatra* was Swapan Dasgupta, a journalist with a doctorate in History from London University. In recent years he had come very close to the BJP leadership but he held no official position. Advani had told me that Swapan had been 'converted' by the Rama *yatra*. When I put that to Swapan he smiled and said, 'I wouldn't exactly say converted. But when I saw the *yatra* in Udaipur, the phenomenal mobilisation of people, the emotional raw energy, it did overcome me. You have to realise that even before Advani took up the Rama issue there was a critique of secularism in some people's minds. There was a feeling that there were double standards, and that Hindus were not being given a stake in the country.

On the other hand there was the enormous degree of condescension of the left liberal historians with their claim to modernity. They dismissed those who recognised that one of the pillars of India is its Hindu inheritance as country bumpkins. Then there was the political hypocrisy of the Congress Party. You must remember the Shah Bano case, a preposterous denial of human rights to acquire a vote bank.'

Shah Bano was a Muslim woman who had been divorced and appealed to the courts for maintenance. Her former husband contended that under Islamic law paying her maintenance for three months was sufficient. The courts upheld Shah Bano's right to maintenance but the government, headed by Rajiv Gandhi, overturned that verdict by passing a bill under which responsibility for maintaining Shah Bano fell on her relatives not on her former husband.

When I asked Swapan why the debate over secularism had gone off the boil he put it down to a new-found self-confidence amongst Hindus: 'In the late eighties Hindus saw themselves as victims, they felt besieged and they also saw their country being left behind globally. Socialism had clearly come to a dead end, and India seemed to be going nowhere. Now Hindus no longer feel beleaguered and there is a cocksure, irrational exuberance about the economic progress we are now making, a feeling we have shown our potential, an excitement at our global exposure.'

'But why have the secularists apparently quietened down too? Why has there been no reaction to the propagation of Hinduism on television?'

'I think that within the Congress Party there has been a greater realisation that secular fundamentalism is an absurd project. If you are over-secular you invite a reaction. If you insist on denying the role of Hinduism in Indian culture you propel Hindus in the opposite direction.'

After the Ayodhya mosque was pulled down there was turmoil within the Congress Party. Arjun Singh, one of the most senior members of the party, led what he himself calls a rebellion against the Prime Minister, Narasimha Rao, for his failure to prevent the attack on the mosque. The subtext of the rebellion portrayed Narasimha Rao as sympathetic towards the Hindu cause.

Just a few months before he died, I went to see Arjun Singh to ask him whether he agreed that the shouting match between secularists and those they accused of being communal had at least declined by several decibels. He had been a cabinet minister in the last government but Sonia Gandhi had excluded him this time. Nonetheless Arjun Singh still retained his prestigious government bungalow in Lutyens' Delhi.

Greeting Arjun Singh, I said, 'It's like the old times when I used to come to you as a political reporter.'

Having just turned eighty, the veteran politician said ruefully, 'Yes, but then I used to get up to greet you; now sadly I can't.' He was sitting in a wheelchair wearing a safari suit. Unlike many other politicians, he didn't think it was necessary to wear traditional handspun clothes to demonstrate his patriotism.

Going back to the period that followed the demolition of the mosque at Ayodhya, I asked him why he had not rebelled openly against Narasimha Rao. He replied very firmly, 'I did rebel,' then after pausing to think he added: 'I didn't want to rebel violently because I was conscious of the fact that ultimately this may harm the party.'

'But you did have the ambition to be Prime Minister?'

'Yes, if you are in politics what is wrong with wanting to get to the top just as you want to get to the top in any other profession?'

'Do you remember me saying you reminded me of a man trying to shin up a greasy pole and time and again slipping down just as he is about to reach the top?'

He laughed. 'No, I don't, but I must put that in my autobiography.'

When we came on to the subject of secularism Arjun Singh reflected: 'It has always been the essence of Hinduism to separate the temporal from the religious. Take Rama himself. His *dharma*, or duty, was to protect the people no matter what they believed in. When belief and politics get mixed, that is where the trouble starts.'

'But that is just what your party is always warning against, communalism as it is called in India, so much so that anyone who talked of Hinduism was likely to be accused of communalism by you. Twenty years ago if you'd had *sadhus* on television preaching Hinduism, having national channels devoted entirely to that as well, you and your party would have been up in arms about it, so why this silence?'

'I believe, hopefully, that the action of people reflects the times – whether they are turbulent and violent or not. The early tradition of India, our natural tradition, that is, being able to keep religion and politics separate, went into decline because of turbulent times. A different psychology developed. Now the idea that India has come into its own takes us very much back to the early tradition.'

At this stage in our conversation a servant in white uniform brought in a small silver bowl and Arjun Singh sipped from it. I thought it was perhaps medicine, but Arjun Singh explained that his wife was in her prayer hall and had sent him a bowl containing water from the Ganges and tulsi leaves. Tulsi is a type of basil considered sacred.

After completing the short ritual, Arjun Singh smiled and said, 'So you see I am a Hindu but as you know I do keep my politics separate from my religion. It is possible.'

Getting back to the main point, I asked, 'If the BJP tried another Ayodhya would they fail?'

'That's why they are going into decline. They thought they could do it again but they have failed time and time again.'

'So why do the Congress continue to harp on and on about communalism?'

To my surprise Arjun Singh, who had been one of the loudest voices in the Congress Party condemning communalism said, 'I don't think it is the correct thing to do. They should get out of this habit and not harp on about communalism.'

So has the final whistle been blown in the secular versus communal shouting match which has dominated Indian politics? It cannot be said that there have been no major outbreaks of communal violence since Ayodhya and the riots that followed the destruction of the mosque. In 1992, there were vicious anti-Muslim riots in Gujarat after a compartment of a train carrying, amongst others, activists of one of the RSS organisations was set on fire. The BJP government in Gujarat, which was fiercely criticised for not taking action to protect Muslims, admits that nearly one thousand people were killed; others put the figure far higher. In 2008 some twenty-five thousand Christians were forced to flee their houses when they were attacked by Hindus in the eastern state of Orissa. Nevertheless, it does seem that prominent leaders on both sides feel the shouting match should come to an end.

Although much of the steam seems to have gone out of the secular versus communal issue, the Congress Party shows no sign of following Arjun Singh's advice. They still lose no opportunity to accuse the BJP of communalism while shouting from the housetops about their secularism. Should other opportunities to stir up Hindu passions come along, should for instance there be repeats of terrorist attacks like the attacks on Bombay in November 2008, or the attack on Parliament in 2002, will the BJP revert to hardline Hindutva again? If India's economic progress falters will the self-confidence Swapan Dasgupta has noticed evaporate? And if any government tackles the economic and social deprivation of the Muslim community, might that not arouse Hindu jealousy? Has India, as Arjun Singh suggested, reverted to the old culture where religion and politics were naturally separate, or could there be a return to tumultuous times?

5 | BUILDING COMMUNITIES

Although religious issues seem to be in abeyance in India at least for the present, and hopefully for a lot longer, the issue of delivery, of governments that work and governments that do not work, is certainly not. Anyone who watches Mumbai, or Bollywood, movies will notice how that industry has picked up on Indians' awareness that all is not well when it comes to governance. There have been a series of satirical films mocking politicians, civil servants and sometimes journalists.

One of the most entertaining is *Well done, Abba!*, a satire on the functioning of government in rural areas, made by one of India's most talented and respected directors, Shyam Benegal. In one scene a father and daughter arrive at a rural police station to report an unusual theft. Their well has been stolen.

'Your what?' shouts the police inspector. 'This is a police station, not a lunatic asylum! A well is *immovable* property! It cannot walk from one place to another.'

'Sir,' the girl says firmly, 'don't you know that the stars, the earth and moon are in constant movement, and if they can move, why not a well? Ours has been stolen and we can prove it!' She produces an immaculate file filled with papers showing that every step in the digging of the well, provided free as one of the government's schemes for the poor, has been followed to the letter. There are all the receipts, the inspection reports of the engineer, photographs of construction, and the written statement of the head of the village council who had visited the well and tasted the water, which was, she said, clear and exceedingly sweet.

The police are forced to investigate and it comes to light that not only the father and daughter's well, but all the wells built under the scheme have been 'stolen'. Villagers take to the streets in protest shouting, 'Our wells are being stolen, and the police is sleeping!' The issue turns into a political storm, debated in the Assembly, and threatening the Minister's position.

Well done, Abba! is highly entertaining not only because the actors' timing is perfect but because the storyline is so close to the truth. Although all the wells existed on paper not one had been dug because at each stage in the bureaucratic paperchase the bureaucrats had to be paid to move the file, and so in the end there was no money left for the wells. What is known in corrupt bureaucratic parlance as 'ghost works' were created.

The story of *Well done, Abba!* is an example of the kind of misgovernance the American academic Lant Pritchett had in mind when he wrote a paper in 2008 entitled 'Is India a Flailing State? Detours on the Four Lane Highway to Modernization'. In my view the answer to that question is yes, India is flailing because, as Pritchett says, 'The capability of the Indian state to implement programmes and policies is weak – and in many domains it is not obvious it is improving. In police, tax collection, education, health, power, water supply – in nearly every routine service – there is rampant absenteeism, indifference, incompetence and corruption.'

Nowhere is it more obvious that India is a flailing state than in the countryside where Shyam Benegal set his film and the majority of Indians still live; nowhere is Lant Pritchett's diagnosis that India's 'head is no longer reliably connected via nerves and sinews to its own limbs' more accurate. The head, which is the Indian state, that is the central and the state governments, has poured trillions of rupees into the countryside to deliver development. The dividends have been deeply disappointing because the state has not been able to control the limbs that are responsible for administering and spending that money.

There have been and still are numerous special schemes for improving the provision of basic necessities in rural areas such as education, health care, housing, and clean water. Described as plans, campaigns, or missions, these schemes are often named after members of the Nehru-Gandhi family, but I can't think of one that has not fallen far short of its target. The result is India's persistently poor performance in the United Nations Development Programme's Human Development Index, which I mentioned in Chapter 2: 'Caste Overturned'.

In the mid-eighties the Prime Minister Rajiv Gandhi, who had come to power after his mother had been assassinated, famously estimated that 85 per cent of development funds flowed into the pockets of corrupt officials, politicians and their allies, the contractors, and only 15 per cent reached the poor. But that level of corruption is not the only problem. There are also the problems of managing the schools, health centres, and other assets that have been created despite all that money disappearing.

Rajiv Gandhi tried to stem this flow by sending funds directly to those for whom they were intended. In 1989 he introduced a constitutional amendment under which development funds would go straight to village *panchayats*, or councils. This bypassed the state governments with their rapacious politicians and bureaucrats, and greatly increased the powers of the village councils. The bill failed to get the necessary majority in the upper house of parliament, and his government fell before he could make another attempt. The amendment that enlarged the scope of what is known as Panchayati Raj was only passed in 1992, the year after Rajiv was assassinated, and I think the outcome would have disappointed him. Corruption at the village level, collusion between the *sarpanch* or elected head of the *panchayat* and the official who is its secretary, has become an all too common feature of Panchayati Raj.

In 2004 the Congress returned to power after eight years in the wilderness. Sonia Gandhi believed the party's success was largely due to its promise to concentrate on improving the lot of the *aam aadmi*, or common man. She therefore made another attempt to deal with the problem her husband had tried to overcome by enacting the National Rural Employment

Guarantee Act, or NREGA. Under this massive scheme any unemployed person, man or woman, over the age of eighteen living in a rural area would be entitled to one hundred days of paid work in a year on development projects. NREGA funds are intended to bypass the *sarpanch* and the *panchayat* secretary and put money directly into poor villagers' purses. But villagers find there are blockages in the pipeline that delivers their wages, and corruption in the selection of the workers and the work they do.

Ever since I came back to India as an adult I have been impressed by the success some NGOs (non-governmental organisations) have in ensuring that the government doesn't flail and does deliver development in the areas where they are working. So I decided to return to Rajasthan to take a longer look at the role that one such NGO was playing in making Sonia Gandhi's effort to put money in the purses of the poor successful.

I arrived shortly after thousands of village councils across the state had met to argue over the projects that were to be taken up under NREGA. The meetings tended to be stormy because much hung on their outcome. Who was going to benefit from the work done by the villagers? Who was going to be responsible for carrying out the work? Were contractors going to have a role? These were questions involving large sums of money and considerable benefits by village standards.

I saw a video-recording of one of these meetings which wasn't just stormy: there was pandemonium for much of the time. Villagers spoke whenever they felt like it, creating a clamour in which it was almost impossible to hear what anyone was saying. Their main target was the secretary, who was sitting cross-legged on the floor in front of a low table strewn with the papers of the different development schemes villagers were proposing. One enraged villager, Kalulal Khateek, did make himself heard. Towering over the secretary he bellowed, 'This *panchayat* doesn't have any morals. The *panchayat* never listens. As for this secretary he never gets any work done. All we get is just him saying, "It will happen." The secretary is a liar.'

Ignoring all attempts to stem the flow of his tirade, Kalulal roared, 'Why isn't a more senior official than the secretary present? Only officials will listen, not this secretary. He won't give anything in writing.'

Another villager thundered, 'When the collector comes he says, "Get the work done in five days!" but the secretary does nothing!'

'Transfer the secretary!' was shouted from somewhere and Kalulal took up the cudgels against him again, asking, 'Aren't you a servant of the public? Ask people what their issues are and write them down!'

Some villagers, fed up with this rumpus, made for the door, others shouted, 'Finish it, finish it!', referring to the meeting. But the meeting continued and eventually after some negotiations things settled down a bit. Throughout all this the *sarpanch* or elected head of the village council sat with her back against the wall, the end of her sari drawn across her face, saying nothing, and making no effort to control the proceedings. The *sarpanch* was a woman from one of the tribes of Rajasthan.

Some *sarpanch* seats are reserved for tribals in an attempt to ensure that they benefit from development schemes like NREGA; that it's not just the dominant castes in villages who are the beneficiaries. There are also seats reserved for women and that is how this tribal woman came to be *sarpanch*.

Coping with all the deeply entrenched vested interests, the caste rivalries, the politics in a traditional male-dominated village, is no simple matter for a woman used to having a husband take decisions for her. Some women *sarpanches* do just that: they are merely nominees of their husbands and some opt out, letting the various groups in the village fight it out for themselves. But some women *sarpanches* do stand firmly on their own feet. I once attended a meeting called by a tribal woman who was the *sarpanch* of her village. She'd called the women of the village together to discuss the problem of drunkenness among the men. The women decided that any man who got drunk would have his head shaved to put him to shame.

NREGA is pumping unprecedented funds directly into villages, and so it's hardly surprising that deciding who should benefit from those funds generates so much heat in a largely rural state like Rajasthan. The concept has its enemies too. There are economists who believe the government can't afford the massive sums of money involved. There are sociologists, as well as economists, who believe that NREGA is just another scheme which will waste money because of the government's chronic corruption and inefficiency. There are politicians and bureaucrats who never like development funds which they don't control. But Professor Sanjay Lodha, a political scientist teaching in the southern Rajasthani city of Udaipur, has researched the impact of NREGA and he believes it is performing its prime function. He was cautious, as academics tend to be, but he did say to me, 'Of course there is some corruption but money really is reaching the people, and this has never happened before. That's why migration from villages to cities is coming down, and wages migrant labour can command are going up because there is now a shortage. At a recent meeting with the Minister for Rural Development in Udaipur the President of the Chamber of Commerce said the government's top priority should be scrapping NREGA. You can understand why, if you know what the impact of NREGA is on wages.'

In the small town of Delwara, less than an hour's drive from Udaipur, Ram Lal Khatik, the *up-pradhan* or deputy head of the *panchayat* told me, 'NREGA is a magic scheme. There's never been anything like it. The big people don't like it, but then they don't like anything unless it benefits them. That's why they are telling journalists and others to spoil NREGA by highlighting very small corruption. They don't highlight the big corruption in other schemes.'

'But surely corruption is a problem in NREGA?' I asked.

Slim and smartly dressed, with that fashionable designer stubble which verges on a beard, and clearly a young man who had learnt to fight his corner, Ram Lal Khatik wasn't going to let me get away with that. He shot back, 'Only some selfish people who put down false names of people. But why do people try to spoil NREGA by talking so much about corruption there? Yes, a *panchayat* secretary was caught ten days ago claiming that thirty people had worked when only five had but, as I say, he was caught. At least in NREGA there is a social audit and corrupt people like this man are caught. I want to know why there is no social audit in other government development schemes.'

One of the most common ways that those who administer rural development schemes make money is by fiddling muster rolls, lists of people who have worked on projects and are therefore entitled to be paid. Those who draw up the muster rolls include fictitious names, names of villagers who have moved away, of villagers who have died, or even villagers who never existed, and pocket the wages of these 'ghost workers'.

In a book called *Making Democracy Work*, which has been widely read by the leaders of Indian NGOs, Robert D. Putnam studied the reasons why regional governments in north Italy functioned well and the north had flourished, while southern governments were lethargic and the south lagged far behind. The government office he describes in Bari, the capital of the Puglia region, could well be an Indian government office and its staff Indian officials:

In the dingy ante-room loll several indolent functionaries, though they are likely to be present only an hour or two each day and to be unresponsive even then. The persistent visitor might discover that in the office beyond stand only ghostly rows of empty desks. One mayor, frustrated at his inability to get action from the region's bureaucrats, exploded to us, 'They don't answer the mail, they don't answer the phone, and when I go to Bari to finish paperwork I have to take along my own typewriter and typist.'

Unresponsive institutions like the regional government of Puglia are, as I see it, one of the fundamental reasons why, for so many Indians, democracy doesn't work. Putnam believes institutions are shaped by history, and by the social context in which they operate. He compares the social contexts of north and south Italy. In the north he finds the civic community 'marked by an active public-spirited citizenry, by egalitarian politics and political relations, by a social fabric of trust and cooperation'. The south, according to Putnam, is characterised by 'vertically structured politics, a social life of fragmentation, and a culture of distrust'.

Traditionally in India society is vertically structured. There is a ladder of castes whose relations with each other, their politics, are anything but egalitarian. To build social trust and cooperation between them means breaking down centuries of mistrust. The traditional Indian family is patriarchal, and the dominant position of elders is reflected in the heads of political families whose sons only come into their own when fathers die. The vertical structure of Indian society was reinforced by the feudal nature of Indian society under the Mughals. The British, by creating a class of landlords known as *zamindars* in a large area of India and by not interfering in the government of the states ruled by Maharajas, reinforced this feudal structure. The British administration was known as the *mai baap* or 'mother and father' government because it encouraged villagers to believe that they should turn to the state to answer their needs and solve their problems rather than cooperate with each other and build up what sociologists would call 'social capital'. After Independence India adopted a highly centralised constitution, and continued with a *mai baap* style of administration.

I had asked the NGO Seva Mandir, or Temple of Service, to help me find out more about the impact of NREGA. Seva Mandir is the leading NGO working in the villages and towns of the neighbouring districts of Udaipur and Rajsamand. Seva Mandir believes that government development schemes can be made effective if villagers form communities to take on responsibility for the development of their villages.

Seva Mandir realises that even if corruption is reduced and more money does reach villages, it won't transform them unless there are communities to match Robert Putnam's description of a successful community. I had a long conversation with Ajay Mehta, who had headed Seva Mandir, and his successor Neelima Khetan before I left for Udaipur. Ajay, who is the diffident member of a family of high achievers, had said, 'We need to ask why the poor are so ineffective in demanding their rights and seeing that what they are given works. But we haven't asked that question, nor indeed have we suggested to the poor that they should be more accountable, take their responsibilities more seriously. Seva Mandir is trying to ensure that villagers realise they have a responsibility for bringing about development and change.'

'Does that mean villagers must exercise their rights and demand development from the state and indeed from NGOs?' I asked.

'Seva Mandir has a commitment to strengthen village people's ability to hold the state responsible for fulfilling its responsibilities,' Ajay replied.

'Yes, but we believe it means more than that,' Neelima chipped in. 'It means teaching villagers that they will never bring about the development and change they have a right to expect unless they become more horizontal societies, and learn to live as communities, not just in their own caste societies. Then they will make demands which benefit the community, and have the strength to see those demands are met.'

'Of course we don't put it quite like that,' Ajay added with a shy smile.

Both Ajay and Neelima are in their understated way deeply committed to the belief they expressed in a joint essay, the belief that 'true development or civilisation is about activating in people a sense of duty towards their community and surroundings, and towards society.'

On my first day in the Rajasthan countryside I found Ajay and Neelima sitting on a rug surrounded by a group of villagers who were members of the village committee Seva Mandir had nurtured. The villagers were discussing the stormy village council meeting they had attended to decide on the work that should be done under NREGA in their *panchayat*, Nayakheda.

Ajay explained, 'The results were rather disappointing. We had been hoping that five proposals which Seva Mandir would execute would be approved and none were.' Under the law the village panchayat has to execute 50 per cent of the NREGA projects but they can call in NGOs or government organisations like the Public Works Department to execute the other 50 per cent. With an NGO like Seva Mandir there will not be any cheating in the lists of workers or fiddling with muster rolls, and the materials supplied will not be adulterated. Villagers know that the same cannot be said for any work executed by a *panchayat* or a government agency.

The village committee had been formed under the tutelage of Seva Mandir to bring different communities together to work for the benefit of the whole community – its ambition was to acquire social capital. The main spokesman was Shiv Lal. Smartly dressed in a cream shirt and grey trousers with a notebook in his top pocket, he looked more like a sleek minor government official than a tribal. But he had not always been so smart. Shiv Lal's father was uneducated and wasn't that convinced about the value of educating his son. So he pulled him out of school and told him to find a job to contribute to the household expenses. While working as a construction labourer Shiv Lal met someone from Seva Mandir who encouraged him to attend one of the NGO's adult education programmes in Udaipur. After a course lasting just ten days Shiv Lal returned home and started teaching in the evening when he had finished his day's work. Eventually joining Seva Mandir as a Forest Worker, Shiv Lal and two of his colleagues became the nucleus of the village committee the NGO wanted to see established.

Shiv Lal's first job had been in the soapstone mine of the local landowner. 'The mine was very deep and dangerous,' he told me. 'There were no security protections for us, accidents were always happening, and I was afraid one would happen to me. Anyhow we never got our wages properly. They were small and the local Thakur paid them as and when he felt like it.'

Thakurs, members of the Rajput caste, are the villains of countless Bollywood movies. The community has complained vociferously about their celluloid image but it looked like a film could easily have been made about the one in Shiv Lal's village. The Thakur was unwell during my visit, and so I wasn't able to meet him, but villagers agreed he looked the part of a feudal lord. Apparently he was tall and well-built with a commanding presence reinforced by an impressive moustache curled up at the ends. Shiv Lal told me, 'The Thakur was jailed for killing eleven people in broad daylight, but managed through his money and muscle power to get released by a court – as happens here,' he added as an afterthought.

Used to ruling over the village as a dictator, inevitably the Thakur resented Seva Mandir's interventions in the village and saw the development of the village committee as a challenge to his status and to the influence he regarded as his prerogative. At the recent NREGA meeting the Thakur had been determined to see that proposals the village committee wanted to be executed by Seva Mandir were not recorded in the minutes. From the start he overawed the *panchayat* secretary, the local official who writes up the minutes, by sitting behind him and placing his sons next to him.

When Shiv Lal came forward with his committee's proposals, the Thakur and his supporters kept on shouting, 'This is our Gram Sabha, our meeting. This is our Gram Sabha. We will not tolerate Seva Mandir here.' Shiv Lal and one of his colleagues tried to speak but they were silenced. The Thakur's sons got the secretary to start noting their proposals in the minutes. Eventually Shiv Lal complained, 'What is the purpose of this Gram Sabha if only rich and influential people are allowed to speak?' At that point one of the Thakur's sons did say, 'Let them speak,' and the secretary wrote down some proposals in addition to those approved by the Thakur. But they were small, personal requests. When the meeting broke up none of the proposals involving Seva Mandir were noted in the minutes.

It hadn't been easy for Shiv Lal, a tribal, to bring villagers of different castes together to form this committee. He had been greatly helped by the persuasive powers of Seva Mandir workers and small but successful initiatives he and two colleagues had undertaken. Eventually the villagers whose trust he had won asked him to be their candidate in an election for the position of *sarpanch*. I asked Shiv Lal whether he had been 'greedy for the chair', a common phrase in India to describe political ambition.

Shiv Lal laughed. 'No, I had no such longing for power. I didn't even want to contest. After all, I didn't have any money and everyone knows that you need it for fighting elections. But I was told others would find the money, I wouldn't even have to buy a bidi.'

'When you decided to contest how did the Thakur Sahib take it?' I asked.

'He was very angry,' Shiv Lal said, with the smile which never seemed to desert him. 'He had put up his own candidate and expected that he would be elected as always happened. Everything he could think of he tried. When I wanted to register myself as a candidate the secretary who issues the necessary certificates suddenly disappeared. There were only three days to go so we hired a vehicle, very rare for us, and drove to the secretary's house and demanded that he give us caste and residency certificates.'

The next day, when Shiv Lal and his supporters went to file his nomination papers, the Thakur's men objected on the grounds that he worked for Seva Mandir. A Seva Mandir coordinator managed to convince the returning officer this was not so. But the Thakur did not give up. On the day of the election he tried to overawe the voters by bringing six vehicles to the polling booth and parking them in what Shiv Lal called 'a threatening manner'.

According to Shiv Lal there had also been 'some trickery at the counting'. Apparently the officer counted three times and eventually announced that he had won by 552 votes, but the official record only showed 35. When Shiv Lal took this up with the returning officer, he had replied, 'You wanted your victory. You've got it. So leave it at that.'

From time to time as we were talking women walked by, swaying elegantly, balancing pots full of water on their heads. Behind me some of their children were drawing pictures in an *anganwadi*, which is a cross between a health and nutrition centre as well as a nursery school. It was run by Seva Mandir. Neelima told me there were meant to be three government *anganwadis* in the *panchayat* but none of them functioned. She remembered a visit by the Collector, the most senior official in the district, who had said to her, 'Do please go on running your *anganwadi*. There is nothing I can do about mine.'

We couldn't leave this meeting without discussing corruption, the subject that dominates all conversations about delivering development. When I asked whether NREGA was generating corruption, everyone wanted to give me their answers. A Brahmin pointed at a nearby concrete platform for holding village meetings and said, 'Look, it was built some years ago but there is only sand inside it, there is no concrete. You can never trust the material which is used when the government does the work.'

I asked whether there had been a problem with muster rolls. A Rajput replied scornfully, 'What do you think? Wherever there is the government there is corruption, so of course there is pressure on the person who writes the muster rolls to do wrong. But we have the strength now to see that he doesn't.'

'What do you mean by strength?'

'I mean us, the villagers, our power. Now we have learnt that we must stand together if we are not to be cheated. But it took time to bring us together.'

One of the major achievements of the village committee has been their campaign to restore common land to the villagers. Here once again the local Thakur came in because he had encroached on the common land, and even sold some of it. He also tried to evict some householders, saying he needed their land to dump the waste from his soapstone mine. Shiv Lal explained that matters came to a head when the Thakur came to see him one night.

'He asked whether I wanted the land or my life. He threatened me: "I have killed eleven people in broad daylight so killing one more won't hurt me." But when I didn't give in he said, "You and your colleagues come to the land tomorrow and see if you take it."'

'That sounds to me like a trap,' I remarked.

'Well, I wasn't a fool,' replied Shiv Lal, the smile finally disappearing from his face. 'Before deciding anything, I and my colleagues went round the village asking people if they were with us. They were. They even said if we were killed they would look after our children. Next day at ten o'clock we went to the land and there was the Thakur with his two sons. He kept talking until five o'clock telling us all that he had done for the village.'

'Did he threaten you?'

'No, he just went on like that. Other villagers were watching, hidden in the sugarcane. After all this talking the Thakur suddenly got up and said, "We'll measure the land. Just let me keep two *bighas*." I was so surprised I immediately agreed. He still has his land and we have ours.'

*

As we drove through the narrow lanes of the village flanked by stone walls to see the land, Neelima explained the significance of recovering common land. She is slight, with close-cropped dark hair, a serious-minded woman who makes no concessions to fashion. Being totally engrossed in her work she tends to use development-speak. She talked to me of 'dependency engendered by the encroachments', of 'patronage-centred access', and 'privileging communities to manage their resources'.

I asked Neelima how Seva Mandir had helped to recover the land.

'Well, we only helped the villagers. We didn't do it ourselves. First of all the tangled land records had to be sorted out, and they were tangled. Then we had to approach the encroachers to persuade them it was in their interests to move off the land.'

'But how did you do that? No one in India, or indeed anywhere else in the world, wants to move off land they occupy.'

'We tried to persuade the encroachers and the rest of the village that they would be better off if the land was returned to common use. We pointed out that watersheds and forest lands could be productively developed, crops grown for the benefit of the whole village, and land provided for everyone to graze their cattle and goats on.'

'The fact that villagers had also encroached means in a way that the Thakur Sahib isn't the only villain of the story. The encroachers are villains too.'

'Yes, that's the point that is often missed,' Neelima said eagerly. 'In so much of the dialogue on corruption, it's the obvious villains who are highlighted – that Thakur Sahib and local officials who collude with him. But the villagers themselves often cheat or cut corners if it's in their interest. We hope our work will persuade them that this is no more ethical than the corruption of those above them that they complain about.'

That still left the question of 'patronage-centred access', which I didn't fully understand. Neelima explained: 'Encroachers can only occupy common land under the patronage of local officials. The officials have to be persuaded to turn a blind eye to what is after all illegal. Encroachers also often have to seek approval from the village elite. Begging for that patronage either from officials or the elite is humiliating and can of course be costly also.'

The common land we had come to see was a large area of tall reddish brown grass which would soon be ready for cutting as hay to feed livestock. All the villagers would then be entitled to harvest it by paying a small sum 'per sickle'. The land was demarcated by a high stone wall. Shiv Lal patted the wall and said with a certain smugness, or it might be fairer to say with justifiable pride, 'The question is what is the difference between this wall and the wall over there put up under the World Bank watershed development scheme? Why did people steal the stones out of that wall, while we haven't lost a single stone of this wall?' He didn't answer those questions but then he didn't feel he needed to. He was so well versed in the Seva Mandir philosophy that he assumed everyone would understand the difference between a wall villagers had built as a community, and a wall that had been built for them.

The next day we drove south of Udaipur, through the Aravalli mountains to a region dominated by tribals. Occasionally we came across patches of forest but for most of the journey we were driving along a valley flanked on both sides by bare, barren mountains.

We came first to the Seva Mandir office in the small town of Jhadol, which is the headquarters of a Block, an administrative unit. There we went to visit the Block Development Officer, commonly known as the officer who blocks development, to discuss a case of blatant corruption involving NREGA funds. As we drove up the slight hill leading to the administrative complex, we passed an archery competition. Bows and arrows are the tribals' traditional weapons. The offices were shabby and in severe need of a coat of paint or at least whitewash. As usual there was little or no sign of horticulture or afforestation in the compound. I thought to myself, as I have so often done in the past, 'It's absurd that state governments put up notices all over the place calling for a Green Rajasthan, or whatever other state it may be, and yet don't bother to green their own premises.'

Inside, the office building was dark and unwelcoming. A peon, or messenger, an essential status symbol for a government officer, was occupying his traditional position, sitting on a stool waiting to be summoned by his sahib. To my surprise, however, Ashok Maheshwari, the BDO, was welcoming. But in order to ensure that we couldn't quiz him too deeply, the small genial official started by telling us he had only recently been posted to Jhadol. Looking at boards on which earlier BDOs were listed along with their dates, I said, 'It looks as though you won't be here for long either.'

He laughed and replied, 'No, I'll be lucky if I last two years. But then that's a long time in a government servant's career.'

The BDO had found time to inspect work done under NREGA and said he had been satisfied in two panchayats but in some others he had suggested they improve the quality of the work and what he called its 'economic feasibility'.

When I asked him what that meant he said, 'Like for example culverts built in areas which didn't benefit many people, when they could have been put in parts of the village where they would have been very useful.'

'So, do you mean the culverts were built in the areas where the big people live?' I asked.

'You wouldn't necessarily be wrong in saying that,' he replied with a smile.

It wasn't long before news of our visit got round and the Programme Officer NREGA came into the office. Subodh Shivpuri was the opposite to the BDO. He was a large man with a substantial stomach, bald but with an impressive moustache. He stood over us clutching his mobile and looking sternly at the BDO, clearly expecting an explanation for what to him was an unwanted intrusion. I had never heard of such an official before, but the BDO seemed to regard him as his senior. He explained anxiously, 'Sir, Seva Mandir asked to come to see me. I can't say no because they have influence in this district.'

I then explained that I was writing about NREGA, and just wanted to find out how it was working. The Programme Officer grunted, 'The *panchayats* haven't been able to understand the object of the project. The projects they propose don't help development.'

'Isn't there a lot of corruption too?' I enquired hesitantly.

'What do you expect?' he replied. 'The *panchayats* don't have any accountants or technical staff. The government hasn't sanctioned any. How can villagers do that sort of job?'

'I've been told of a case where an official as well as a *sarpanch* were discovered cheating on muster rolls. The *panchayat* is called Bichhiwara. What has happened about that?'

The Programme Officer looked angrily at the Seva Mandir Block Coordinator and replied abruptly, 'An FIR has been registered with the police,' and then walked out. The BDO relaxed and we continued our conversation.

He agreed that the main problem with NREGA was the lack of professional staff to help villagers plan and execute the schemes. He thought each panchayat should have at least one junior engineer and one social scientist.

'What about the problem of powerful people in the villages bagging the projects?'

'That happens. It's very difficult for us to stop. These people have political connections and if we complain against them that won't help anyone because we will just be transferred – as you well know,' he added, laughing.

*

We set off to see some land which had been reafforested by another Seva Mandir-nurtured committee. A jackal slunk across the road and disappeared through the leggy, purple-flowering shrub known as *be-sharam*, or the shameless one, because it will grow absolutely anywhere. Eventually we turned off the tarmac road onto a bullock cart track to reach the hamlet of Nayahola and meet the village committee. The concrete revolution hadn't yet reached Nayahola. The small houses were built of mud or stones plastered with a mixture of mud and cow dung. The tiles looked as though they might slip off the sloping roofs at any moment. Maize was laid out to dry in the small courtyards. The members of the committee were sitting under a mahua tree. Tribal communities distil the liquor they are so fond of from the mahua's fleshy, sickly sweet flowers. One tribal once told the distinguished anthropologist Verrier Elwin that hell for him would be miles and miles of forest without a mahua tree.

The village committee was discussing the local forest guard, an employee of the Forest Department. According to them, he was clearly hand-in-glove with contractors who were excavating boulders from land the village committee had greened. Whenever the villagers complained, the forest guard rang the contractors on their mobiles and warned them to clear off before he arrived. So he was able to say that he had not seen anything to back up the villagers' complaint. Eventually the village committee took matters into their own hands and fined two of the contractors.

There were eleven members of the committee. Most of them were comparatively young, including their chairman, Devi Lal. Only one elderly member was dressed in the tribals' traditional loose-fitting clothes with a turban, the rest were wearing shirts and trousers. I asked Devi Lal whether boulders were still being stolen from the reafforested land after they had fined the contractors.

'The situation is better,' he said. 'The contractors are not so blatant. But they sometimes send their tractors in after dark.'

'What about the people who drive the tractors and load the trolleys? Do they come from the village?'

'They used to, there were two drivers and five labourers, but we threatened them with isolation.'

'Do you mean *hookah-pani bund* – not smoking a hookah or drinking water with them?'

'We told them we wouldn't join their ceremonies or allow them to celebrate festivals with the rest of the village. We were very serious; we even said we wouldn't attend their family funerals.'

As we drove to see the afforested land we passed the contractors' boulders, now broken into stones used for road-building and neatly piled along the verges. Young saplings were taking root on the land and the grass was recovering, but there were brown scars where boulders had been removed.

There was a sad story about the saplings. One of Seva Mandir's star workers, Jalum Chand, had been in charge of the afforestation and a relative had owned the nursery which had supplied the saplings. When a bill for 30,000 saplings reached Seva Mandir, which was responsible for executing the scheme, someone thought there was 'some black in the daal', as the Hindi saying goes. Thirty thousand saplings seemed an awful lot for the 250 acres that had been replanted. On investigation it was discovered that only some 7000 saplings had left the nursery. This was a personal tragedy for Jalum Chand, who had received an award from Seva Mandir for his outstanding contribution to their work. At that time he was considering whether the social capital he had acquired was sufficient to make an attempt at a political career.

Seva Mandir believes in being open about incidents of corruption amongst its workers so I was taken to meet Jalum Chand. He did not appear to be particularly repentant or ashamed as he greeted me with a broad, self-assured smile, a baseball cap – which apparently never leaves his head – shading his round face. He took charge of the villagers, hustling them to organise a mat to sit on and to my embarrassment insisting that a chair should be brought for me. It appeared that the scandal had not diminished the status he had won for himself in the village when he was supervising the forestry project. He was, he told me, still connected with Seva Mandir but at a different level of involvement. When Seva Mandir had dismissed Jalum Chand he had been deeply resentful and threatened to accuse the NGO of mistreating him because he was 'a poor and helpless tribal'. But it seemed clear that he had by now acknowledged his fault and made a new start.

After taking away Jalum Chand's job, Seva Mandir had drawn a line under the incident. So we didn't talk about the scandal. We discussed the work that had been done in his village and the villages around, and the problem of deforestation. I told him about the village committee meeting I had just been to and of course he already knew the whole story.

'They will find it very difficult to get rid of that forest guard,' he said. 'The Forest Department always defends its own people and they always take the side of the big people with money. Of course there are some good forest officers, but they just get transferred because they stop the others making money. It is very bad because with the expanding population we need more forests not less.'

When I asked him what could be done he replied without blinking an eye, 'The people will have to defend the forests.'

Although he had slipped up once I thought he would be among the defenders, if for no other reason, to avoid forfeiting his status in the village.

In two days I had seen the obstacles villagers had to overcome even when they had taken on the responsibility for developing their villages. On the third day, in the town of Delwara, where I had earlier met the deputy leader of the *panchayat*, I was to see how building communities could work in what is known as a 'peri-urban area', not a category I had ever heard of before. Apparently it means 'a transition zone where urban and rural activities are juxtaposed'.

Personally I would have called Delwara a small town. It has a long history, and was originally called Devkul Paton Nagri or the town of the gods. Almost every street still has a temple, either Hindu or Jain, many of them very old. There is also a substantial mosque and the mazaar or shrine of a Muslim saint, Kasim Ali Baba. Hindus as well as Muslims pay their respects there. The town is built on a hillside and above it stands one of Rajasthan's magnificent fort-palaces, now a heritage hotel. Seva Mandir has nurtured a Citizens' Development Organisation here and one of its undertakings has been restoring some of Delwara's built heritage including one of the town's most important sources of water, a deep well approached by flights of stone steps.

The committee of the Citizens Development Organisation had assembled to meet me. I learnt that in addition to the restoration work they had installed a solid waste disposal system, as well as establishing street cleaning and waste collection too. Lavatories had been built, septic tanks installed, and piped water provided in some areas. Over half the families of the town had agreed to contribute to pay for the waste collection.

The organisation had to get its projects approved by the panchayat. I wondered whether that presented the same sort of problems that village committees encountered. A vocal Muslim woman, Mehrunissa Sheikh, who was joint secretary of the organisation, told me they had discovered a way round that: 'We found that if only one or two of us went our projects got bogged down, but if we went as a body, we were listened to.'

By joining the committee, Mehrunissa Sheikh had defied the tradition among Muslim women that they stayed at home, and, what's more, she had encouraged others to do the same. I asked her whether the clergy had objected. She replied, almost disdainfully, 'Of course and because of tradition, and because we were women, we couldn't talk to them. So we told our husbands, "You go and talk to them, you tell the Maulanas what we are saying." We haven't heard from the Maulanas since.'

The treasurer of the committee was a Muslim with a long white beard and wearing traditional white clothes and a prayer cap. When I asked him what he felt about women breaking the tradition of staying at home he smiled and said, 'They came out, what more can I say?' Then after a long pause he added, 'No one can stop them.' It certainly appeared that he was right.

As so often, the Dalit *basti*, or quarter, was on the edge of the town. There I met the person who impressed me most in Delwara. She was a Dalit woman named Durga. Young, strikingly good-looking and self-confident, she was neither obsequious nor surly, as those born into communities which have been humiliated for centuries can understandably be. Durga had been elected the leader of a committee, or a cooperative might be a better way of putting it, that had gone into the garment business. They embroidered and sewed clothes which were then purchased by the commercial wing of Seva Mandir.

Durga is a name of one of the most awe-inspiring deities of the Hindu pantheon. Once her young namesake had money, she had been able to inspire awe in the local marketplace.

'Our image has gone up in the market,' Durga told me. 'I tell shopkeepers that we are people with money now so you have to respect us. Otherwise we won't do business with you, we won't buy from you. I can now get a loan from a miserly moneylender without having to deposit my jewellery as security. You know how mean and careful with their money they are. What's more, I also tell other women not to put up with discrimination. There is no need now, I say.'

The small group of women with Durga shook their heads from side to side in agreement.

'We can now eat like other people too,' Durga went on excitedly. 'Before, even looking at a chapatti made from wheat flour made us happy. We were limited for most of the time to millets, because they're cheap. Now we can afford *halwa*, we can even have it twice a day if we feel like it.' *Halwa* is a sweet dish made from a rich mix of wheat flour, clarified butter and sugar.

When I got a chance to get a word in, I asked whether Durga and her colleagues suffered any discrimination from their husbands.

'Certainly not,' she shot back. 'We don't allow our husbands to tell us what to do now that we are earning our own money. We make sure there is no discrimination against us anywhere by anyone. My mother wasn't allowed to travel anywhere. I have been to Bangalore for an exhibition of our work. Now Delhi and Mumbai won't be enough for me, I want to go abroad too.'

I told Durga she should come to see me when she came to Delhi. She laughed and said, 'Delhi, why Delhi? I'll come to see you in London one day. And next time you come here I'll serve you food on the dinner service I got for my Diwali present. Who could imagine *me* eating off a dinner service!'

I started to say my goodbyes, but Durga interrupted me.

'You are not going before I tell you the most surprising thing of all. Who would ever think I would have gone into the shares business but I have.'

This did seem to be too good to be true so I asked, 'Which company?'

The answer came back without a moment's hesitation: 'Fabindia.'

Fabindia is a remarkable retail company set up to provide an outlet for goods produced by artisans, and concentrating on selling in the Indian market. William Bissell, the son of the founder, is managing director of the company. I referred to his book *Making India Work* in the introduction. Since William took over, the business has expanded dramatically. It is now twenty-five times bigger than it was in 2002. But Fabindia has never been a purely commercial affair. For William's father, John, ensuring the welfare of the artisans producing goods for him was the purpose of doing business. William has maintained that tradition, and introduced a scheme whereby artisans now become shareholders. Seva Mandir has been selling Durga's work to Fabindia and that is how she now, much to her delight, owns shares.

Durga is now more capable of standing on her feet and ensuring she gets what is due to her. This is because she is a member of what Robert Putnam would consider a successful community. Seva Mandir hopes that its policy of building self-confident communities capable of 'holding the state responsible for fulfilling its responsibilities', as Ajay Mehta said, will spread to other parts of Rajasthan and indeed the rest of India. This would bring about fundamental changes in India's traditionally vertical society. Changing the attitude of the poor in this way can obviously be an effective method of pressurising governments to deliver on their promises of development. But Ajay and Neelima's vision goes beyond that. They hope villagers will come to realise that development isn't just about demanding resources and power. It's also about using them ethically, not breaking laws and cutting corners to steal from each other, as those who steal from them do.

6 | FARMING FUTURES

India can rightly be proud of its best NGOs, such as Seva Mandir, and its dedicated activists who have fought corruption in the government's schemes for the welfare of the rural poor. But perhaps the best way to do that is to reduce the role of the government in delivering welfare, including health and education, and rely more on the private sector and the market.

Joseph Stiglitz, the Nobel Prize-winning economist, proposed a new vision for America in his book *The Roaring Nineties*, which analysed those switchback years with their economic ups and downs, their booms and their busts. It was a vision 'somewhere between those who see government having a dominant role in the economy and those who argue for a minimalist role; but also between the critics who see capitalism as a system that is rotten to the core, and those who see the market economy as unblemished, a miraculous invention of man that brings unprecedented prosperity to all'. After the global economic crisis of the last decade I suspect that the number of those who regard the market as unblemished has decreased, and in India at least only doctrinaire communists and socialists would welcome the return of the dominant role the government played in the economy before the reforms of the last twenty years. But there is still a debate in India over the balance there should be between the role of the market and the role of the government, and indeed the role of NGOs such as Seva Mandir.

The private sector and the market have played the dominant role in the remarkable growth of the Indian economy over the last twenty years. That has led many to believe they can best provide the education, health care and employment that India needs most if it is to deliver development to those who so far have gained little or no benefit from economic growth. But even those who advocate the private sector and the market's case most vociferously acknowledge that the government must have some role.

Nandan Nilekani, the co-founder of Infosys, one of the most successful of the IT companies which have done so much to change the world's view of India, is a passionate advocate of the private sector and the market. In his book *Imagining India: Ideas for the New Century*, he says the economic reforms 'have brought the private sector into the economy and handed them the responsibility for growth'. But he is not pinning his hopes on the private sector alone. In education he looks for 'a truly competitive market between government and private schools'. When it comes to health care, Nilekani suggests that the state should be one among many providers. Indians should have vouchers, publicly financed, that would enable them to choose their provider. But at present, as Nilekani admits, many of the private doctors in the rural areas and the slums are quacks. So there will have to be a wholesale change in private as well as government hospitals and health centres. Furthermore the government will have to institute a regulator to ensure that quacks no longer dupe the public, and there will have to be a wholesale change in the way that regulation is carried out.

In 2010 it was discovered that the government couldn't regulate medical education, let alone medical practice. The head of the Medical Council of India, which is responsible for regulating the training of doctors, was arrested for taking bribes to certify private medical schools were up to standard. Then in 2011, when a pilot landed her plane nose-wheel first at Goa airport, it was discovered that she had paid for her licence rather than passing her exam. In the investigation that followed it emerged that she was not alone.

Not surprisingly, Nilekani sees a major role for IT in improving the quality of everything the government does. But at the same time he warns: 'When it comes to computerisation within the state we cannot build new systems over a creaky base – we have to first reinvent our state processes to increase our efficiencies rather than merely computerising what is already there.'

Since writing his book, Nilekani has resigned from the company he co-founded and taken responsibility for the ambitious government scheme of issuing every Indian with an identity card. This he believes has the potential to dramatically improve the delivery of public services, and cut out the bureaucratic hassle and corruption that goes with obtaining the many identity cards a citizen of India requires at present. Inevitably some civil liberty groups fear the identity cards will be used to increase surveillance and invade privacy.

The private sector does have a strategy that has made two of the tools of development more widely available than would ever have been thought possible twenty years ago: telephones and computers. The strategist was the American of Indian origin, C.K. Prahalad, who started his career in a battery plant in Chennai and was Professor of Corporate Strategy at the Ross School of Business in Michigan when he died in 2010. The aim of his strategy was to transform the poor of the world into active consumers. Prahalad's seminal book was called *The Fortune at the Bottom of the Pyramid*. He envisaged the global market as a pyramid. At the top of the market was the small proportion of global customers who came from the affluent class in developed countries. At the bottom level of the pyramid were the poor who, until Prahalad came along, were normally regarded by businesses as not having the money to be considered potential customers. Prahalad's aim was to turn the poor into a market that had to be very different from the traditional markets in which companies had sold their products or services. The primary requirements were credit and income-generating opportunities. The two went together. He also pointed out that it was no use trying to sell products to the poor which they couldn't afford, and so products had to be tailored to the purses of those at the bottom of the pyramid.

Indian manufacturers have taken Prahalad's advice and devised a way to reach the bottom of the pyramid. The strategy is called cost-engineering. With the unsavoury reputation that financial engineering has now acquired, cost-engineering might sound a bit dodgy. Some might think it is just another form of cost-cutting, the panacea most consultants and managers prescribe for falling profits. But cost-engineering is neither dodgy, nor just another way of cost-cutting. The first stage in cost-engineering is to assess the spending power of a segment of the market that cannot afford a product at present prices. Designers then evolve a similar product that segment can afford.

Cost-engineering has already produced the world's cheapest mobile phones and the world's fastest-expanding mobile phone market, growing from 5 million connections in 2001 to over 700 million by the end of 2010. The principle has also been applied to call charges, reducing them to levels within the spending power of those who buy the cheap phones. Students at one of the elite Indian Institutes of Technology, always known as IITs, have done some cost-engineering themselves and designed a computer which costs only thirty dollars.

But cost-engineering is not going to help deliver the most fundamental need of all – food for the large number of Indians who go to bed hungry every night. At the time of writing, the government was considering a National Food Security Bill to specify the legal entitlement to rice or wheat of every family below the poverty line. M.S. Swaminathan, the agricultural scientist known as the father of the Green Revolution, has said, 'The bill will mark the fulfilment of Mahatma Gandhi's call for a hunger-free India.' But Swaminathan warned that a sustainable food security system could only be developed with food grown in India; the government could not rely on imports to make up for any shortfall in domestic production. The fact that some 60 per cent of Indians are still dependent on the land for a living makes tackling agriculture even more crucial.

Unfortunately Indian agriculture is a laggard. The output is growing very slowly, being held back by outdated farming technology, old-fashioned marketing that benefits middlemen more than farmers, lack of storage for crops after they have been harvested, and inadequate returns for farmers. Swaminathan has called for 'a small-farm management revolution'. Agriculture in India is in such a deep crisis that between 1997 and 2010 a quarter of a million farmers committed suicide because they accrued debts they felt they had no hope of repaying.

The northern state of Punjab is the breadbasket of India, and renowned for its progressive farmers, but even there agriculture is in trouble Occupying only 1.5 per cent of India's land the state produces 20 per cent of the wheat Indians consume and 11 per cent of the rice. In the sixties Punjab was in the vanguard of the Green Revolution, which ended the country's humiliating dependence on American Food Aid. But now Punjab farmers' incomes are declining, they are having to bore wells deeper and deeper to reach the water they need for irrigation, they have invested too much capital in equipment that they hoped would make their farms more profitable, and they have planted wheat and rice so regularly that the soil is suffering from bearing the same crops year in year out. In addition to the damage caused by the failure to rotate crops, the soil has been poisoned by overdoses of chemicals to increase yields, keep pests at bay, and kill weeds.

The private sector believes it can provide the storage and the efficient market that farmers need, 'from farm to fork' as mass retailers like to call the process they implement. The method the private sector advocates is contract farming, which it believes will provide supply chains that guarantee markets for farmers, and the technical assistance they need to improve their yield. The central government believes contract farming can at least be one answer to the agricultural crisis. It is given priority in the government's approach paper to the next Five Year Plan for the economy.

There are different forms of contract farming, but the one most favoured involves a company providing farmers with seeds or seedlings, advice on cultivation and a guarantee to purchase the produce at a price agreed in advance. Quality is crucial. The crop must meet the standard set by the company.

PepsiCo, the American multinational best known for slugging it out with Coca-Cola to be the biggest player in the carbonated-drinks market, was the pioneer of contract farming in Punjab and is still the leading contractor. I remember in the eighties hearing the then Prime Minister, Rajiv Gandhi, telling a rally in Punjab that Pepsi were coming to the rescue of farmers by establishing a factory to process tomatoes. He had to sell the project hard because in those days there was still strong opposition to foreign multinationals. This was part of a deal Pepsi did in order to be allowed to bring their bottled drink into India, and challenge an Indian cola which had dominated the protected market. In return the multinational did establish a tomato processing plant in Punjab and set about assuring produce for it by contract farming. But after a few years Pepsi sold the plant.

PepsiCo's explanation is that the tomato season in Punjab was limited, tomatoes could not be stored for long even in cold storage, and so the plant was uneconomic. PepsiCo's critics suggest that it never intended to run the plant for long, and that Rajiv Gandhi had been led up the garden path. Whoever is right, when I was in Punjab looking at contract farming I saw fields of tomato plants packed tightly together. The seedlings had been provided by PepsiCo and so had the technology. So the multinational had clearly not entirely deserted the tomato farmers although they no longer provided them with a market.

PepisCo has also experimented with contract farming for chillies, peanuts, basmati rice, and potatoes. They are still in the rice business, but growing potatoes is by far the most important operation from their point of view because of the four plants they have making crisps and other potato snacks.

I visited Punjab at the beginning of May. The farmers had just harvested their wheat. Many of the fields were charred black after the stubble had been burnt off, although this practice is officially frowned on. Punjab farmers are said to be over-capitalised but a few farmers were still using bullocks to pull their carts laden with the last sheaves of straw. I stopped to talk to labourers putting the finishing touches to a structure made out of straw sheaves that looked like a giant thatched beehive. It is the traditional store for the finely chopped straw that provides fodder for buffaloes and cows. The structures are certainly much more picturesque than the ugly rolls of straw packed in black plastic that mar the beauty of the British countryside.

The labourers had come from the state of Bihar hundreds of miles away to the east. For many years now Punjab farmers have been dependent on labourers from Bihar and other poorer parts of India. Yogi Rai Yadav, diminutive, wizened and toothless, had been coming to Punjab for years. He was intending to stay on for the transplanting of the paddy. I had been told that Punjab farmers were facing a shortage of labour because Biharis could now stay at home and earn money under the government's National Rural Employment Guarantee Scheme. Planting a ladder against the straw beehive, Yogi said, 'I don't trust that scheme. I need assured money. So I come here. It's wiser than trusting the government.'

On the outskirts of the town of Nabha, the capital of one of Punjab's erstwhile princely states, we turned into a new housing colony and drew up outside one of the smart modern houses. The architecture and ornate wrought iron gate would not have been out of place in one of Delhi's many middle class neighbourhoods. I had been invited there by a group of Sikh farmers, and was greeted by a prosperous-looking young man who was my host's son.

'You have a beautiful home,' I said as we climbed the stairs to the first floor.

'Yes, but it still belongs to the bank,' he replied.

'You would rather live in the town than in your village?'

'Much better electricity supply in the towns,' he replied, swinging open a door to reveal the group of farmers sitting waiting for us, all big men who between them seemed to fill the room.

After we made our introductions we got down to brass tacks. These were men who took their profession very seriously. I asked them why this cycle of growing wheat and rice prevailed even though farmers knew that they needed to diversify their crops for the sake of their soil's health.

Lakhvinder Singh Rai, a highly articulate farmer who demonstrated his points by referring to diagrams on his laptop, explained, 'There is this tendency to grow rice and wheat because they are the crops for which the government guarantees a minimum price. If I grow something else, as I am told to by the government, what will I do? If I grow carrots or alfalfa where would I sell them? Even with cauliflowers there are no buyers for bulk supplies.'

'But isn't that where contract farming comes in, with its guaranteed prices?'

'No,' Lakhvinder Singh said firmly. 'For a start around here they are only interested in potatoes, nothing else. If I do grow potatoes what happens? From one acre I will get sixty to seventy quintals of potatoes. But PepsiCo will say, for instance, they only want potatoes over a certain size and then use that as an excuse to only accept thirty to forty quintals from me because they don't want any more. Then what do I do with the rest? Like a beggar I go to the market, plead with people to buy them, and grab whatever I can get. We are worse than cobblers. Even they have the power to say I have made a pair of shoes and will sell it for no less than one hundred rupees.'

'So have you stopped contract farming for PepsiCo?'

'If Pepsi has a surplus then there are quality cuts. If Pepsi needs the potatoes then everything is fine. If not I'm turned back at the factory gate. I've had experience of that, and after that bitter experience I am only going in for seed potatoes.'

'Not the table potatoes Pepsi needs for making crisps?'

'No.'

Another middle-aged Sikh farmer, Gurinder Deep Singh, who wore a canary yellow turban, was anxious to weigh in against PepsiCo.

'My experience was very bad,' he said. 'The first year they took half my potatoes. The next year they refused most of them, saying they were not sugar-free – that is, the sugar content was high. Can you imagine? I was in California working as a driver and so my wife had to drive the trolley to the factory gate and had to deal with Pepsi. She had to face that shameless behaviour. After that I left contract farming.'

'Never to go back?'

The reply to that was also a definite 'no'.

After a cup of tea, we travelled further west through the flat plain of Punjab to meet another group of farmers in Rampura Phul, a small town in the district of Batinda. They told me PepsiCo contract farming had failed in their area and that was why the multinational had gone to Nabha.

The meeting was held over lunch in the house of a farmer politician called Sukhdev Singh Dhillon. The elderly Sikh, like so many politicians in India, had indulged in *dal-badal*, or party-changing, moving from the Sikh religious party, the Akali Dal, to Sonia Gandhi's Congress. He felt there had to be 'proper rules' for contract farming and there were not, and claimed that PepsiCo didn't always fulfil its part of the bargain, rejecting potatoes 'when it suited them'. But he admitted that farmers didn't always play fair either, saying, 'If my contract gives me one rupee a kilogram and the price in the market goes up to twenty-five I will certainly sell at twenty-five, and there is great fluctuation in the market. So this does happen.'

After several other farmers had criticised contract farming, one man who had remained silent spoke somewhat hesitantly in favour of PepsiCo, with whom he had been working for some five years. There was vocal disagreement all round, which he replied to defensively: 'I spoke in favour of Pepsi from my experience, so what is wrong?'

I spent the night in the city of Chandigarh, the capital of two states, Punjab and Haryana. The next morning I set off to hear the PepsiCo side of the story, driving along the broad boulevards of the city designed by the famous French architect Le Corbusier and the only one of his urban plans that was implemented. The boulevards are flanked by houses set back from the road and low-rise red brick lines of shops. The two state governments' offices are massive concrete buildings, blackened by some fifty years exposure to the winds blowing off the nearby Himalayan foothills and the dust of the North Indian plain.

The uniformity of Le Corbusier's plans has been preserved for the most part, which gives Chandigarh an orderly, almost antiseptic appearance. But this appearance vanished as I entered the urban sprawl that has grown up around Le Corbusier's city. The crisis in agriculture and the failure of government schemes for creating jobs in the countryside have inevitably attracted villagers to the city in search of work. Planning seems to have ended with Le Corbusier.

Some miles outside Chandigarh I met Nischint Bhatia, the Executive Vice President in charge of the PepsiCo's Indian Agro Business. He was going to introduce me to some of the farmers under contract to the multinational. Nischint was the son and grandson of farmers, and had read Agriculture for his first degree, before going on to gain an MBA. Speaking with assurance, the manner that brooks no doubt, and the slight

American twang corporate executives adopt in India, he told me, 'We are the biggest contract farmers in India and Punjab is our biggest operation. Potatoes have always been grown here in Punjab but there were no potatoes of processing-quality grown until we came along. It was a case of water, water everywhere but not a drop to drink. We are also the most successful in contract farming because we believe in building a bond with the farmers by keeping in touch with them throughout production. Those who work with farmers will get a better result than those who just purchase produce.'

'You may be the biggest but that is still not very big. Here in Punjab I am told that only just over two and a half per cent of the acreage is under contract farming.'

'Well, even some two per cent is a beginning. We can't solve all the problems of agriculture. They are enormous. Five million tons of potatoes gets wasted in India every year, and that's just potatoes, because of lack of storage and food processing. We can't solve all the problems of the poor either, which our critics seem to expect us to do. But even if we can have a one per cent impact we should do it.'

'You talk of wastage. Some farmers who were with you, but are no longer, complained that you rejected potatoes on grounds of quality when it suited you, that is to say when you already had enough potatoes to keep your plant going.'

'We have twelve thousand farmers throughout India, with a ninety per cent retention rate, so you must have looked very hard to find those we haven't retained,' the Pepsi Executive said with a smile, and then went on: 'We rarely say the quality is bad, and only to those who don't take care of the crop while it is growing.'

When we reached the first group of farmers brought together by Pepsi, we were greeted with the hospitality that Sikhs are so famous for. The farmers planted turbans on our heads and put saffron-coloured cotton shawls called *saropas* around our necks, both traditional symbols of respect and welcome. As we were talking, what are called snacks, but in Punjab are usually in reality a full-scale meal, appeared. Although I'd had my customary big breakfast I couldn't resist a very large, crispy samosa.

Jitendra Singh, one of the few farmers we came across who was not a turbaned Sikh, was the most vocal Pepsi supporter: 'Farmer is safe in contract farming,' he said carefully but firmly. 'We know what we are going to get in three months. If you are cautious and listen to their advice there will be no problem of quality or rejection. If we could we would do one hundred per cent contract farming.' He thought for a moment and then went on, 'But if everyone goes in for contract farming there will be a problem.'

We were crowned with turbans again by the second group of farmers we met and ushered into the drawing room of Bhagwan Singh's sprawling joint family home deep in the countryside. The lawns and gardens outside were immaculate, while inside the furniture and fittings were typical of the style of decoration a friend of mine once described as 'Punjabi Baroque'. One shelf was loaded with trophies won by the family in local sporting events.

His brother, who was an important local figure, the Chairman of the Market Committee, was away but Bhagwan Singh, a huge man with piercing eyes and an expression that commanded respect, was impressive enough. The samosa I'd already eaten meant I didn't put up much of a show when faced with the second round of snacks that morning, but I did enjoy the iced lassi, the chilled yoghurt drink Punjab is renowned for because of the high quality of its milk.

Bhagwan Singh also upheld Nischint's contention that problems with quality and the rejection of potatoes were rare: 'There is no difficulty with under-grading,' he maintained. 'Until now they've never rejected our crop. Pepsi gives us doctors, does soil testing so we don't overdose with chemical fertilisers. With potatoes they come every few days and we can contact them for help. If it wasn't for them we wouldn't plant so much potato, we would make losses if we did. We would go back to the paddy and rice cycle. For example this year potatoes slumped in the market to the very bottom but Pepsi paid us five hundred and fifty rupees a quintal.'

A young, round-faced and mild-mannered farmer, Jitendra Singh, stepped in to add his support: 'I made one crore twenty-two lakhs turnover last year from potato. Fifty per cent of that was profit. My younger brother is in America. I applied for a visa with my Pepsi earnings and got it, no problem. A ten-year visa.'

That was an achievement he was proud of, and justifiably so because the US immigration officials in Delhi take some convincing before they accept that visa applicants have an assured income.

The last meeting with farmers was held out in the open on a threshing floor surrounded by huge beehives of straw, and stacks of plastic crates full of tomatoes. Over fifty farmers were sitting on chairs waiting for me. Some of them had travelled long distances to get there.

It was here I met Dr Sankhayan, a PepsiCo agricultural scientist responsible for helping farmers to produce the crops the company needs. He was more like a missionary than a multinational executive. 'Our mandate is to increase production, lower production costs, and save water,' he told me earnestly. 'We don't pay more money than the market but we increase revenues by increasing productivity.'

I asked the agricultural scientist about those farmers who had their crops rejected ostensibly on the grounds that they were not up to standard but actually because the company had no need for them. Dr Sankhayan maintained that they were strict on anything that was in the hands of the farmers, such as water and sugar content, but liberal when it came to any problems caused by the weather. When I suggested that bad weather potatoes might produce bad weather chips, he laughed, 'No, no. It doesn't come out quite like that.'

The farmers were particularly happy about the technical assistance they received from Pepsi. 'They are always ready to help when we face a problem,' one said. Another told me, 'My water use has gone down, so I am saving on diesel for my pump.' A third declared very firmly, 'Pepsi does give us a proper assurance that they will buy. No government has done this. Pepsi has.'

I asked how it was that they needed advice from Pepsi when the government and the agricultural universities had officials whose job it was to advise them. A tall, elderly Sikh, with a capacious turban tied somewhat eccentrically, stood up and said in excellent English, 'The government extension officers are corrupt – that's why they can't be of any help guiding us as to what crops are to be sown, how much fertiliser is to be used, how much water, and introducing us to new techniques. All the works of the government are corrupt through and through.'

Dr Sankhayan whispered to me, 'He is regarded as a *sant* and called Kartarpur Baba.' 'Sant' and 'Baba' are both titles of holy men. Kartarpur Baba went on to speak about Indian agricultural scientists and complain that they were not allowed to go abroad to attend conferences. 'They are like frogs in a well,' he said. 'They don't know what is going on in the rest of the world.' From there the Baba turned his attention to old age and exhorted me to realise the value of being old. I wasn't quite sure why he thought I wasn't realising the value of being seventy-four, but decided not to enquire further.

As we drove away from that meeting I said to Nischint, 'I am impressed by the zeal of your colleague Dr Sankhayan. I would say he seems more like someone working for an NGO than for a multinational.'

'Yes,' he replied. 'His latest mission is to persuade farmers to sow rice seeds directly and bypass the back-breaking, labour intensive and expensive process of transplanting seedlings. He's persuaded us to provide fifty of the machines newly designed for direct sowing.' Now that

Biharis are not so willing to travel to work in the fields of Punjab mechanisation has become more important than it used to be.

All the farmers I had spoken to said contract farming only worked because they had large farms by Indian standards, but Nischint had an answer to that. He told me that in West Bengal, not far from Kolkata, PepsiCo had six thousand five hundred farmers who between them had only three thousand acres. 'Here in Punjab one farmer contract will bring you one hundred and fifty acres. There for fifty acres you need one hundred farmers. It's strange that we, an American multinational, are loved by farmers in Bengal, which has been ruled for years by the Communist Party.'

At the end of the day I couldn't deny that the evidence PepsiCo had presented to me was impressive and so were Nischint and Dr Sankhayan. But it was clear that contract farming the Pepsi way involved constantly keeping in touch with the farmers and that must be costly. Any company that thought it could just come along, sign some contracts and expect the farmers to deliver would be in for trouble. Contract farming must surely also require a different culture to the hard-nosed sales and marketing that are the activities that normally define the ethos of a company like PepsiCo.

With only just over 2.5 per cent of the acreage of Punjab, India's most advanced agricultural state, being contract farmed by the private sector, it's too early to judge how this system will fare. Making this judgement is further complicated by the fact that potato is the only crop which has been contract farmed on a reasonably large scale. Attempts at farming other crops in Punjab have been less successful. Some advocates of contract farming say it will increase rapidly once modern retailing takes off in India and so they are urging the government to lift restrictions on the big foreign retailers such as Walmart and Tesco investing here. But others like Manjeet Singh, the director of the Centre for the Study of Social Exclusion and

Inclusive Policy at Punjab University, do not believe contract farming should necessarily expand. He said to me, 'Contract farming is based on belief in the market and I don't agree that the market will solve the problems of Punjab. People draw the conclusion that the market is a leveller, but it is not. Experience elsewhere suggests that in the end contract farming benefits the buyer and reduces prices rather than supports them. Unless the government is there to prevent cartels and to ensure that agreements made are honoured, contract farming will not be in the farmers' interest.'

Knowing the effectiveness of the government, it seems to me that if contract farming does expand, the farmers will have to protect their own interests by coming together in cooperatives or some other form of collaboration.

Whether contract farming takes off or not, it's clear that agriculture can't produce all the jobs that are required to provide sustainable livelihoods for Indians living in the countryside. It has to be supplemented by other opportunities to earn income. C.K. Prahalad said the primary requirements for his bottom of the pyramid theory to work were income-generating opportunities and credit. Both are provided by micro-credit schemes which lend money to those whose credit rating is so low that a normal bank wouldn't consider them, and in theory at least insist that the money they lend should be spent on income-earning projects. Microfinance has been applauded internationally. The founding father of microfinance, Muhammad Yunus, and his Bangladeshi Grameen Bank were awarded the Nobel Peace Prize 'for their efforts to create economic and social development from below'.

In India microfinance was particularly successful in the southern state of Andhra Pradesh until some of the NGO lenders developed a private sector model. In 2010, the largest for-profit private sector lender in Andhra Pradesh, SKS Microfinance, amazed the market by raising the equivalent of 350 million dollars when for the first time it sold shares on the stock exchange. Shortly after that, reports of borrowers committing suicide started appearing in the press. It was said that the borrowers, who were all women, had been put under pressure by the agents of the micro-finance companies to keep up their loan repayments. The competition to lend had been so fierce that women had been persuaded to take several loans, and some had borrowed from one lender to repay another.

There followed a series of setbacks to microfinance. Opposition politicians, seeing the suicides as a chance to embarrass the government, mounted a campaign to persuade borrowers not to repay their loans. The retail banks, which had been funding the microfinance companies, got cold feet and stopped lending to them. In some cases the banks asked for their money back early. The government reacted by introducing controls on microfinancing which threatened to strangle the business.

Wanting to learn more about this crisis because it seemed to illustrate how dangerous the market can be if the government does not ensure that it's regulated, I went to see Gurcharan Das who has been a champion of microfinance for the last twelve years. It was a cold winter day in Delhi and he was sitting in his book-lined study wrapped up in a scarf and with a peaked cap to keep his head warm.

I last came to his house to interview him about a book he had written called *The Difficulty of Being Good: On the Subtle Art of Dharma*, a study of the great Hindu epic the Mahabharata. To write the book Gurcharan had gone back to his Alma Mater, Harvard, to brush up his Sanskrit. But Gurcharan was very much a businessman as well as a scholar. He had been the CEO of the Indian subsidiary of the multinational Procter and Gamble, and took early retirement to write when he was the Managing Director of Procter and Gamble Worldwide in charge of strategic planning. He was now on the board of the not-for-profit educational NGO funded by SKS Microfinance.

Gurcharan maintained that the regulations the government were imposing would mean death for the microfinance industry. 'Can you believe it?' he asked. 'We are being asked to get clearance for every loan, that means getting pre-approval for millions of women for millions of tiny loans.'

I suggested that would lead to widespread corruption because officials would only sanction loans if they were bribed.

Gurcharan agreed readily and went on to say, 'There are other regulations which will make doing business impossible. It all reminds me of the dreaded Licence-Permit Raj which we were meant to be getting free from. I wrote a book called *India Unbound* about this freedom and now we seem to be being bound again.'

'But surely there was a problem, and something had to be done,' I said.

'Well, let's take these suicides first,' Gurcharan replied. 'They are a terrible tragedy but I don't believe they were caused by professional microfinance companies like SKS, which would not have been so successful if it hadn't won the trust of its customers over the last ten years. If rogue companies or NGOs have been indulging in malpractices and encouraging women to get in debt and then using strong-arm tactics to get them to repay, they should be punished. Why kill the ethical ones? Because of the regulations the banks already are not lending. Our customers are not repaying, the recovery rate of loans has dropped from ninety-eight per cent to twenty per cent, and our shares have fallen in value too.'

'But this surely isn't just because of the new regulations. There has been the politicisation of the issue, with opposition politicians telling your customers not to repay their loans.'

'Yes, that's true. But I think this whole crisis has been whipped up because the government is angry that companies like SKS are doing much better than their microfinance scheme. Although the government offers loans at a lower rate of interest, people come to us because there is no hassle, no delays, and no corruption. Just look at how corrupt the government's retail banks in the rural areas are and you can imagine what it would be like getting a microfinance loan from a government scheme.'

The microfinance crisis was discussed in the academic weekly magazine *Economic and Political Weekly*. The magazine's editorial ended with an outright condemnation of the private sector, asking, 'How many more of the poor have to be pushed over the edge before the powers-that-be realise that for-profit microfinance has no purpose other than to reap the highest returns on the backs of India's poor?'

In his article in the same edition, an independent researcher, M.S. Sriram, was critical of the management of the top for-profit microfinance companies' management, complaining of 'greedy executive compensations and short-sighted behaviour'. But he hoped that the government and the Reserve Bank, India's central bank, would find ways of regulating microfinance which would not kill the for-profit model. Like Gurcharan Das he was very critical of the regulations the government of Andhra Pradesh had introduced, saying, 'It has shown its inability to target the errant microfinance institutions and has instead come down heavily on the entire market.'

I have often attended meetings of women's groups organised by NGO microfinanciers and not once has there been any pressure to borrow. The most recent occasion was a meeting of a group managed by an NGO called TARA, which stands for Technology and Action for Rural Advancement and is a sister organisation of one of India's most admired NGOs, Development Alternatives.

TARA has a centre in the countryside of a region called Bundelkhand. It's in the heart of India, some 400 kilometres south of Delhi. Bundelkhand is crossed by broad rivers, and rich in history and monuments, including the famous temples at Khajuraho. But the terrain is barren and strewn with rocks. The soil is unproductive and earning a sustainable living there is particularly challenging.

Bundelkhand is also a land of Maharajas. The most senior is the Maharaja of Tikamgarh, Madhukar Shah, a scholarly historian and the custodian of one of the major temples of Ayodhya. Another is Narendra Singh, the Maharaja of Sarila. Unwisely in my view, his publishers wouldn't let him call his autobiography *An Elephant for my Pram*. Its pedestrian title, which doesn't do justice to the colourful contents, is *Once a Prince in Sarila*. In this book, he tells the story of being a model, or perhaps I should say a dummy, Viceroy. He was aide-de-camp to Lord Mountbatten, who didn't have time to spend hours posing for his official portrait. So the young ADC stood in for Mountbatten while the artist painted his robes and their elaborate adornments. From time to time the real Viceroy came to check that the medals, the sash, and all the other regalia were in the right place. When Mountbatten wasn't looking, Narendra had himself photographed in vice-regal dress, probably the only Indian ever to have done so. The photograph, next to Mountbatten's, is published in his book. From this beginning, Narendra Singh went on to be a diplomat and a very successful businessman.

In a village near the TARA Centre in Bundelkhand I found a group of surly, suspicious looking men sulking behind a building and peeping round the corner periodically to see what their wives were up to. The wives were members of a group that TARA had established. They were sitting on the ground in a circle discussing loan applications. When I asked what they had achieved through such small loans I was told that they had built thirty-two houses, which had replaced mud buildings with tiled roofs that leaked during the monsoon.

The motivator of this group was Kaushalya, a young woman, little more than a girl. I wondered how she commanded respect from the members of the group who were all considerably older.

'I have been educated up to middle school,' she explained. 'They respect education and especially when I started teaching in this village they respected me. Out of that came not just one but three groups.'

'Why three?'

'That's what they wanted,' she replied, 'and anyhow the groups are not meant to be very big. So it's better to have three small groups than one big one. This is not a business where you are meant to get bigger and bigger. If we grow we must grow naturally,' she added with surprising firmness.

SKS is a business and there perhaps lies the fundamental difference between its microfinance lending and Kaushalya's.

Development Alternatives and TARA have also pioneered an NGO scheme for implementing Prahalad's bottom of the pyramid policy. They design machines that are suitable to local needs and distribute them to people who use them to build up small but profitable businesses. At the TARA Centre in Bundelkhand I was shown some of TARA's technology, including paper made from denim scraps, bricks that don't require firing made from fly ash, a waste product from coal-burning thermal power stations, and stone dust turned into concrete. All simple and easy to replicate technologies. But I saw the technology that impressed me most when I was taken out to the villages.

There we came across some two hundred and fifty cows in a very large pen. They were strays that would otherwise probably have been slaughtered. The breeds varied, as did the colours – some were white, some brown, and some grey. Their dung was fed into a bowl measuring sixty cubic feet and converted into biogas. The gas drove a fifteen-kilowatt generator. There is always a demand for power in rural India because even when villages are connected to the grid the supply of electricity is more than likely to be erratic. The slurry which emerged from the plant was mixed with compost created by vermiculture – literally worm-eaten vegetable waste – to make what I was assured was 'a very powerful combination'. I had seen small cow dung gas plants often before, but I had never seen a monster like this one.

When I met Ashok Khosla, who founded Development Alternatives back in 1983 to provide the poor with sustainable livelihoods, I suggested that there were similarities between his model and Prahalad's.

'Well, there are in that we both aim to serve the bottom of the market,' he replied, 'but I believe Prahalad and the private sector have got their economics upside down. Although they talk about the need to provide credit and that is true, their emphasis is on supply when what is needed is creation of demand. It's not the products that are missing; it's the purchasing power. Unless you can figure out a way to increase purchasing power, you are not going to reach those right at the bottom of the pyramid and there are an awful lot of them. Purchasing power is obviously best increased by providing people with ways of earning a living.'

Khosla is a man of many achievements. Born in 1940 into an academic family, his father a professor and his mother a lecturer, he read Science at Cambridge, and went on to get a PhD in Experimental Physics from Harvard. A member of the team that designed and taught Harvard's first course on the environment, Ashok seemed destined to follow an academic career in America. Instead he became involved in running Indian and international environmental organisations, winning numerous international awards and holding prestigious positions both in India and abroad. When he turned to entrepreneurship, and founded Development Alternatives, he retained his interest in the environment. He had recently been elected President of the International Union for the Conservation of Nature. But Ashok Khosla wears his prestige and achievements lightly.

Short and stocky, he usually dresses in crumpled kurtas, and likes to tell the story of bumping into a foreign friend at an international airport who was so surprised to see him in a suit that she exclaimed in a loud voice, 'Oh, Ashok – this is the first time I have seen you dressed!'

When it came to the private sector, Ashok Khosla said, 'They do have tremendous access to capital, and can do things very fast. They can bring technology and institutional innovation into the field, but they are driven by the profit motive and numbers. Mind you, with a population of more than a billion, I suppose being obsessed by numbers is not a bad thing.

But the profit motive does tend to distort decisions, to exclude any consideration for welfare.'

'What about contract farming?'

'Well, the missing link for farmers is the market, but the trouble with contract farming is that people like Pepsi are fair-weather friends. They take stuff when they want it. What are needed are long-term contracts. I agree you can't depend on the traditional local markets but contract farming – the way it's practised – is pretty brutal.'

As I expected, Ashok didn't have much time for the government.

'Government is hugely expensive,' he said. 'There are long delays and massive leakage too. People don't realise that it's not just the leakage that makes government expensive. If you take the building of a check dam for water harvesting, we do it for between a third to a quarter of the price the government does, even if you don't count the cost of all the leakage of funds which inevitably takes place.'

Ashok Khosla went on tell me about a government scheme to persuade villagers to buy cooking stoves that did not fill their cramped homes with smoke. The government had offered a subsidy of one hundred rupees on each stove. He dismissed the scheme scornfully, saying, 'Can you imagine villagers going through all the bureaucracy of the Block Development Officer and then tramping all the way to the District Headquarters and facing the bureaucrats there just to save one hundred rupees? No wonder no one bought the stoves. Look also at the government in the business of food distribution. Their fair price shops have been hijacked by babus and their cronies.'

So then I came to Ajay Mehta and Seva Mandir's patient community building. Ashok Khosla was very sympathetic towards this but he didn't think the dominant castes would ever let go. Explaining Development Alternatives' strategy he said, 'We are more mechanical. While we believe that the structure of society needs to be broken down, we think the answer is to give people the means to be more prosperous and so be able to claim their dues. And if you are worried about social equity, making sure the benefits are shared equally, we put the responsibility on the villagers. We say, for instance, we will give you a well on condition that everyone is allowed to use it.'

Finally I asked Ashok about the much-vaunted private–public partnership, the government providing the resources and the NGOs or the private sector delivering the development. For instance the government providing vouchers for education and the private sector the schools.

'It would be nice, wouldn't it, but where do you see it working?' he asked. 'The problem is that it's the natural tendency of the bureaucracy to trust only those in the system. What's more, they want to control the spending and allocation of resources for obvious reasons. They particularly don't trust NGOs because they show the government up for what it is. Look what the Finance Minister did recently – slapped income tax onto civil society and left it to the petty bureaucracy to decide who should be exempted, knowing full well how the petty bureaucracy operates.'

After much travelling and talking, I myself remain convinced that delivering development is a matter of balance. Advocates of the private sector often say 'if only the government will get off our backs ...' That's all very well but there has to be some regulation and the government must be ultimately responsible for providing that. Moreover, there are at present huge gaps in the services provided by NGOs and the private sector that the government has to fill. Those gaps may narrow but they will never be entirely filled. Furthermore, the farmers who had their crops rejected by Pepsi would agree with Ashok that contract farming can be brutal.

The government used to think of itself as the *mai baap*, the mother and father of everyone, the universal provider. But its past record has shown that it cannot fulfil that role, so it does need to hand over resources and responsibilities to the private sector and to NGOs.

The NGOs will always have a role as pioneers, like Seva Mandir, and as providers, like Development Alternatives, but they can never replace either the private sector or the government. As for the private sector, I personally believe that it will need to be restrained. If commerce is given free rein the damage that contract farming and 'farm to fork' retailing could cause to small farmers and shopkeepers could well lead to rioting and other protests that would be costly in the disruption they might cause to economic activites, and violent.

To me the one thing India needs to avoid is imitating practices first adopted in Western countries without adapting them to Indian circum-stances. I know it's selfish to want to keep my friendly neighbourhood shops, the chemist, the grocer, the butcher, and the sabzi or vegetable-wala I know so well, but they do serve a social purpose, keeping commu-nities together, and they deserve a living just as much as I do. Besides, just think of the pollution it would cause if everyone did their shopping by car, as they do in the United States.

7 | THE ENGLISH RAJ

Whether the government, the private sector or NGOs should deliver development is a question which will not have much relevance unless India's wealth continues to grow to pay for that development. English is one of the advantages India has which are said to be propelling it to economic super-power status. There are all those Indians who speak excellent English. It's the mother tongue of the elite and effectively the offical language of the central government. Then there is the growing number of parents who now aspire to give their children an education through the medium of that language. But is the craze for English an unmixed blessing?

Back in the sixties the British regarded Indian English as something of a joke. The comic actor Peter Sellers had mocked it so comprehensively that I found it well nigh impossible to get the BBC to allow anyone with even the faintest Indian accent on the air. In India, we native English speakers laughed at quaint phrases like 'please do the necessary and oblige', or more simply 'please do the needful', and 'it is suggested that the meeting be preponed', which appeared regularly in Indian official correspondence. A senior British diplomat once suggested that his PA should find some less geographically specific way of answering the telephone when he couldn't take the call than saying, 'Sahib is not on his seat.' Much to the diplomat's dismay a colleague told him that his PA had misunderstood the instruction and been even more specific. He'd told the colleague, 'Sahib is in the lavatory.'

Now with Indian writers carrying off the major literary awards, and Westerners in the IT and BPO industries talking of being 'bangalored' when they are replaced by English-speaking Indians, Indian English is anything but a joke. But could the very success of English in India 'bangalore' India's own languages? The linguist Professor David Crystal speaking in Delhi said, 'A language is dying every two weeks somewhere in the world today. Half the world's languages will no longer be spoken in another century. This is an extremely serious concern, and English has to share the blame.' Others put it less politely, describing English as a killer language.

But should India worry if English kills off some of its twenty-two officially recognised and hundreds of its not-so-official languages? Perhaps the answer is no. In his book comparing the future of India, China, and Japan, the former editor of *The Economist*, Bill Emmott, said India fell short of China in almost every measure except the ability to speak English. So why shouldn't India build on its one advantage? One practical reason is because, looking back over the history of India since it became independent in 1947, it is clear that any threat to Indian languages can provoke a violent backlash.

When India became independent it seemed essential to designate an official language and the obvious candidate was Hindi because it was the most widely spoken and, mixed with Urdu, had become the unofficial lingua franca of the Raj, known as Hindustani. But those who spoke other Indian languages were not at all happy because they feared Hindi would become a killer language.

In the fifties India's first Prime Minister, Jawaharlal Nehru, faced challenges from violent protests by Telegu speakers in the south and Punjabi speakers in the north demanding that they should have their own state with their language as the official language. Bombay, now renamed Mumbai, the commercial capital of India, was paralysed for a week during riots over the demand that it should be the capital of a Marathi-speaking state. In the southern city of Madras, now Chennai, the English daily *The Hindu*, which could by no means be called sensationalist, described the violent protests there against Hindi as 'a mass uprising'. The paper reported police trying to disperse 'riotous mobs' by beating them with canes, with lathis or lead-tipped staves, and by opening fire. Twenty-two people were shot dead in one day and the mobs took their revenge by burning two police officers alive. Some protesters immolated themselves. Railway stations were captured, suburban train services suspended, and mainline services seriously affected. Post offices were set on fire and shops looted. Schools and colleges closed.

As the riots continued the army was called out, the last resort in a country which at that time was acutely aware of the dangers of involving the military in civilian affairs. Two ministers of the central government tendered their resignations and in Parliament opposition members from Tamil Nadu ranted against 'the bloodthirsty Chief Minister', accused the government of 'indiscriminate firing', and asserted 'there has been no rule of law in Madras state, only the law of the jungle has prevailed'.

The Prime Minister, Lal Bahadur Shastri, broadcast to the nation assuring the people of Tamil Nadu that Hindi would not be imposed on them, but the riots continued. Indira Gandhi, then just a comparatively junior minister in Shastri's government, upstaged him by rushing to Tamil Nadu and helping to bring the situation under control. Inder Malhotra, one of India's most respected political correspondents, remembers Shastri being very annoyed that Indira had jumped over his head, but she was unapologetic. She told Inder Malhotra she didn't consider herself just the Minister for Information and Broadcasting but 'one of the leaders of the country', and went on to say, 'Do you think this government can survive if I resign today? I can tell you it won't. Yes, I have jumped over the Prime Minister's head and I would do it again whenever the need arises.'

By going to Madras, Indira Gandhi demonstrated the courage and political astuteness that were to be the hallmarks of her career as Prime Minister. She was astute because as a North Indian she realised that involving herself in the affairs of a southern state would strengthen her claim to be a leader of the whole country. At the same time she was well aware of the deep feelings that had been aroused by what the people of Tamil Nadu saw as a threat to their language, Tamil. That awareness stayed with her when she was Prime Minister and so she insisted that Tamil Nadu should be the only state in which the government television service's national news in Hindi would not be broadcast.

India has a tradition of syncretism, of adopting and adapting rather than opposing. When a follower of Mahatma Gandhi died while fasting in protest against the government's refusal to create a state where Telegu would be the official language and Nehru reluctantly accepted the demand, he feared that 'India was becoming a land of fortresses with walls built round them', and warned Indians: 'We have disturbed the hornet's nest and I believe most of us are likely to be stung.' However, the hornets eventually returned to their nest and India adapted to its many languages because the government became wise enough to realise that it was best to allow Hindi to spread naturally as a link language rather than force the pace.

Now that Tamils know Hindi is not going to be imposed on them they are no longer mortally afraid of it. There is even a demand to learn Hindi in Tamil Nadu. C.N.V. Annamalai is General Secretary of the South India Hindi Promotion Organisation in Chennai. On the walls of his office hang pictures of the distinguished Indians who have supported its work. They include Mahatma Gandhi, Indira Gandhi and her son Rajiv. But in spite of this powerful support, promoting Hindi in Tamil Nadu used to be an uphill task.

Annamalai, an impressive, well-built man whose brow was smeared with gray sacred ash, said, 'I am a pukka Tamilian from Kanchipuram, a city that has existed since the Vedas, and I've always been proud of that, but when I was young and said I wanted to learn Hindi because Gandhi would have wanted me to, I was accused of not being a Tamil. I was threatened and all my school friends turned against me.'

'What about now?' I asked.

'There are no problems now. There are three hundred schools in Chennai now where Hindi is taught as a second language. Here we find more women come than men and when you teach one woman you teach a generation.'

Annamalai said the turning point came with the extraordinarily popular Hindi television serials of the Hindu epics the Ramayana and the Mahabharata in the eighties. 'People here wanted to understand the series so they started to learn Hindi.'

There are other reasons for the gradual spread of Hindi. In spite of the popularity of Tamil films, Bollywood's all-pervasive Hindi movies and their songs have a following in Tamil Nadu. Hindi widens the job market, extends educational opportunities, and it's an asset in the tourist business now that so many Indians are travelling within their own country. My Hindi-speaking Tamilian taxi driver pointed out, 'North Indians are very happy to find someone in the south speaking Hindi. They give bigger tips.'

But it would be unwise to make too much of Tamilians learning to live with Hindi and assume that therefore they will not object to the incursions of English. The lure of Hindi is insignificant when it's compared with the attraction of English. English is seen as the gateway to the world, while Hindi is only the gateway to North India, so while there may be Tamils learning Hindi as a second language, there are far more Tamils learning English. So far however there are no signs of a widespread backlash against English, in spite of its reputation as a killer, but there are Tamils who are very concerned about its impact on their language.

Some twenty years after the anti-Hindi riots, I met a man who had devoted his life to Tamil publishing because he feared his language's development was being stunted by the dominance of English among the elite. He had said to me, 'English is not a healthy thing. It limits the possibilities of the expression of experience. Unless we do most of our communication in Tamil a large section of the people will not be able to understand wide areas of experience. There will just not be enough Tamil works or indeed words for them.' Since I wanted to discover how the demand for English, which has grown because of its advantages in the new fast-expanding economy, was now affecting Indian languages I decided to go back to see Ramakrishnan of Cre-A publications.

Driving through the streets of Chennai, I could see everywhere signs of the new economy – shopping malls, international brand names, international fast-food chains as well, old buildings that had been knocked down and replaced by new monstrosities, and of course cars, motorcycles, scooters and unwieldy buses, all tangled up in traffic jams.

When I came to the gleaming white basilica that stands over the crypt where the relics of the apostle St Thomas the Doubter are preserved, I saw a large notice – in English of course – announcing that his resting place was now an international shrine. I thought to myself, 'So even poor old St Thomas has become a victim of the global commercialisation.' Mind you, if the legends about St Thomas are true, he must have been quite an international figure himself to get from Palestine to India and then cross the country to preach in a place which the two British founders of Madras described as 'no-man's-sand' when they arrived there. One legend indicates that St Thomas' preaching did not go down well and that he died a martyr, but according to another legend he was accidentally shot by an arrow from a hunter's bow. He is said to have remained an international figure after he died. Edessa in Iraq, the Greek Island of Chios, and the Italian town of Ortona all claim to have relics of St Thomas.

Eventually I reached the office of Cre-A, where I found Ramakrishnan at his desk. Sturdily built, but by no means stout, he had barely aged over the past twenty years, but he was even more pessimistic than he had been earlier about his language, Tamil.

'English has become an even greater threat with this boom in IT while Tamil has not exploited IT,' he said and went on to explain: 'There are no Tamil spell-checks, there is no hyphenation, no dictionary on the net. That's because everyone thinks English is the only language of IT and so now there is a craze for education in English, with both children and parents saying there is economic value in English and not in Tamil, and everyone seems to think life is all about economics.'

Ramakrishnan lent back and glared at me.

'You look as though you are blaming me for the damage English is causing,' I said.

He laughed. 'No, not really. It's not you English who are to blame. Actually we Tamils are to blame for not looking after our language and seeing that it develops.'

Cre-A's office is a small first-floor residential flat on an avenue lined with rain trees in south Chennai. In spite of its size, it's not cramped but neat and orderly, like Ramakrishnan himself. He always insists that he is not an academic, but I remembered him as having the tidy mind of an academic and the ability to spend hours paying attention to details that would drive me with my much more limited attention span to despair. My memory was confirmed by the two books on his desk. Both were dictionaries: one the *Oxford Advanced Learner's Dictionary* and the other Cre-A's own *Dictionary of Contemporary Tamil*.

As a preparation for writing this chapter I had just read *Spoken Here:*

Travels Among Threatened Languages by Mark Abley, who believes 90 per cent of languages will be extinct by the end of this century. He described English as being the Walmart of languages, 'convenient, huge, hard to avoid, superficially friendly, and devouring all rivals in its eagerness to expand'.

Tamil should be in a strong position to put up a fight against English. It is one of only two Indian classical languages and it is still spoken, while the other, Sanskrit, is somewhat like Latin in Britain, only used by scholars and priests. The earliest history of Tamil is inevitably disputed, but it goes back to at least 300 BC. Medieval Tamil religious poetry, suffused with love for the Gods Shiva and Vishnu, is widely acknowledged to rank with the greatest religious literature in the world. Today Tamil is spoken by some sixty million Indians. It's also the language of northern Sri Lanka and is spoken extensively in Singapore and Malaysia. So I suggested to Ramakrishnan that there was no evidence to suggest that Tamil was being devoured by English.

'That's not the point,' he shot back. 'I quite agree that English is a language that can kill but it's also a language which maims, and that is our problem. We have a great past, a glorious tradition, and we are not going to be wiped out, but we are not addressing the problems of the present and future of Tamil. What we have to do is to ensure that Tamil remains capable of generating knowledge.'

'So how is English preventing that?'

'Whatever new knowledge is generated comes to us via English. It's borrowed from English. People work in English. Tamil was capable of generating knowledge. Today even many academics think half in Tamil and half in English, and then they produce a pedantic language, Tamil with English sentence patterns.'

With his mop of grey hair, Ramakrishnan always reminds me of a fighting cock, ever ready to go into battle. He has been a fighter all his life. His mother would get him to carry milk for anointing the images of the gods in the temple and he would get angry because he felt it would be much more useful to give the milk to the poor. Ever since then he has been fighting against religion. He fought against tradition by living with a partner for sixteen years, until she died of cancer. They never married, much to the disapproval of Ramakrishnan's family. For the thirty-five years he has been in publishing he has been fighting for Tamil and his job has become his passion.

Ramakrishnan's weapon in the fight to ensure that Tamil continues to develop as a language in which knowledge can be generated is Cre-A's own dictionary of contemporary Tamil.

Opening the dictionary, Ramakrishnan showed me a message from the designer of its special font: 'No formalities needed for this font. It is a gift from me to you. Thanks for your inspiration.'

Ramakrishnan said, 'This is another example of how Tamil has failed to develop. There is a chronic lack of fonts so I had to get one specially designed.'

Ramakrishnan was the editor as well as the publisher of the dictionary, and it took twenty-eight years to complete. It has already been expanded once but it hasn't been a great commercial success. In fact Ramakrishnan said he would never have gone into dictionaries if business had been his only criterion.

One reason the dictionary hasn't done better business is the pedantry and intellectual snobbery of the Classical Tamil purists. They disapproved of the dictionary when it was first published, accusing Ramakrishnan of promoting slang. A professor of Tamil, who took shelter behind a pseudonym, wrote a review in which he said, 'Under the cloak of "contemporary" and "standard written Tamil", the tragedy of stabbing Tamilians with his own hands has once again been staged.' Tamil academia has, not surprisingly, ignored the new expanded version of the dictionary. Ramakrishnan says, 'It's been like the Tamil saying "if you drop a brick in a well it stays there".'

But Ramakrishnan was not disheartened. 'Whatever the reaction,' he said, 'I know I and my team have undertaken a vital task. This is the only dictionary of contemporary Tamil, in fact the only contemporary dictionary of any Indian language. The intention is to make Tamil more capable of generating knowledge, and to help people read, write and understand modern Tamil. I accept that it won't change the situation overnight, but I hope it will bear fruit in forty or fifty years' time.'

Ramakrishnan didn't have much hope that the government of Tamil Nadu would help to hasten the day when his dictionary would bear fruit. Apparently the government purchases a lot of books because it has one thousand six hundred libraries, but they are not valued by their quality, the amount of work that has gone into them or by the publishers' suggested prices. Those who purchase books for the libraries have just two criteria, the number and the size of the pages. Ramakrishnan refuses to have his books treated as commodities and so he doesn't sell to the state libraries. There is a government Tamil Development Directorate but it is bogged down in the purist pursuit of trying to eliminate any Sanskrit words from its word bank.

It's a measure of the lassitude of Indian governments that there has been so little official attention paid to ensuring that Tamil keeps up with the times and remains a language in which knowledge is created. In the wake of the riots against Hindi, the DMK, a Tamil regional party appealing to Tamil pride, ousted the Congress Party. Ever since then Tamil Nadu has been governed by that party or the party which broke away from it.

The DMK traces its origins to the Self-Respect Movement in the nineteen twenties. It considered Tamil so central to Tamilians regaining their self-respect that the language was promoted to the status of a goddess, Tamil Tay. According to this movement it was North Indian Brahmins with their language Sanskrit who undermined Tamilian self-respect. Under the British Raj the Brahmins certainly dominated Tamil Nadu, and succeeded in cornering the jobs and educational opportunities that came with the British. In 1913, 75 per cent of the graduates of Madras University were Brahmins although they represented only 3 per cent of the population.

The Brahmins also undermined Tamil self-esteem by claiming to be innately superior intellectually. This claim was widely accepted by the British. In *A Book of South India*, the author, J.C. Molony, a British civil servant, said the Brahmins dominated politics and 'lucrative employment' because of their 'intellectual superiority'. Tamil Brahmins' intellectual ability is still admired today in banking and in IT, where 'Tambrams', as they are known, are considered a class apart.

It's not surprising that the founder of the Self-Respect Movement, E.V. Ramasamy Naicker, known as EVR, was a fervent advocate of Tamil and virulently opposed to what he called 'Brahminical Sanskrit'. He had a particular dislike of Gandhi, and accused him of being Brahminical. EVR demonstrated his dislike by living life in flagrant contradiction to Gandhi's principles, deliberately cultivating a reputation for indulging his appetites rather than curbing them, as the ascetic Mahatma so publicly did. As for religious faith, which was central to Gandhi's life, EVR coined a slogan: 'He who created God is a fool, he who propagates God is a scoundrel, and he who worships God is a barbarian.'

The DMK and its rival the AIDMK both still claim to follow the ideology of the original Self-Respect Movement, including its respect for the goddess Tamil Tay. They both owe a tremendous debt to Tamil because they spread their message through Tamil films. The founder of the AIDMK was a legendary film star turned politician, M.G. Ramachandran. After ten years in power, during which Tamil Nadu did not exactly prosper, MGR's film fans still remained so loyal to him that several immolated themselves when they heard he had died. His successor, Jayalalitha, a formidable lady, was a film star closely associated with

MGR. At the time of writing the Chief Minister was the DMK's M. Karunanidhi. He was renowned as a Tamil film-script writer and a poet and was known as 'the protector of Tamil poetry, music and theatre', but Ramakrishnan didn't think he was doing much to protect the Tamil language from the threat posed by English.

'How can Karunanidhi claim to be concerned about Tamil when it is not even taught as a compulsory subject in many schools?' he asked angrily. 'Even in the schools run by the government it is only compulsory up to class five, and children don't have to take any exams until class eight.'

'So why has Karunanidhi lost interest in Tamil, surely it's still a potent political issue?'

'No, it's not. It's not just the tremendous demand to learn English which has taken the steam out of the Tamil issue. Karunanidhi himself was involved in two historic campaigns against Hindi but now in Tamil politics there is not a whimper against that language. It's happened ever since the Tamil parties joined coalitions in the central government in Delhi and realised the value of Hindi as well as English in national politics.'

'So you are fighting against two killer languages.'

'You could say that. Do you know that in English medium schools many children choose Hindi not Tamil as their second language?'

Ramakrishnan believed the answer was to insist that all children should be educated in Tamil medium up to the sixth class.

That was also the view of a Tamilian who, although armed with a PhD in Electronics from Maryland University, had given up the prospect of a lucrative career in America to return home and campaign for better education. Balaji Sampath, a large, balding, middle-aged man with a casual attitude to shaving, was now heading an NGO called AID India, which trained teachers in government schools and devised educational aids for them. He took me to the Lloyds Road Corporation School to see some of the aids his society provided to government schools. On the way he told me the lure of English was so strong that parents had come to believe if their children were educated in Tamil medium schools they would become second-class citizens.

There were no surprises about the school. It was a series of square concrete boxes, built in the uniform Indian government style, around a rectangular court. The monotony of the architecture was relieved by a magnificent tree in one corner of the courtyard, which I thought was a rain tree but was told very firmly it wasn't. No matter how poor the education may be, in any Indian school the children are almost always immaculately turned out and the Lloyds Road school was no exception. The boys all wore light blue checked shirts and dark blue trousers and the girls light blue checked blouses and dark blue skirts. Some of the girls had strings of jasmine flowers clipped to their heads or entwined in their plaits.

In one of the classrooms nine-year-old children were sitting in different groups, making use of educational aids designed by Balaji's colleagues. There were boys counting imitation currency notes to make up sums of money which corresponded with the figure on a card each was holding. Balaji said, 'They should have learnt this in the second standard and now they are at the fourth.' One particularly eager boy came up to me to show me a word he had made on a card designed to improve vocabulary, and a girl rocked gently as she read aloud in a sing-song voice. She was reading a story from the Panchatantra, a collection of Indian animal fables. Another girl could only read by spelling out the letters from a specially designed reading book. 'You see how standards vary,' Balaji said, 'but these girls are nine and they should all have been able to read by the age of seven.'

Balaji went on, 'Probably all the parents of these children would have preferred to send them to an English medium school but they couldn't afford it. Ask them what their fathers do.'

One drove a scooter rickshaw, two worked for the company which collected the garbage. There was a father who erected *pandals*, the tented pavilions which shelter guests at weddings and other functions, and another who cooked biriyani. One boy was not too clear about his father's occupation. All he knew was that his father went to some office.

'There, you see.' commented Balaji. 'There are three categories of school in Tamil Nadu – elite private schools providing a good education in English, private schools where parents spend money they can ill afford to provide a bad education in English, and government schools like this teaching in Tamil, which only parents who can't afford to pay for their children's education patronise.'

'And this is because Tamil is seen as second best?'

'Very much so. But what is worse is that the children from the inferior English schools emerge knowing neither English nor their mother tongue properly. Although the government schools have better-trained teachers, better facilities and are free, parents opt for the inadequate English schools.'

After hearing these woeful stories about the demand for English and its impact on Tamil, I was surprised to read a report in the newspapers about the launch of a new university course in media studies to be taught in Tamil. It was to be taught in Loyola College. Founded by the Jesuits, it was an oasis of order surrounded by the chaos and cacophony of Chennai traffic, a green lung in a city choked by congestion and pollution.

The original building might best be described as colonial Palladian with three storeys each lined by arches in a different style. The chapel appeared to be a smaller version of the cathedral which stands over the tomb of St Thomas. Both are shining white, is built in the same late-nineteenth-century high Gothic style, and have similar spires a hundred and seventy-five feet high. In the shadow of the chapel a man knelt in prayer in front of a tomb in the graveyard where former Jesuits from the college are buried. The uniform, plain tombstones are inscribed with the name of the Jesuit, the date of his joining the order, the date of his death, and his age. Behind the small graveyard students jogged round and round a football field. Outside the west door a young woman practised riding a scooter, evidence of how far Chennai, regarded as the most conservative of India's four metropolises, had come.

The media school was in one of the more modern buildings on the campus. Vatican Radio had an office there. The director, Father S. Rajanayagam, was one of the fifteen Jesuits teaching in the college. The Jesuits spread throughout the world are commanded by their General based in Rome, and their constitution has been described as 'military and autocratic', but there could be no one less military in appearance than Father Rajanayagam. His beard was unkempt, as was his hair straggling down below his shoulders. He was wearing a blue denim jacket and cap and creased white cotton pyjama trousers. A fervent advocate of Tamil, he believed in tackling English head on, by exploiting the advantages Tamil still has.

'Why misguide the youth by telling them English is the solution to get good employment?' he asked. 'Tell them it's only one of many solutions. Why not make what appears to be a handicap a strength, and give the youth the opportunity to exploit the opportunities Tamil offers? That's why we started this course. Tamil newspapers have a far larger readership than English ones and they need people who can write in Tamil. You can't compose a radio jingle if you don't think in Tamil. Advertising agencies are always saying they can't find people who will think and sell concepts with Tamil cultural values.'

The new course was part of the Jesuits' option for the poor, and in India that means an option especially for the Dalits or former Untouchables, and the tribals or indigenous people. Father Rajanayagam's aim was to recruit students from poorer backgrounds who hadn't had the opportunity to study English and he intended to give preference to the Dalits and tribals who applied to join the course. He admitted that this would be 'a daring venture' because many of those admitted would inevitably not have had a good education so far.

Tamil was very dear to Father Rajanayagam. He had written two books in which he had evolved a Christian theology rooted in Tamil culture. He was also a Tamil poet, novelist, and short story writer. I was surprised to hear that he had published a collection of Tamil feminist poems jointly with a woman professor who is a friend. I wasn't surprised that he too was disappointed by the Chief Minister and his colleagues' lack of zeal for their own language.

'How can Karunanidhi lead the movement against Hindi and come to power on its back and then educate his grandsons and granddaughters in schools where Hindi is taught?' he asked. 'How is it that all DMK leaders send their children to English medium schools?'

Chennai has one of the country's five original IITs, or Indian Institutes of Technology, the prestigious engineering and scientific colleges set up after Independence with foreign help to supply the scientists and engineers needed to build 'the new India' Nehru dreamt of. The IITs have certainly fulfilled the ambitions of their founders. They have produced a regular flow of world-class graduates, so world-class that many of them are snapped up by other countries. America's Silicon Valley owes an enormous debt to India's IITs. IIT Chennai would have been an obvious place to discover whether Indian languages were losing the capability to generate knowledge, and whether we needed to worry about that, but the two people I knew I could discuss this with were both teaching in IIT Delhi.

I failed at my first attempt to get into the Delhi IIT campus because the gate I used to drive through had been closed for security reasons. It took a little time to persuade the all-too-typical security guards that merely blowing a whistle and waving me away wasn't very helpful and that it would be nice to be told which gate I could drive through. Eventually I reached that gate and drove through the extensive campus to the main building, which could at best be called functional, but I suppose that is no bad thing for an institution where the emphasis is on the functional. After walking down a very, very long corridor with identical classrooms on both sides I came to the office of Rukmini Bhaya Nair, the Head of the Department of Humanities and Social Sciences.

Rukmini is an academic with a formidable reputation. In the laudation, or commendation, she received when she was awarded an honorary degree from Antwerp University she was praised for her 'synthesis of the humanities'. The core of that synthesis was described as 'narrativity', telling stories to define who we are. So I suggested to Rukmini that it was important to make sure India's different languages were kept alive so that the stories they told could be preserved. She agreed.

'India has so many cultures and they have been expressed in its different languages. The languages keep them alive, and keeping the languages alive becomes particularly important because so much of this culture is oral still. Mind you, we are the greatest repository of scripts in the world too. So Indians are always illiterate because there are some of their scripts they cannot read. But that doesn't mean we should allow the scripts to fade away any more than we should allow the languages to do so.'

'But you teach and write in English, and isn't it English which is threatening these languages, and I assume these scripts too?'

'Yes, and I have said some pretty harsh things about English.'

Rukmini then showed me a long poem she had written called 'Ode to Our Languages'. It seemed to me very harsh on English:

English, smart, jackbooted, of our languages
the one we fear the most [...]
To this divinity we have willingly sacrificed
Our children, to it we kneel, babbling.

'So are you not afraid of English?' I asked.

'Well perhaps not, at least in India's case. I wouldn't deny that English is eating up or you could say cannibalising other languages. But it's possible that here in India we have ways of living with English without being eaten by it. I notice this in my students because they are schooled in at least two languages, English and their mother tongue. The way they swap from English and Hindi shows their confidence.'

That still left the problem that exercised Ramakrishnan so much, the question of the development of Indian languages so that they remained capable of creating knowledge. Rukmini suggested I put that question to her students, and promised to let me sit in on a class she was teaching after lunch.

Lunch was in Rukmini's small flat on the campus. The wall of the outside staircase leading to her flat had been smeared with whitewash that had seen too much water, someone had scribbled in chalk over the door of the servants' quarters, and the whole building had the air of neglect that pervades government buildings in India. When I asked Rukmini why the elite, modern IIT couldn't do better when it came to maintenance she said, 'Whenever I complain about maintenance it is implied that I should not be addressing myself to such mundane matters. I am told, "You are not being sufficiently serious about your academic subjects."'

There was further evidence that the minds of the IIT's governing body are on higher things than mere administration when we got back to the main building on the campus where Rukmini was to teach her class. One of the lifts was not working, and the other lift got stuck between floors with us inside it.

When we eventually reached the classroom we found eighteen young men and six young women sitting around a table, all of them 'freshers'. Rukmini introduced the question of English by asking how many of them had been educated in their mother tongue. All had been educated in English medium schools and coaching institutions which crammed students for the highly competitive IIT entrance examination. The students came from all over India, including the remote and mountainous northern area of Ladakh on the Tibet border.

When I asked whether they had learned their mother tongue properly although they had not been taught it, one student from the south said, 'Not in my case.' A fervent advocate of Hindi said scornfully, 'Some people can't do basic things, can't count for instance in their mother tongue.' No one demurred.

The Hindi speaker appeared to be the only student who read books in his mother tongue. Yet almost all of them spoke affectionately of their own languages. One student said, 'We love our mother tongue because it signifies home, family, love.' Another agreed and said, 'We want to be proud of our mother tongue but we don't want to say so in public. People don't necessarily want to speak in English, but they feel forced to.'

The Hindi speaker intervened: 'I certainly do say I'm proud of my language in public and I speak it rather than English.'

Then I asked whether science could be studied in any Indian language. Even the Hindi speaker admitted that was a problem. No one had an answer when I asked why science could be studied in Russian or Japanese, if it couldn't be studied in an Indian language. But then one student remarked, 'Why should we worry? English is an Indian language,' and everyone, Rukmini and myself included, laughed.

But when I went to see Amitabha Bagchi, a young mathematician who teaches the maths of computer science in IIT, he told me, 'It's not true that Hindi cannot be used to create knowledge. What is true is that in maths and science there is the notion of a global audience and your work has to be original. That means it has to be in English.'

Amitabha graduated from IIT Delhi and then spent six years at Johns Hopkins University in Baltimore before returning to teach in his Alma Mater. I asked whether he had felt it was his duty to come back to India where salaries were so much lower and international prestige harder to come by.

'Oh no,' he replied with a laugh. 'There was no high-minded motive about my return. It wasn't patriotism or love of my country, not that I don't love it. The only way I can explain it was just the knowledge that Delhi was the only place I could live in.'

Amitabha told me he sometimes found Hindi more effective than English in putting over particularly difficult points in lectures and tutorials while some students only felt confident asking questions in Hindi. However, although he felt Hindi could be used to create knowledge, Amitabha did not think that in the long run it would be used in maths and science. But he went on to say, 'I don't think that matters. Different languages have different strengths and in the popular sphere Hindi is unchallenged. It's the language which has street cred here in IIT. Even now when I meet my college friends we speak in Hindi, and if someone speaks in English he gets mocked.'

With the popularity of Hindi, there is evidence to suggest that the question of language comes full circle here. Maybe in North India it's Hindi which is the language that is maiming English. In an English novel called *Above Average*, which Amitabha wrote about his days as a student in IIT, a friend became a *yaar*, attempting to attract a girl became *line maro*, getting into a fight became taking *panga*, and blacks in America became *kaloos*.

But Amitabha didn't think the emergence of Hinglish mattered. 'I'm opposed to the snobbery of much of this talk about Hinglish,' he said. 'I think in India it's a natural development for Hindi words to be used in English and English in Hindi. The Indian Urdu poet Akbar Allahabadi used English to evoke humour and Bashir Badr has used English as pronounced in Urdu to give an everyday feel to his poetry.'

The reverse process took place throughout the British Raj. Any English dictionary contains words which came into the language through the Hinglish that the British spoke during the Raj. Bungalow is believed to derive from the Bangla- or Bengali-style houses the early British built. Gymkhana is a hybrid from an abbreviation of the Greek gymnasium and the Urdu suffix *khaana* which means, amongst other things, house. Pyjamas, pundits, pugs, as in pugmarks, all came into English from India, as did bangle and bazaar. When I was young my ayah, or Indian nanny, would call me a badmash and I was delighted to find that both those words have found a place in my English dictionary.

So many English words are entering Hindi that scholars are now studying Hinglish as a language in its own right. One scholar, Rita Kothari, associate professor at the Mudra Institute of Communications in Mumbai, has said, 'Hinglish tends to be dismissed as the preserve of those who know neither English nor Hindi well. It now deserves its due as the popular idiom, one that has helped us shed our colonial hangover and appears to be emerging as a sort of link language.' But there is no comfort in that for Tamils such as Ramakrishnan, and for those who love all the other regional languages spoken in multi-lingual India. As far as they are concerned, Hinglish is a combination of two killer languages and perhaps all the more dangerous for that. Maybe the answer for Ramakrishnan is to expand his dictionary of contemporary Tamil into a dictionary of Tamish?

I can understand why Ramakrishnan would regard the encouragement of Tamish as a step too far in keeping his language up to date. But the market for Tamil speakers which Father Rajanayagam has identified, the circulation figures for Indian newspapers showing that there is only one English language daily among the top ten, the rest being Indian language papers, and the money being invested in regional language television, all indicate that Indian English is not 'bangaloring' other Indian languages. However, although they don't seem to be likely to number among the languages English is going to destroy, they are likely to be maimed, their development stunted, unless children are educated in their mother tongue, at least in the earlier stages of schooling.

With those words I thought I had reached a reasonably balanced conclusion to this discussion about the impact of English on Indian languages, but I should have remembered that discussions in India have no end, there are indeed no full stops in India. My complacency was shattered a few weeks later when I received an unusual invitation to a foundation day and dinner. The invitation was to celebrate the foundation of 25 October as English Day and was sent by Chandrabhan Prasad, the Dalit activist behind the survey I discussed earlier that showed how Dalits' lives were changing for the better in Uttar Pradesh.

Chandrabhan thinks English should 'bangalore' all Indian languages. So fervent is his admiration that, taking a leaf out of the book of the Self-Respect Movement in south India, he has consecrated a temple in which English is the deity. In posters he and his supporters have distributed, the Goddess English is modelled on the Statue of Liberty but holds a fountain pen instead of a torch in her upheld hand. A computer stands at her feet. The poem on the posters ends:

> With Goddess English the baby will not grow up
> to serve landlords,
> The baby will not grow up to skin dead animals,
> The baby will not grow to raise pigs,
> The baby will not grow to chase field rats,
> The baby can grow into an adjudicator,
> The baby can grow into an employer,
> into a benefactor.

Chandrabhan's opposition to Indian languages springs from the belief that they prescribed and still preserve the laws of caste which have oppressed Dalits for so long. In his four-page invitation he quoted a heroine of the Dalits, the nineteenth-century Savitribai Phule, as saying: 'Through English, casteism can be destroyed and Brahminical teaching can be hurled away.' In a more imaginative vein Chandrabhan wrote of Manu, the ancient Hindu law-giver hated by Dalits for promulgating the laws of caste: 'Manu didn't go to an English school, he remained English illiterate all his life. With entire India turning English, Manu would under-graduate to a monkey at the Times Square knowing not where to go, what to do ... Friendless and frustrated Manu would have all options closed.'

Unfortunately I was out of Delhi on the night of the dinner but I arranged to have lunch with Chandrabhan a few weeks later. I asked him why he felt English could do away with caste.

'Because it has no links with Indian culture, tradition or metaphysics,' he replied. 'You have to realise that language is not autonomous. It is linked to culture and so Indian languages are linked to caste. If English becomes the one national language it will link India together without caste. Caste, as you know, divides India.'

But can it really be right that a language imposed on India by her colonisers, a language which for so long was the entry ticket to the elite of the country, an entry they guarded jealously, be the national language? Are all the traditions and the culture preserved by Indian languages rendered valueless or even worse by caste? Chandrabhan would say yes. He believes, 'Tradition is nostalgia, which is a psychological weapon of the dominant.' I would say that is taking opposition to caste one step too far. But then I haven't suffered the oppression that Dalits have.

A few weeks after meeting Chandrabhan I received another reminder that India is a land in which one can never say 'that's it'. Earlier in this chapter

I reported criticism of the Chief Minister of Tamil Nadu, Karunanidhi, for being lukewarm about his state's language, Tamil. Just when I thought that with the Goddess English this chapter was done and dusted, I learned of a vast World Classical Tamil Conference that Karunanidhi's government had sponsored. It was held at Coimbatore, a large industrial city in Tamil Nadu.

In a newspaper article the two chairmen of the conference described it, in the English that has become an Indian language, as, 'one of the grandest conferences ever conducted attended by some of the tallest research workers'. The timing of the conference was not surprising. The state assembly election was due in six months. Clearly the Chief Minister believed that the electorate did take great pride in their language. That confirmed my belief that the Goddess English will never kill Indian languages, she will learn to live with them. But surely more than that is needed. Sanjaya Baru, the editor of the *Business Standard*, a daily widely read by those in industry and commerce who have a vested interest in expanding the role of English, surely got it right when he wrote, 'Every educated Indian must be proficient in her mother tongue. A two-language policy – mother tongue and English – must be made compulsory.'

8 | ENTREPRENEURSHIP UNLEASHED

The remarkable developments in India's corporate world over the last twenty years have highlighted the advantages India has when it comes to doing business – its entrepreneurial flair, and managerial talent. The second is remarkable in a country where the government mismanages so much.

Outside the Mumbai Stock Exchange a bronze bull, charging, tail up, head down, and unfortunately reminiscent of the Merill Lynch bull that met such a sorry fate during the sub-prime crisis, represents the self-confidence of the Exchange. Since 1991 it has grown from a purely Indian affair, with foreign investors excluded by law, to a truly international marketplace. Now international fund managers feel they must have Indian investments in their portfolios. Processes have been modernised and regulation has improved because the Exchange has been allowed to make its own rules instead of having them devised by bureaucrats who, although possibly strong on economic theory, didn't understand market practices.

The companies quoted on the Stock Exchange have developed into successful competitors in the global market. But not all the bureaucratic constraints on them have been removed. Government policies are still not implemented transparently. Ministers and bureaucrats have too many discretionary powers to bend those policies for their own benefit too. And businessmen and women have not been above using influence – would be a polite way to put it – in order to persuade ministers and bureaucrats to bend policies in their favour. Nevertheless India does now have some remarkable companies.

The Reliance Group is India's largest private sector enterprise. It started in textiles and has grown into the largest polyester yarn producer in the world. Among other Reliance interests are oil and gas exploration and production, petrochemicals, plastics, retail and infrastructure. Then there is the Aditya Birla Group, a twenty-nine-billion-dollar multinational operating in twenty-seven countries and earning 60 per cent of its revenue from outside India. Its interests are very varied, spanning aluminium, copper, cement, acrylic fibre, financial services, retail, and much else.

The group pays particular attention to corporate social responsibility, as the term goes. Each plant has to involve itself in welfare activities. I have made films for the group about micro-credit schemes, education, health and veterinary services, provision of drinking water and even mass weddings provided by its companies to the people living around their plants. Aditya Birla is by no means the only group to show that Indian companies can operate internationally. Meanwhile, the large number of global automobile brands seen on the Indian roads shows that it's now possible for foreign manufacturers to set up in business here.

But, as I said, all is not well with Indian business. In particular there are frequent allegations that business is responsible for much of the political and bureaucratic corruption that plagues the country. I decided to look at one group to illustrate the positive and negative sides of the business ledger in India, and I chose Tata. The Tata Group is India's largest conglomerate, its interests are also the most varied, its history the most fascinating, its shareholding the most unusual. Tata is also a remarkable example of the way that Indian companies have expanded over the last twenty years, and within the group is India's largest IT company. IT is the field where the most remarkable developments have taken place. At the same time the group has not been above controversy. It is one of the business houses whose role in a major scandal in the mobile phone business is under investigation.

*

I first went to visit the Tata headquarters in Mumbai in November 2008 when a bear was rampaging through the trading floors of the Stock Exchange and the Indian rupee was falling. The *Business Standard* reported exports shrinking for the first time for five years, automobile companies cutting output, airlines threatening job cuts, the Security and Exchange Board of India conducting a survey 'to probe investor apathy', and harassed business executives turning to gurus for spiritual comfort.

Despite this there was no sign of any panic in Bombay House, a four-storey, early twentieth-century stone building with clean classical lines that contrast with the extravagance of the ornate Saracenic-Gothic Bombay the British built. Hidden in a narrow street round the corner from the Stock Exchange, Bombay House is the headquarters of the Tata Group.

Before the Indian economy opened up in 1991, Tata only had limited interests outside India. By the time I visited Bombay House the group had operations in over eighty countries, and had bought well-known international companies such as Daewoo, Jaguar and Land Rover, and the Anglo-Dutch steel manufacturer Corus. But unlike the Stock Exchange's bull there was no emblem of success outside Bombay House. When I arrived there I couldn't see any sign of who occupied the building so I had to ask the security guard standing in the porch whether this was indeed the home of Tata Sons.

Jamsetji Nusserwanji Tata, the merchant turned industrialist who founded the group in the nineteenth century, was renowned for his reticence. When he died *The Times of India* wrote, 'He was not a man who cared to bask in the public eye. He disliked public gatherings, he did not care for making speeches ... He sought no honour and he claimed no privilege.'

The current Chairman of Tata Sons and therefore of the Tata Group is the great-grandson of the founder and renowned for his reticence too. Ratan Tata, a bachelor living in a Mumbai flat, shuns the celebrity culture of today's India. Educated at Harvard and Cornell Universities, he has spent his entire working life with the family group, starting as a blue-collar worker on the factory floor of Tata Steel's mill.

Inside Bombay House I found an unostentatious, sober way of doing business. The dress code was dark suits and discreet ties. Senior executives had tastefully furnished offices, a long way from the functional work stations seen at the highest level in some companies where good taste would be considered frivolous and the ethos demands creating the impression of sacrificing everything to efficiency and being permanently busy. In spite of the turmoil on the Stock Exchange, and the consequent fall in the value of many Tata companies, three executives heading major companies in the group and others who were directors of Tata Sons found time to meet me during the two days I was there.

It was clear that Tata Sons did not subscribe to all the shibboleths of modern management. The cult of youth was not followed. The retirement age for directors was seventy-five. Staying with one company was not considered evidence of a lack of ambition and initiative. There have been only five chairmen in the one hundred years since Tata Sons was founded. One of them, J.R.D. Tata, served for fifty-three years, steering the group through the Second World War and the difficult post-Independence decades of the Licence-Permit Raj. All the top management of the hugely successful IT company Tata Consultancy Services had been around for four decades. I learnt that Tata did not believe it was necessary to pay absurd salaries to retain the loyalty of its top executives.

But for all Bombay House's reticence, the brochure I was given describing the group said its purpose was 'to grow aggressively in focussed areas of business'. Ratan Tata had taken over as Chairman in 1991, the year India faced bankruptcy and the Prime Minister, Narasimha Rao, took advantage of the crisis to force India to face up to the fact that the Licence-Permit Raj had to be dismantled. The new Chairman used the freedom the group was at last given to fulfil its purpose by growing aggressively. The areas Tata's one hundred companies now operate in vary from providing Information Technology services in forty-seven countries to selling tea bags in even more; from manufacturing steel to crafting fine jewellery. Tata makes the world's cheapest car. Its chemical group is the third largest producer of soda ash in the world. Much of Mumbai's electricity is generated by Tata. It provides for travellers wanting to live in the height of luxury, owning, amongst other grand hotels, the renowned Mumbai Taj, a landmark for passengers approaching India's commercial capital by sea. The group also has hotels with no frills for those travellers who have meagre budgets. It has a presence in financial services and in retail too.

When he set out, Ratan Tata decided it was necessary for Tata to become less reticent and to make the most of the good name built up over more than one hundred years by creating a unified brand that is promoted by all the group companies. So now, in the open square just down the road from modest Bombay House, no one can miss the Tata logo emblazoned on a gleaming white skyscraper. It houses the international telecommunications business Tata took over from the government – privatisation that would have been unimaginable during the Licence-Permit Raj.

So how does the reticent tradition of the apparently old-fashioned Bombay House fit in with the companies it controls which are committed to aggressive growth and ostentatiously promoting the Tata logo? I got a clue when Alan Rosling, the Englishman who was the only foreigner on the board of Tata Sons, winced as I described Tata as a conglomerate. 'Conglomerate is rather negative,' he said. 'We would describe ourselves as a diversified business house.' Tata Sons is like the head of a house and the companies it controls are treated like members of a family. All have independent boards and Tata Sons is there to guide and support them rather than direct or govern them. Ratan Tata took over a collection of companies so independent that they had, in his view, become a commonwealth rather than a group of companies. He feared that his predecessor

J.R.D. had taken Tata Sons' tradition of easy-going patriarchy so far that the group was in danger of disintegrating.

Tata Sons is also there to ensure that the unique traditions of the group are upheld. No matter how competitive the struggle to grow may be, how necessary aggression may be, all companies have to subscribe to the Group Purpose. It is not just the usual increasing of shareholder value, although from the founder onwards all Chairmen have realised they have a duty to shareholders. Tata's purpose is to 'improve the quality of the communities we serve through leadership in sections of national economic importance'. Some 65 per cent of the shares of Tata Sons are held by philanthropic Tata trusts. Tata companies also accept the group values which include: 'What comes from the people goes back to the people many times over.'

Tata's purpose and values are inherited from the group's founder, Jamsetji Tata, who, after making a fortune from trading and the textile industry, went on to risk that fortune in ventures that he hoped would enable India to catch up with the industrial and technological revolution taking place in Europe and America. When a statue in his memory was unveiled in Mumbai, *The Times of India* said, 'to his mind wealth and the industry which led to wealth, were not ends in themselves, but means to an end, the stimulation of the latent resources of the country, and its elevation in the scale of nations'.

Jamsetji was acutely aware that before it was colonised the Indian subcontinent had been one of the great manufacturing areas of the world, and that it was missing out on the industrial revolution because it was only allowed to develop on British terms. Those terms favoured the interests of Britain rather than India. So Jamsetji set out to pioneer steel-making, and hydro-electric generation, both of which schemes only matured after he died. He did complete his third pioneering venture, the building of the Taj Hotel. Legend has it that Jamsetji vowed to build the best hotel in Bombay after he had been turned away from a hotel which only welcomed white guests. However, Sharada Dwivedi, who has researched the history of the Taj, says, 'Jamsetji was too proud a man to visit such a hotel. It is more likely he gave such an outstanding hotel to his city because of his deep love for Bombay, a city he was proud of.' Unfortunately the Taj was not an instant success and became known as Tata's White Elephant until the Second World War rescued it from that unfortunate sobriquet.

But the Tata Group would not be where it is if it was so high-minded that it scorned behaving as other businesses do, if it was so philanthropic that it forgot the need to make profits. When he opened an extension to one of his cotton mills, Jamsetji Tata said, 'We do not claim to be more unselfish, more generous, more philanthropic than other people. But we think we started on sound and straightforward business principles, considering the interests of our shareholders, our own, and the health and welfare of our employees the sure foundation of our prosperity.' Ratan Tata, the present Chairman, has taken radical and difficult decisions after consulting McKinsey, considered the arch high priests of modern business methods. He has brought about the first internally imposed restructuring in the group's history. But in the epilogue he wrote to the history of the company he said, 'I would hope that my successors would never compromise and turn to soft options to meet their ends, and never allow the Tata Group to join the growing number of companies in India which have shed their values, forgotten about their integrity and closed their eyes to maintaining ethical standards.'

There are two obvious reasons why the Tata Group should have been able to help India fulfil the dream of its first Prime Minister, Jawaharlal Nehru. It was the same dream as Jamsetji Tata's – the dream of India recovering from missing out on the industrial revolution because of the lost years of Imperial rule, of India becoming one of the great industrialised nations of the world. Both Nehru and the Tata Group believed this could best be done by developing basic industries. Jamsetji Tata and his successors had laid some of the foundations for the fulfilment of that dream. There is no doubt that J.R.D. Tata, who was Chairman of the group for the first forty-four years of India's Independence, would have built more on them, had it not been for the Licence-Permit Raj. Looking back on the years of Nehru and his daughter Indira Gandhi towards the end of his own life, J.R.D. Tata said, 'My one sorrow and regret is that the government had, from Jawaharlal Nehru's time and at least up to a couple of years ago, not allowed many of us imbued with enthusiasm and hope to do enough.'

The second reason why Tata could have contributed so much more to the growth of the Indian economy in the early years of Independence is their history of pioneering and of persevering when the going got hard. In his foreword to the official history of the group, J.R.D. Tata wrote of its 'remarkably consistent propensity, perhaps unavoidable in any pioneering and risky venture, for getting into difficulties in the early years of new projects, and ultimately retrieving them by enormous and prolonged effort backed by a dour determination not to admit failure'.

The history of Tata Steel is an example of this ability to pioneer and persevere, which could have been so valuable when Nehru had to start industrialising India almost from scratch. It was in 1882 that Jamsetji Tata conceived the idea of founding India's first steel plant, but he had to keep it alive for seventeen years before the British Government liberalised their policy and granted him a licence to prospect for iron ore. He then paid for two expensive failures to find iron ore in sites suitable for manufacturing steel.

Eventually he was told of an iron deposit which had been discovered in the central Indian princely state of Mayurbhanj. The deposit was conveniently near coalfields. It's often forgotten that some of the Maharajas administered their states more progressively than the Raj administered British India, and the ruler of Mayurbhanj was one of them. He had the foresight to see how his state would benefit from the steel mill and the railway it would bring with it, and offered liberal concessions to Tata. Eventually an adequate source of water was also discovered, but Jamsetji died three years before that. His son Dorabji, who succeeded him, met with much discouragement, and not a little racial prejudice. Sir Frederick Upcott, the Commissioner for the Railways – potentially a major customer – poured scorn on the idea that Tata could manufacture steel rails to British specifications, and committed himself to 'eat every pound of steel rail they succeed in making'. It was his words he should have eaten when Tata exported 1,500 miles of steel rails to Mesopotamia during the First World War.

Dorabji originally attempted to raise money to finance the project on the London market, but Rudrangshu Mukherjee, the historian of Tata Steel, says, 'There existed enormous problems, mostly to do with racial bias, in raising capital in London.' Eventually Dorabji succeeded in doing what at that time appeared impossible – he raised the capital he needed by selling shares in India. But that wasn't the end of his money worries. Tata Steel flourished during the First World War but after that the directors overreached themselves with their expansion programme and Dorabji had to pledge his entire fortune, including his wife's jewels, to tide the company over its difficulties.

Chemicals was another basic industry that India did not develop under British Rule, until in 1939, eight years before Independence, Tata Chemicals was formed. At that time India was almost entirely dependent on imports for chemical salt products. True to Tata form, the company had more than its fair share of difficulties. Its first consignment of turbo-generators was sunk at sea during the war. The second consignment wandered from Sweden to Moscow and then the Gulf, before eventually landing in Bombay. A foreign consultant poured cold water on the whole project, saying, 'You are in the wrong place doing the wrong job; the sooner you get out the better.' It took sixteen years for Tata Chemicals to prove him wrong and make a profit, but then there was another setback. In the sixties the plant and its township on the coast of the western state of Gujarat almost ran out of water. The problems posed by a persistent shortfall in the monsoon were overcome by a crash programme of innovative technology which reduced the need for water, recycled fresh water, and used sea water.

Karl Marx had forecast that the arrival of railways would industrialise India. He got that wrong because the British saw to it that the manufacture of railway equipment, which could have industrialised India, took place back at home. As Independence was approaching, Tata were able to start manufacturing steam locomotives in an old railway workshop which they had bought. What's more, they did not tie themselves to Britain's apron strings. In its heyday the Tata Engineering and Locomotive Company (TELCO) manufactured one hundred locomotives a year and 98 per cent of their parts were Indian. Steam lasted longer in India than in most other places but Tata could see that it would have to go and so they turned to manufacturing commercial vehicles. The Tata tradition of getting into trouble hit the company at the start of the new millennium, just as they were planning to move into manufacturing cars as well as commercial vehicles. The market for commercial vehicles suddenly collapsed. There were as yet no cars to sell, but the car project's costs had mounted up. The company showed a loss for the first time.

Ravi Kant, of Tata Motors, as TELCO has become, was one of the Managing Directors of a Tata Group company who had not spent most of his working life there. A graduate of one of the prestigious Indian Institutes of Technology, he joined Tata Motors from the electronics multinational Philips.

Ravi Kant's fastidious appearance – neatly brushed white hair, notably well-cut suit, and stylish but unostentatious colour combination – was matched by the neatness of his mind. Facts and figures, memories of the past, and plans for the future he recalled without any hesitation.

Remembering the market collapse facing the company when he first joined in 2000, he said, 'It was a rude awakening. It chastened the whole organisation, and forced us to rethink our whole future and come up with a new strategy. We had to stop the bleeding.' The new strategy did staunch the flow of losses. Ravi Kant said, 'We consolidated our presence in the Indian market. We revamped our product. We revamped our market. We revamped everything. As a result the turnover of the company had increased from two and a half billion dollars to twenty-four billion. More than fifty per cent of that revenue, perhaps nearly two-thirds now, comes from outside India.' The revenue from abroad has been boosted by international purchases, in particular the purchase of the bankrupt Korean manufacturer Daewoo. Under the Licence-Permit Raj, Tata Motors would never have been allowed to purchase Daewoo, or the upmarket Jaguar or the all-purpose Land Rover. The strict controls on foreign exchange and on investing would have seen to that.

The automobile industry is the most often quoted example of the pernicious effects of the Licence-Permit Raj. Industrialists had to obtain a licence to invest, and existing manufacturers didn't want any new competitors. They had ways of seeing that new licences were not granted, and so for many years one car, Hindustan Motors' legendary Ambassador, reigned virtually unchallenged on the roads of India. It was an Ambassador that I drove into the back of a tractor in the incident I described in the introduction.

The Ambassador was originally designed and manufactured in the late forties in Britain as the Austin Cambridge and the Morris Oxford, and its technology was transferred to India. Sturdy, with the high clearance necessary for negotiating potholed roads and bullock-cart tracks, the Ambassador looks like a bowler hat on wheels with its rounded roof and its stubby bonnet and boot. For a short while an Indian version of the

British Triumph Herald did make an appearance during the Licence-Permit Raj, but it proved too delicate for India's roads and Indian driving. The only rival to survive along with the Ambassador was a small square Fiat but it really wasn't up to much more than city driving, and became the standard Mumbai taxi.

For ten years an abortive challenge to the Ambassador was mounted by Indira Gandhi's younger son Sanjay. His sole qualification was an unfinished apprenticeship with Rolls-Royce in Britain. Although her son had no business experience, in 1970 Indira persuaded her cabinet to license him to manufacture 50,000 cars annually, when other experienced manufacturers, including Tata, had been refused licences.

The excuse the government had given for rejecting other applications for licences was that cars were luxuries and India's scarce resources should not be wasted on them. Sanjay got round that one by saying he would make a people's car, a car ordinary people could afford to buy. But inevitably there were cries of foul play. The leader of the right-wing Hindu Jan Sangh, Atal Bihari Vajpayee condemned the decision as 'corruption unlimited'. A Communist member of parliament was more poetic. He described Indira Gandhi as 'the fountainhead of all corruption in India'. Indira Gandhi replied, 'It is obvious that some people are opposing my son's project and attributing all sorts of irregularities to it merely to malign me ... In fact nothing irregular has been done and no favour shown to the project ... There is nothing wrong in a young man proving his capacity.'

Unfortunately for Indira, her son did not have the capacity to develop and manufacture his car, which he called Maruti after the Hindu god of the Wind. In 1980, ten years after receiving his licence to manufacture the Maruti, Sanjay Gandhi crashed his plane while performing aerobatics and was killed. The Maruti was still not on the road. To keep Maruti in existence Indira Gandhi nationalised the company. But that did not overcome the problem of the people's car which had to be produced if

Sanjay's memory was not to be associated with a project that had been an abject failure. To solve that problem, Indira waived the strict restrictions on foreign investment by allowing the Japanese motor manufacturer Suzuki to buy a major share in the nationalised Maruti. Suzuki effectively took over the running of the company, which did then produce the first people's car in India.

Tata Motors have shown that India could have built its own modern, bottom of the range car years ago without any foreign collaboration if it hadn't been for the Licence-Permit Raj. After Suzuki effectively took over Maruti, Tata were still refused a licence to collaborate with Honda and so they decided they would have to make a car without any foreign collaboration. When they came out with a small car called the Indica it proved very successful in the market. Ravi Kant is very proud that the trend set by the Indica has continued.

'We manufacture Indian cars,' he said. 'That's more than China does. Their cars are all produced by joint ventures with foreign companies. We worked backward to design our cars. We survey the market, analyse who will be our customers and what they will want, as well as what they can afford to pay. So with the Indica we discovered that customers wanted a car as roomy as the Ambassador at the cost of a Maruti and we gave them that.'

Tata had now moved even further downmarket with their plans to build what they claimed would be the cheapest car in the world, a car called the Nano. It was about to hit the market. I asked Ravi Kant what had been the reaction to the Nano.

'When other manufacturers saw it they were shocked. They didn't believe it could be done,' he replied.

'Who will be your customers this time?'

'When you look at families on a two-wheeler, a husband and wife and two children, you can see it's very unsafe. The family is exposed to the elements and of course to pollution and it's very uncomfortable too. So then you discover that eight million two-wheelers are sold every year. To work out the price we found that two-wheelers were sold for about 42,000 rupees and the cheapest car was about 200,000 so we went halfway and came up with a price of one hundred thousand.'

Although Tata Motors' potential was wasted for so many years by the restrictions the Licence-Permit Raj imposed on them, Ravi Kant told me there was a positive side to that story,

'Because we were not allowed to import components, the commercial vehicles we made were 99 per cent Indian. That meant we had to devise ways of being self-sufficient. When we came to manufacture a car on our own we couldn't have done it without the competence that we had already developed. But on the other hand it has to be said that during the Licence-Permit Raj we didn't develop our product as we should have done. You see, we were in a sellers' market because our production and our rivals' production was limited by the government. So there were always more customers than vehicles, and there was no pressure to improve the product. That was a gap which had to be filled after the economy was liberalised.'

As he was short, thickset, and determined, I had thought Ravi Kant might be pugnacious. I wondered what he would feel about having to spend time talking to a journalist when he had much more important things on his mind with his company facing difficult market conditions. But I was wrong. Ravi Kant was extremely polite and as he showed me out of his office he said, 'It's good to talk to someone like you because it takes your mind off all the bad things which are happening.'

Tata Steel was one company that was particularly suited at Independence to play a major role in Nehru's dream of building the basic industries which would be the foundations of a new modern India. But the Licence-Permit Raj saw to it that the company's potential was not realised.

Jamshed J. Irani joined Tata Steel in 1968, after working with British Steel. He became Chief Executive Officer in 1991 and retired ten years later. But he was still a non-executive director of Tata Steel and some other Tata companies so he retained an office in Bombay House. Through the large windows I could see a verandah packed with plants. 'Our not very successful attempt at gardening in Tata House,' Irani said with a broad grin.

Relaxed, and avuncular, now in his seventies, Irani told me what his life was like in the last ten years of the Licence-Permit Raj.

'I had to go to Udyog Bhavan, the offices of the Ministry of Industries in Delhi, at least twice a month if not more. Secretaries and Ministers would condescendingly give us time. They never said yes at the first meeting, we would have to go again and again because there were always "a few more questions". Now when I go to the same ministry I don't need a prior appointment. There is no one in the corridors. Before it used to be like Grand Central Station.'

'What impact did this have on the company?' I asked.

'We failed entirely to modernise because of the Licence-Permit Raj. You couldn't get permission for anything. On at least one occasion we were told to pull down a product line we had put up. At the same time we couldn't get a proper price for what we were able to produce. Every year the Bureau of Industrial Costs and Prices would grant us a small increase in price and tell us we were lucky to get that. J.R.D. Tata told me we had only been allowed to manufacture steel because we were in place before Independence. The thinking was that all steel should be in the public sector.'

'And how is it now?'

'We feel as free as any company in America. The decisions are ours and the money is ours. People often blame corruption for the problems of the old Raj but it was lethargy more than corruption that caused the problems. Civil servants being unwilling to take decisions.'

But I had recently heard the director of a foreign company saying that India was still one of the most difficult countries in the world to do business in. When I put this to Irani he said, 'Well, I have to agree there is still a certain amount of lethargy about. The Finance Minister has said this country won't progress until the politicians learn to say no and the civil servants to say yes. He is right, the politicians say yes to every populist demand they think will get them votes, and the civil servants tend to say no because that's less risky than saying yes. The government is unable to follow its own dictates. There are plenty of good rules now but the government is short on application, so people who want to misuse those rules and create trouble can get away with it.'

In the years of comparative freedom that Tata Steel has enjoyed, it has modernised, expanded, and become a multinational. My next appointment was with the Managing Director, B. Muthuraman. I once flew with him from the headquarters in Jamshedpur to Mumbai and found him a most friendly man, and a great talker without any of the airs and graces one might expect from someone so senior. I wasn't disappointed this time. Muthuraman greeted me with a smile so broad that it split his face and crinkled his eyes. With his neat wavy white hair and uniform dark suit he looked like a benevolent bank manager of the old school. When I told him this he laughed and said, 'I don't know whether such figures exist today.'

Muthuraman joined Tata steel in 1966, and so had twenty-five years in the Licence-Permit Raj and now he had enjoyed seventeen years of 'freedom'. He calculated that when the government controlled the prices, Tata Steel and the Nationalised Steel Authority of India had between them effectively given away five hundred billion rupees. 'Those were sums which could have modernised and expanded production, introduced new products, and been spent on research,' he said.

It took Tata Steel time to recover because it was in such a poor state when it was released from the chains of the government controls. B.

Muthuraman said, 'All plants were outdated. We had no idea how to market. Our decision-making process was hopeless because we didn't have to make decisions. The government made them for us. There was no research and development and no proper supply chain. One consultant told us, "You look ugly and you may well not survive."'

It took nine years for the company to revive. During that time the workforce was cut back from 78,000, making two and a half million tons of steel, to 35,000, producing seven million tons. The plant was modernised, IT and marketing were reorganised, and well-defined decision-making processes put in place so that by 2000 the company felt ready to expand.

Five years later, the Chairman and the Chief Executive Officer of the Anglo-Dutch steel manufacturer Corus came to talk to Tata Steel about the possibility of evolving strategies to work together. As these talks evolved Corus came to believe that it might be best to be taken over. B. Muthuraman was involved in these talks and he told me, 'Corus saw India as a growth story and they realised that we had a firm base here with good access and good markets. The courtship lasted one year and we met ten to fifteen times.'

'So was it a smooth marriage?' I asked.

B. Muthuraman laughed, 'Not really. In the end we had to bid for the bride. There was an auction with CSN of Brazil bidding against us. The auction in London lasted from nine-thirty at night our time to five-thirty in the morning. There was an hour between the bids. I watched with Ratan Tata while our man in London bid. CSN confused us by varying the amount by which they upped their bid for each Corus share. It varied between one penny and eight pence. We had a simple formula go up by five pence at a time, and eventually we won out.'

The founder of the House of Tata was determined to manufacture steel because he realised that would at last make India a player in the industrial revolution. J.R.D. Tata foresaw the IT revolution and was determined that

India would not be left behind again. So in 1968 he founded Tata Consultancy Services, normally known as TCS, to ensure that India found a place in the new world of Information Technology which was in its infancy. He was fortunate to find an engineer called Faqir Chand Kohli to head TCS in its early days. Kohli was a visionary with remarkably accurate foresight. He told the Computer Society of India: 'Many years ago, there was an industrial revolution; we missed it. Today there is a new revolution – a revolution in Information Technology which requires neither mechanical bias nor mechanical temperament. Primarily, it requires the temperament to think clearly. That we have in abundance. We have the opportunity to participate in this revolution on an equal basis; we have the opportunity even to assume leadership in this revolution. If we miss this opportunity those who follow us will not forgive us for our tardiness and negligence.'

By the time I met S. Ramadorai, Faqir Chand Kohli's successor, he had been Chief Executive Officer of TCS for thirteen years, and the company had become the largest IT consultancy services and solutions company in Asia, with offices in Britain, America, China, and Japan among other countries. I met Ramadorai in a multi-storey residential building well away from Bombay House and the commercial heart of the city. The spartan flat he was staying in was a company guesthouse.

The CEO had been with TCS for thirty-seven years and so remembered the early days.

'We had no access to capital,' he said. 'The tariffs were very difficult and it took three years to get a licence to import a computer. There was a condition that you had to export five times the landed value of the computer otherwise you would have the machine confiscated. The dedicated lines we opened up to customers gave us enormous problems because they were a government monopoly. As a result we had to physically send tapes and disks. I remember that when I was doing business in Britain I used to post two sets of them back to India, one from Feltham and one from Trafalgar Square to make sure one got through.'

The CEO was from the southern state of Tamil Nadu, renowned for its serious-minded, highly intelligent intellectuals. Lean, thin-faced and bespectacled, Ramadorai seemed to fit into that bracket. He told me that his main interests were reading and music. But underneath the serious appearance there lay a sense of humour. He was particularly amused by my description of the days of socialism and central planning as the Neta-Babu Raj – *neta* being a leader or a politician and a *babu* being a bureaucrat.

'That's good,' he said. 'It was your netas and babus who caused all the trouble. For instance, by stifling the economy, they drove all the talented young engineers out of the country. How could they stay here when there were no opportunities for them? We knew we had to get them back otherwise we wouldn't do anything of any relevance. Nothing existed inside India except for lots of Neta-Babu Raj.'

'Yet the IT industry did manage to spring up much more rapidly than any other,' I said.

'Ah, but you see, that was in part at least because the netas and babus were not involved. They didn't know what was going on, because we didn't need the government for anything except visas to bring in foreign consultants. They probably wouldn't have understood it if they had known what was going on.'

Ramadorai was all too well aware that the advantage he and other Indian IT companies had fought to establish was threatened by the poor standard of so many Indian universities and the danger that the supply of young engineers would not meet the growing demand. So he was sending TCS engineers to more than three hundred colleges to help their faculties, in his words, 'come up to scratch'. He'd also established a programme that trained science graduates to become software professionals.

'We don't just suck from the system,' Ramadorai explained. 'We contribute to the system, we have a commitment to nation building.'

I managed to return to the subject I was particularly concerned about for one last question, asking Ramadorai, 'Would you say that the Neta-Babu Raj is no longer a problem? Many businessmen say it does still create difficulties.'

'Dealing with multiple government agencies is still a problem but the situation has improved. There has been an enormous improvement. We now do a lot with the government, for instance we have just taken on passports. I am very optimistic, having lived here for thirty years, seeing opportunities as they arise. You have to work within constraints. You have to fix problems, not complain about them.'

I had gone to meet the Tata senior executives at the start of my travels for this book because I wanted to catch those who had experienced the bad old days before they retired. As I was finishing this book, I asked to meet a director of Tata Sons to discover how the group had fared during the two turbulent years through which the global economy had just passed. I also wanted to know whether the board was still confident about the future of India, and as happy as they had been about the acquisition of Corus Steel and Jaguar-Land Rover. I was invited to discuss these questions with R. Gopalakrishnan, an executive director of Tata Sons, chairman of three Tata companies, vice-chairman of another Tata company and director of three more.

Once again I walked up the steps and through the rounded Roman arch that leads to the marble-floored reception area of Bombay House. From there I was escorted by a messenger in immaculate white uniform to R. Gopalakrishnan's office. Opposite the lift was a bronze bust of J.R.D. Tata, the patriarch who had steered the group through the dark days of the Licence-Permit Raj. I wondered what he would think of today's Tata, which had expanded from being an almost entirely Indian group to a multinational earning 65 per cent of its revenue from abroad. Would he worry that in the hurry to expand Tata was losing the ethos he had nurtured, the ethos that had been established by the founder?

R. Gopalakrishnan, always known as Gopal, was sitting behind his spacious, semi-circular desk. 'Will you sit opposite me, or would you prefer to sit over there?' he asked, pointing to a sofa set, with a portrait of Jamsetji Tata, the founder of the group, on the wall behind it. I was happy to sit at the desk.

An engineering graduate, Gopal had spent thirty-one years with the Indian subsidiary of the international multinational Unilever. Twelve years ago he met Ratan Tata, who invited him to join the board of Tata Sons as an executive director. A natty dresser, with his matching shirt and tie, fashionable rimless spectacles, and neatly trimmed greying hair, Gopal talked in polite but staccato sentences, giving instructions to his personal assistant before our discussion started.

I started the interview by asking what the last two years had been like for Tata.

'We've been through a bloodbath,' he admitted frankly, but then he added, 'We have come out looking good. There has been all this global turbulence but because of the changes made by Ratan Tata we have had the advantage of a strong domestic basis. That has put us in a unique position to use all the skills we have acquired in cutting flab here in our foreign companies, which hadn't had to do that for some time. It's like a guy who had a horsewhip and he had not been using it. Mind you, I wouldn't like my foreign colleagues to think we came in with a horsewhip,' he hurriedly interjected and went on, 'but suddenly it became very useful. The benefits of that are beginning to show in cost-cutting and rationalisation.'

I then got a breakdown on developments on the domestic front, which included setting up a plant in thirteen to fifteen months for the very small car, the Nano, that I had talked about on my earlier visit, and plans to expand steel production by six to eight million tons. 'When the rest of the world was looking bleak we were looking to invest more capital,' Gopal said.

The troubles that Tata had faced at its iconic Taj Hotel on the waterfront in Mumbai had evoked not only national but global sympathy. On 26 November 2008, heavily armed terrorists – members of a Pakistan-based organisation called Lashkar-e-Taiba – had burst into the opulent heritage hotel firing at random. They roamed through the building killing guests and staff, setting off explosions, and lighting fires. It was one of ten coordinated attacks, in which at least one hundred and sixty-six people died. National Security Guards and other forces only regained control of the Taj on 28 November. During the attack Indian television networks showed pictures of smoke billowing out of the massive grey stone building.

Part of the hotel was reopened in December of that year but it wasn't until 15 August 2010, the sixty-third anniversary of India's Independence, that the hotel was fully restored and formally reopened. Gopal said the attack had been an emotional blow but the financial blow had been softened by insurance: 'It was as if all my family furniture was lost. Although I got it all insured that didn't make up for losing all my memorabilia. It was a period which tested the leadership of this company to show we can not only survive but how stoically we are able to bear misfortune, to take it and still carry on, as Job must have done in the Bible.'

The tragedy of the Taj wasn't the only setback that the Tata Group had suffered over the last two years. They had to move their Nano project from the eastern state of Bengal to Gujarat on the other side of the country because of a dispute over the land on which they had started to construct the plant. The oppositions took full advantage of the dispute to embarrass the government. Other major projects had been held up by land disputes or projects that environmentalist organisations strongly disapproved of. I suggested that Tata's difficulties indicated that, in spite of the economic reforms of the last twenty years, India's problems of governance were far from resolved.

'There is a problem of governance in this country,' Gopal readily agreed. 'There's a problem of political, civic and corporate governance. But I believe this is an inevitable part of a maturing democracy. In fact I would say an inevitable part of a maturing democratic capitalism.'

He then continued with one of the allegories he was so fond of: 'It's just like human beings can't go straight from childhood to adulthood without going through adolescence, and any adolescence brings with it certain symptoms. Because a young man is difficult in adolescence it doesn't mean the young lad is no good. The symptoms of our adolescence are an apparent, no not an apparent, a real lack of governance, almost anarchy.'

Gopal hurriedly corrected himself again: 'No, I wouldn't say anarchy because that might get confused with the Russian form of anarchy. We do have rules of law, a constitution, but there is corruption. Mind you, I've been looking at Britain and America, I have collected so much material that I might be reading for a PhD, although I certainly don't intend to do that. The situation in both places was absolutely horrible. There were statements made at that time like, "There is no future if these kinds of things carry on." In a sense this gives me some comfort that all is not lost.'

'But when America and Britain were going through what you call their adolescence things moved much more slowly. How much time do you have?'

'That's a very interesting point. If America and Britain had fifty or seventy years, we only have fifteen to twenty. But I do believe that when my head touches the pillow for the last time, which God willing will be in fifteen or twenty years, we'll have got out of this. I am that optimistic.'

Gopal, like most people in business, bases a great deal of his optimism on communications technology's ability to make government much more accountable and less corrupt.

Although an enthusiast for technology Gopal said it was not 'a silver bullet', and then went on to explain: 'The government still has to bring in a clear set of decisive rules. You can't have a computer that partly understands what you mean. That means bringing in a clear-cut set of decisive rules. Nor can the government ignore the people's aspirations. This is a most important part of democracy. The froth of people's expectations must bubble up from the bottom.'

It's always seemed to me that the aspirations of the business leaders, aspirations to be able to be as competitive, creative and productive as business anywhere else in the world, should make them cheerleaders of the campaign for reforming the government. When I asked Gopal whether he thought the business community was sufficiently vocal he replied: 'Absolutely not. Business leaders are deeply concerned that the government will use its powers against them. The government has such powers that if it chooses it can spray its weapons at you. You can be in utter misery. Our institutions are politicised, as you know, so everyone prefers to keep quiet. Equally unfortunately, government still has too many powers that enable it to grant favours to industrialists too. It's the characteristic of the crony capitalism stage we are passing through that the government still has controls that enable it to offer favours.'

By now my time was up but Gopal agreed to have breakfast with me the following week after his early morning game of tennis at the Mumbai Gymkhana Club.

Smartly on nine o'clock I walked into the club to be greeted by Gopal, this time looking even nattier in a bright lime-green shirt and tie. We sat down on the verandah of the club looking out on Azad Maidan, a large open park in the centre of Mumbai, where young cricketers were sharpening their skills in nets, supervised by bowling and batting coaches.

Shortly before my interview Gopal's chairman, Ratan Tata, had given an interview to a television network in which he warned the government that if it didn't uphold the rule of law India could become a Banana Republic.' He went on to describe Banana Republics as being 'run on cronyism'.

I started our conversation by suggesting that it was very atypical of Gopal's normally taciturn chairman, who rarely spoke to the press, to be so outspoken.

'It is atypical,' Gopal agreed. 'Ratan is not a man who courts controversy or publicity. For a man who values his privacy as much as he does, going public like this is very unusual.'

'Well, his remarks bring us back to the crony capitalism we were talking about earlier. Ratan also seems to suggest the threat to India is cronyism.'

'Yes, you see the characteristic of crony capitalism is that there are no rules and no clear policy. If there is no policy, scarce resources like land, water and spectrum lend themselves very easily to crony capitalism. Take land, where we have had our difficulties. In India we are still dependent on a nineteenth-century act. We always blame the British so this comes in very handy. Because there is no proper policy, politics have developed in such a way that the government has become the arbiter, and it is not beyond reproach.'

Ratan Tata's outburst had been prompted by the press publishing recorded extracts from telephone conversations of a prominent lobbyist, Nira Radia. One of the conversations made public was with Ratan Tata himself. I heard part of that conversation on the net. Most of it was a monologue by the lobbyist who was attempting to explain why the Telecommunications Minister, Andimuthu Raja, was not accepting Ratan Tata's view of the correct way to allocate spectrum for mobile telephone companies. At one stage however I heard the gruff voice of Ratan Tata saying, 'I am surprised that Raja, after all you supposedly did for him, is playing this game.'

India was in the middle of two scandals that were rocking the political and business worlds. The first scandal that was being investigated was the apparent embezzlement of massive funds by the organisers of the Commonwealth Games that had taken place two months earlier. The organising committee was headed by a senior politician from the ruling Congress Party.

The second scandal concerned this allocation of spectrum – the electro-magnetic bandwidth required for operating a mobile phone network. The Telecommunications Minister had issued spectrum at a price so low that the government auditor estimated he had lost the country the equivalent of some forty billion dollars. At the same time the Minister had devised a scheme for the allocation of the scarce resource which unjustly favoured some companies. Tata is a big player in the mobile phone business. I pointed out that it had been suggested the Radia tapes showed Ratan Tata was indulging in crony capitalism because he wanted spectrum for his mobile phone operations.

'No, that's not so. Two things have frustrated Ratan, although he has never told me so. The first is that telecommunications has become the temple of crony capitalism. The second is that the oligarchs are in the play.'

'Who do you mean by oligarchs?'

'You will have to work that one out for yourself, but think of Russia and the oligarchs there.'

'But why did Ratan Tata hire a lobbyist, and one with whom he dealt personally. That seems atypical too?'

'When your business is put to disadvantage, frustration starts building up and Ratan came to a situation, I suspect, when he said, "I can't handle this any longer." The mere fact that a man who values his privacy so much gets muddled up with a lobbyist speaks of something. He's saying, "I don't seem to have any other way. It's my shareholders' money." That's why he behaved in an atypical way. But he wasn't pleading for special favours. He was trying to ensure that his company was fairly treated. All the lobbyist was doing was to explain to the Minister that all the changes he was making in the allocation of spectrum were unfair to the existing players. After all, what is a lobbyist for? In India PR is a bad word but what is wrong in employing a PR firm?'

By now we were well into our breakfasts. Gopal, a vegetarian, had ordered fried eggs, and I had ordered bacon to go with mine. But eating did not slow Gopal's pace. He hurried on to another of his analogies.

'Doing business in India can be particularly frustrating because there are so many people who can say no to any project, so many ministries and other regulators. It's like having ten linesmen around a tennis court, any of whom can shout 'out' with no consequences to him. No one is allowed to say "now the game score is this". How does the umpire work? How can you play that sort of tennis?'

'With all the problems that business faces in India and bearing in mind that sixty-five per cent of your revenue now comes from outside India, have Tata ever thought of deserting this country, of being no longer recognisably Indian?' I asked.

'I can understand someone wondering whether we are going away from India but I can honestly say that I've never seen any suggestion of this in Ratan Tata. He is too much of a nationalist to let the thought of leaving India pass through his mind. He has never discussed it. This is the soil that we were nurtured in and we will continue to cultivate this soil and grow things here, but we have money and we have ambitions so we go to other soils as well.'

'Well then, do you believe that you are going to get the India you want – an India where there are clear-cut policies, where there are not all those people, those linesmen as you put it, who can stymie you, an India where there are not the flip-flops in policy Ratan Tata talked about, an India which could never be said to be in danger of becoming a Banana Republic?'

'Yes I do,' Gopal said firmly and went on, 'There are the reasons I gave you earlier, particularly the effect technology will have, but I also believe there is great hope in the present crisis. In fact I always wish India to be in a crisis. We have benefited from every crisis. We are children of a god called crisis.'

Gopal listed several crises including the food shortage in the sixties when India was said to be living from ship to mouth because it was so dependent on American Food Aid. That crisis was followed by the Green Revolution, which made India virtually self-sufficient in food. Then there was of course the foreign exchange crisis of 1991 when India hovered on the brink of bankruptcy. The Prime Minister Narasimha Rao and his Finance Minister, the present Prime Minister Dr Manmohan Singh, used the argument that there was no alternative to ram economic reforms down the throats of politicians and bureaucrats. They didn't want to do away with the Licence-Permit Raj that they could manipulate for their own benefit. It has to be said there were many businessman too who didn't want to see that version of crony capitalism disappear.

Gopal then went on with another of his analogies: 'Take this telecom controversy. Things are coming to a head. Finally everyone is standing up and speaking. Ratan Tata spoke first, but then Deepak Parekh, another much admired businessman, spoke out, now the Prime Minister and Sonia Gandhi have both spoken. I believe in India you have to be like a surgeon who says this cyst isn't ripe enough for me to operate. We can only operate at the right time – that is, when the cyst is ripe. In the Bhagavad Gita the God Krishna says he will reappear when everything is in disarray and I think that's what happened.'

Gopal was carrying a book with him which had a picture of Hanuman the Monkey God on the cover. It was the part of the epic the Ramayana in which Hanuman goes on a mission to meet the God-king Rama's wife who has been abducted by the Demon-king Ravana. I asked Gopal why he was reading this particular part and he replied, 'In our belief system if you have something which is enormously difficult and challenging, you start reading this section because it gives you the *shakti*, the courage, to do whatever you have to do. I'm not saying I'm doing this, but a lot of things are happening now which I'm trying to see the positive side of. I feel India is at a very important turning point.'

Whatever may emerge about Tata's role in the allocation of spectrum for mobile phones it has to be said that the controversy would never have arisen if the government had evolved a clear and transparent policy for distributing it and the Minister had not been given such wide discretionary powers.

When I got back to Delhi I discovered that the largest and oldest body that represents business interests in India, the Federation of Indian Chambers of Commerce and Industry, always known as FICCI, had broken its long silence on the issues of bad governance and corruption. After a stormy meeting, in which some argued that it would be foolish to take on the government, it was agreed that FICCI should issue a statement about recent events. The statement said, 'We are deeply concerned about the potential damage to brand India and the Indian story due to brazen acts of corruption by a select few. To preserve India's robust image and keep the growth story intact, FICCI calls for transparency, accountability, and probity in our system of governance. We urgently need rules and regulations that do not allow rent-seeking. Therefore FICCI believes that anybody found indulging in corrupt practices either as payee or recipient, must be punished in a fast-tracked process.'

When I read the statement I thought, 'At last business does seem to be raising its voice against bad governance and corruption, so maybe Gopal is right. Perhaps the cyst has ripened and the doctor will operate.'

9 | A FORGOTTEN LAND

Tata is not the only group that is having difficulties over acquiring land in India caused by a conflict between development and the environment. Much of India's mineral wealth lies beneath forests, like the forests of Jharkhand. Put quite simply, the question is, 'Do you save the forests or mine the mineral?' Disputes between environmentalists and industrialists are severely delaying the development of industries such as steel and how these disputes are resolved could have a profound impact on India's future, particularly the future of the poorest Indians.

In almost every case of land acquisition there is also a conflict between the interests of the companies and the interests of those living on the land. One of the problems here is India's abysmal record of resettling families driven off the land to further the cause of development. If people losing their land were assured of a decent second chance in life they would not be so reluctant to go. Near the open-cast coal mines of Singrauli in central India, which are spread over more than two thousand square kilometres, and feed so many power stations that Singrauli is now known as Shakti Nagar, or Power Town, I was taken to see some housing built to resettle tribals who had been moved off their land to make way for one of the power stations. The houses were little more than tin shacks, cheek by jowl, standing in straight lines, with no shade, no horticulture at all in fact. There was one pump, so at least clean water was available. But when the resettled tribals complained to the officials accompanying me that they had no electricity they were told, rudely, 'You can't afford electricity, so you can't have it.' They had lost their land and livelihood to provide the rest of India with a basic facility they were never going to enjoy.

In the North Eastern state of Arunachal Pradesh a storm is now brewing over plans to harness the rivers which flow through the Eastern Himalayan mountains, threatening not just livelihoods of those who live there but vibrant cultures too. The North East is another part of India where the record of governance is particularly poor. So Gilly and I went to Arunachal Pradesh to see how this clash between development and the rights of people to live their traditional lives was playing out.

Partition left the region of India known as the North East tenuously connected to the rest of the country by a narrow passage just twenty-one kilometres wide. The passage is sandwiched between Nepal and Bhutan in the north and Bangladesh to the south, and is usually called the Siliguri Corridor, Siliguri being the town in the plains below Darjeeling that stands at its western end. The Indian army knows this strategically vital corridor as the Chicken's Neck. Since Independence, the army has spent a great deal of time battling separatist insurgencies and ethnic uprisings in the North East. The rest of India has gone about its business largely ignoring the problems of this remote and troubled region. Indians are great travellers but comparatively few visit the North East unless they are sent there in the service of the government or to manage the tea gardens and oil industry of Assam.

It's in the North East that the great Himalayan range comes to an end. The jagged mountains of the Eastern Himalayas, divided by deep, narrow ravines, lie to the north of the Brahmaputra valley, the main feature of the region. The range eventually turns southwards and, as though it's finally exhausted by stretching all across India, Nepal, and Bhutan, peters out in softer, greener, more gentle hills. The Brahmaputra valley is the home of plains people known as Assamese and large numbers of Bengalis too, many of them migrants from Bangladesh. Numerous different tribes live in the mountains and hills.

Although most Indians pay little attention to the North East it is an area that is vital to India's defence. Beyond the mountains of the Eastern

Himalayas stands Tibet and it was through those mountains that the Chinese army invaded India in 1962, reaching the outskirts of the town of Tezpur, the army's base, on the banks of the Brahmaputra. With the Indian army in disarray, many in the North East thought India's first Prime Minister, Jawaharlal Nehru, was saying farewell to them when during the invasion he said in a broadcast, 'My heart goes out to the people of Assam.' But the Chinese withdrew without advancing further into the Brahmaputra valley.

Back in 1914, China's delegation at a conference called by Sir Henry McMahon to define the Indo-Tibetan border along the Eastern Himalayas had agreed with the line accepted by the British and Tibetan delegates. But then the Chinese government repudiated this decision. To this day China does not accept the McMahon line and claims that the mountains on the northern rim of the Brahmaputra valley are its territory.

Sanjoy Hazarika, an Assamese journalist who is one of India's most respected commentators on the North East, is scathing about the rest of India's attitude to his homeland. In his book *Strangers of the Mist*, he has written of 'the hollowness of the so-called mainstream of Indian society and its total and inexcusable neglect and lack of interest in areas outside its dusty heat-battered borders ... India's North East remains a peripheral area drawing attention only when violence erupts, when massacres, riots, curfews and agitations spiral out of control.'

The North East's infrastructure, poor even by Indian standards, its lack of industrial investment, the failure to capitalise on the outstanding natural beauty that could make it a major attraction for tourists, all suggest that Sanjoy Hazarika is right. The government of India itself, in a document called Vision 2020, admitted, 'At Independence the North East Region was among the most prosperous regions of India. Sixty years on the region as a whole and the states that comprise it are lagging far behind the rest of the country in most important parameters of growth.'

Separatist uprisings and ethnic clashes in all but one of the North

Eastern states are one of the reasons for the region getting left behind. Subir Bhaumik, until recently the BBC Eastern India correspondent, himself from the North Eastern state of Tripura, has been reporting on the region for nearly thirty years. With the burly physique of a bear, a booming voice and unbounded energy, Subir has travelled to the most remote areas and those worst affected by insurgency. I remember a BBC editor who couldn't believe the extent of his contacts, and so travelled with him to check that they actually existed. When he came back he said to me, 'Subir really does seem to know everybody in the North East.'

Subir's detailed analysis of the region is contained in his book *Troubled Periphery: Crisis of India's North East*. He writes, 'The North East has been South Asia's most enduring theatre of separatist guerilla war, a region where armed action has usually been the first, rather than the last, option of political protest.' One reason for this, Subir points out, is the variety of people living in the area. There are four hundred and seventy-five ethnic groups and sub-groups, speaking over four hundred languages and dialects. Another reason he gives is that 'the North East is seen as India's "Mongoloid fringe", where the country begins to look less and less like India, and more like the highland societies of South East Asia'. Furthermore the North East was never part of any of the empires that ruled over large areas of the subcontinent until the British came along.

The first separatist uprising in the North East was in the Naga Hills, on the eastern border of Assam. The Nagas were tribes renowned as headhunters. After a decade of what was no more successful than a holding operation by the Indian army, the Nagas were parted from Assam and given a separate state of their own. That was not enough to end the insurgency. In 1972 other tribal states were carved out of Assam, but this did not bring peace to the region either and, by the early eighties, as Subir Bhaumik puts it, 'the entire region was gripped by large-scale violence'. The separatist uprising in the small tribal state of Mizoram was so intense that the army ordered 80 per cent of the population to leave their villages and relocate along the main road to isolate them and deny the insurgents their support. The airforce bombed some Mizo villages.

Ethnic riots also took place in Assam and its neighbour, the small state of Tripura, in the early eighties. The target of the rioters was Bengali settlers, many of them from Bangladesh, who had migrated into Assam and Tripura. The opponents of the Bengali migration in Assam boycotted the election to the State Assembly in 1983 so effectively that one Congress candidate won by polling a mere three hundred votes. On several occasions during the campaign the police fired on rioters, killing a total of one hundred and thirty people. In one incident in the village of Nellie, on the highway leading west from Guwahati, the main city of Assam, three thousand Bengali Muslims were massacred by tribals.

Throughout the eighties murder and extortion were rife in Assam, the only part of the North East with anything but a basic agricultural economy. The tea companies of Assam were particular targets. The owner of one tea company was shot dead, and a government investigation found that Tata and other companies that owned tea gardens were paying protection money to the separatist insurgents, the United Liberation Front of Assam. Some companies even showed the amount they had paid in their accounts.

By the end of the 1990s the central government had reached a settlement with the Mizos and was talking to the Nagas. The violence in Assam and Tripura had died down, although the Bengali migrants were still an issue. But in Manipur the Assam Rifles had not been able to curb the activities of the separatists who had splintered into several different groups more interested in extortion and other criminal activities than in achieving their stated goal of independence from India. When I visited Manipur in 2005, I found rocks that were plastered with the words 'Assam Rifles, friends of the Hill People'. But it was difficult to tell who was the more unpopular – the separatists because of their kidnappings and extortion, or the Assam Rifles because of their exercise of the extensive powers they enjoyed under the Armed Forces Special Powers Act. That act gave even a non-commissioned officer the power not just to search and arrest, but also to shoot on sight. In 2004 a group of Manipuri women undressed in the middle of the state capital Imphal in front of the historic Kangla Fort that was occupied by the Assam Rifles. The women were carrying placards that read 'Indian army come and rape us'. They were protesting against the alleged arrest, rape, and murder of a woman by the Assam Rifles. The Assam Rifles did quit the Kangla Fort and the act was reviewed, but not withdrawn. The most remarkable non-violent protest against the act is that of another Manipuri activist, Irom Sharmila, who has been on indefinite hunger strike since 4 November 2000. Arrested by the police for attempted suicide, still a crime in India, she is force-fed through a tube passing through her nose to her stomach. She remains determined even after ten years without drinking or eating.

The one area of the North East that remained peaceful in the troubled eighties was the state of Arunachal Pradesh, which consists mainly of those mountains through which the Chinese had invaded, with only a small section of the state south of the Brahmaputra. In part because it was so peaceful, and so never in the news, I didn't visit Arunachal Pradesh until 2010, forty-five years after I first came to India as an adult.

As well as being peaceful, Arunachal Pradesh is also one of the least developed areas of India. Most of the state is still not directly interconnected by road. To get from the oldest town, Pasighat, to the capital Itanagar travellers have to come down to the plains, drive for six hours through Assam and then re-enter Arunachal and climb up to Itanagar. The roads Arunachal does have are not in good condition. When I asked a taxi driver whether it was true that it took eighteen hours to cover the four hundred and sixty-five kilometres between the Assamese town of Tezpur and the historic Tibetan monastery at Tawang in the north-west of

Arunachal he replied, 'You are lucky if you do it in that time. It's not even a pukka road, for much of the way it's *kaccha*.' *Kaccha* means a road that is not covered with tarmac. One of the lines of the Chinese advance in 1962 was from Tawang to Tezpur and for strategic reasons the road surface should have been made good enough to efficiently transport troops, equipment, and supplies many years ago.

There is no airport in Arunachal Pradesh. A helicopter service does link Itanagar to the nearest major airport at Guwahati, but I was warned against it on the grounds that I was likely to be bumped off to make way for someone considered more important. The only alternative to the helicopter is a six-hours-plus drive from Guwahati.

Arunachal Pradesh has no trains although the railways try to convince the people of the state that they do have one. It's called the Arunachal Express but it isn't an express. It dawdles through the night along a branch-line track that hasn't yet been upgraded from metre- to broad-gauge at an average speed of thirty-seven kilometres per hour. This so-called express never actually reaches Arunachal. It only gets to some stations in Assam near the state border.

Arunachal Pradesh does, however, have the densest forest cover of any Indian state. Because it's mountainous it has a wide variety of forests too. There are tropical forests and subtropical forests in the lower reaches, pine forests higher up, and alpine forests at altitudes between four and five thousand five hundred metres. Now the central government is making a real effort to develop Arunachal Pradesh, but will that development undermine the tribals' unique culture and destroy the ecology of the state?

I was invited by an old friend from Arunachal, Mamang Dai, to spend some days with her exploring the state and discovering why it had been so neglected and what the impact of the government's plans to rectify that would be.

Not wishing to risk the humiliation of being thrown off the helicopter, Gilly and I drove to eastern Arunachal Pradesh through Assam, passing some of the tea gardens for which the state is famous. The rains that bring on the plucking season's first flush of shoots were late, and many of the bushes had begun to wilt visibly in the hot sun. We stayed for a night on the Talap tea estate, and at around nine o'clock the next morning, a dusty SUV drove into the bungalow compound carrying a slightly windswept Mamang, a 'niece-in-law' from her family home, and a driver. They had travelled from Itanagar, a journey which had involved an overnight stay after they got stuck in a sandy riverbed for two hours.

We have known Mamang for more than thirty years. She is a writer, a poet, and a storyteller who is renowned as one of the 'voices of the North East'. Writing in English, she brings neglected Arunachal to the notice of English-speaking Indians. Slim and ageless, softly spoken, compassionate and humourous at the same time, she belongs to a prominent family of Arunachal. Her father is a senior retired member of the Indian Frontier Administrative Services formed in 1956 to provide a body of civil servants who had a special aptitude for work in frontier areas and were prepared to make a lifelong career of it. Naturally he had been delighted when Mamang became the first woman from Arunachal to pass the highly competitive exam for entry into the elite Indian Administrative Service that is the backbone of India's administrative system. But Mamang always had a rebellious streak, and walked out of the IAS before she had completed her training to pursue other interests.

'I do hope you are happy with my idea to start your trip,' she said over breakfast in the bungalow. 'It is a unique occasion, and will allow you to see another aspect of the state.'

Mamang's idea was that we should cross into Arunachal and head for Namsai, a small town not far from the tea estate, to attend the inauguration of a new Buddhist pagoda. This area of the state is south of the Brahmaputra and is home to the Khampti tribe, who trace their ancestors to the Shans of Thailand. They are Buddhists of the Theravada School, or School of the Elders. The Buddhist tribes living north of the Brahmaputra follow the tantric-influenced Mahayana School that is practised in Tibet. So to see a Khampti Buddhist festival would be different from anything we would experience elsewhere.

After breakfast we set off down increasingly bumpy roads towards the Arunachal border. There a surly policeman was critically examining our permit to enter the state when he suddenly noticed that Mamang was sitting in the car. His attitude changed immediately: 'Oh they are with *you*,' he said, 'Please go ahead.' It was the first of many incidents which proved how widely known and admired Mamang is in her home state.

There being no hotels in Namsai, Mamang had managed to book us rooms at the Forest Rest House, a Raj-period wooden bungalow on stilts, where we stopped just long enough to change into clothes smart enough for the inauguration. Banners fluttered in the wind along the route to the new golden pagoda, which had been built on a forested hilltop above a curve in a river. At the bottom of the hill, a fair had sprung up selling balloons, toys and all manner of useful and decorative items, including lethal-looking swords. Many of the women shoppers wore the distinct costume of the Khamptis, a handloom black sarong, wrapped round at the top with a length of green handloom cloth with a patterned stripe, and topped with a blouse and shawl.

Despite travelling as fast as was possible, we had missed the morning ceremony, where the guest of honour had been the Thai Ambassador to India, but were in time for a sumptuous Khampti lunch, hosted by the moving spirit behind the new pagoda, Chowna Mein. He was a minister in the Arunachal government, who was obviously proud of his community's traditions and connections with Thailand. The menu consisted of an array of Khampti specialities, including a fish soup made only by the men of the tribe, salads and spinach of forest herbs, cane curry and a preparation of algae. I must admit I found the white and green algae too slimy for my taste, but Gilly seemed to relish it.

After this banquet we visited the golden pagoda with its giant seated image of the Buddha, and watched the thousands of visitors place offerings before the statue and light incense. The crowds grew larger and larger. Everyone was waiting for the afternoon's Ya-Fra or traditional religious procession.

The procession that eventually assembled on the hilltop was led by two drummers dressed as cockerels with gigantic red combs and ferocious beaks, incongruously strutting around in sneakers. Next came a line of young women. Their tightly wrapped handwoven black sarongs had vertical shocking pink stripes and their long-sleeved blouses were a matching pink. They carried offering vessels wrapped round with flowers, and behind them a gong suspended from a bamboo pole carried by two men resonated like a church bell. It was followed by the centrepiece, a pick-up truck well disguised as a chariot and pulled by two ropes held by hundreds of people, most of them women. On top of the cab stood a white canvas pyramid, decorated with orange marigold garlands. In the back two large red parasols with silver trimmings, symbols of spiritual authority, shaded a collection of figurines of the Buddha and a group of ochre-robed monks. Over the monks towered a wire tree, shaggily festooned with innumerable 'leaves' of ten-rupee currency notes. As the chariot approached a steep descent, I moved smartly away, afraid the human brakes might not be able to prevent it careering into the bazaar below, but it reached the bottom safely, passed the stallholders squatting on the ground in front of their wares, and made its way slowly to the river.

The most beautiful part of the celebrations, an offering of five thousand lotus candles, took place after nightfall. We joined the minister, the Buddhist monks and what seemed an army of women on a creaking bamboo jetty just above the level of the river, and helped light the candles and launch them midstream. Each candle had its own paper lotus. They floated away from us, an armada of twinkling lights, a Milky Way on the dark waters of the river. Above, the Golden Pagoda was flooded with light and all around was silence.

Mamang too found much of this new, as even she was not familiar with the traditions of all the tribes of Arunachal. She spoke to the Khamptis she met in either English or Hindi. Arunachal's tribes have so many different languages that there wasn't one that could be chosen as the state language. Instead it was decided that the national language of Hindi should be the state's link language even though none of Arunachal's tribes spoke it as their mother tongue.

When the British annexed the Brahmaputra valley in the nineteenth century they found some of the tribals living in the hills south of the Brahmaputra troublesome and so they annexed most of them too. But they had little trouble from the tribals living in the mountains north of the Brahmaputra so they left them alone, and promulgated Inner Line Regulations in 1873 to prevent outsiders entering the mountains without special permission. These restrictions, which also applied to the part of Arunachal we were visiting, were retained after Independence and are still in force.

The restrictions on outsiders were introduced because the Raj thought the best way to administer the tribals was to let them continue to live their lives according to their traditional customs. But if the tribal way of life was to be preserved it had to be protected from outsiders who would disturb it – unscrupulous traders, exploiters of the natural resources, land-grabbing settlers, extortionate moneylenders, missionaries and of course politicians. It was vital for the Raj to keep this strategic area bordering Tibet free from the disruptive Independence movement. The Raj wasn't very keen on missionaries either.

There were also idealists among the British officials who believed that there was a nobility about the tribal way of life and that it should be preserved. They were accused of being influenced by anthropologists, who were not liked by some members of the pre-Independence legislative assembly. In a debate on what were then known as excluded areas, the anthropologists were accused of wanting to keep the tribals 'uncivilised' and 'in a state of barbarism'. And why would they want to do this? Their critics in the Assembly said, 'To add to their blessed stock of scientific knowledge.'

Although the people had been left almost entirely to themselves, the British did explore the northern mountains, locate the main routes from Tibet, and establish a bridle road an army could advance along. During the Second World War, although the Chinese were allies of the British, they made bellicose noises about Tibet, which they had earlier lost control of. They also drew maps showing not just the northern mountains but part of the Assam valley below as Tibetan and hence, in their view, Chinese territory. This led the British to resume exploration of the mountains and attempt to establish the McMahon line clearly.

After the Second World War my uncle, Tim Betts, was appointed political officer of the Subansiri area of what is now Arunachal Pradesh. It was a delicate mission. He was to establish the government's presence without alarming the tribals. A platoon of the Assam Rifles accompanied him, but the soldiers' task was limited to ensuring the security of the track leading from the plains to the headquarters which Tim had established and guarding the area in their immediate neighbourhood. In the rest of the area which Tim had was told to 'guide, advise and control the tribal people'. He was forbidden to use force.

With the Chinese still causing concern to the British Raj, Tim also had to find out as much as he could about the routes from Tibet that had not been explored. He was to learn from hearsay and traders coming from Tibet about possible routes invaders might take. In order to build up defences in the mountains bordering Tibet, Tim was also charged with finding a route for a road up to the Apatani valley five thousand feet above sea level and surrounded by nine-thousand-feet-high mountains. The Japanese invasion of Burma and the Naga Hills had taught the government that no matter how difficult the terrain might be, if it was undefended it could not be guaranteed to provide protection.

Tim and his wife Ursula lived in the Subansiri area from 1945 until Independence in 1947. They had met under most unusual circumstances. In the war Ursula was the only woman officer in V Force. It was a guerilla formation put together to persuade the Naga tribals living in the hills south of Arunachal not to go over to the Japanese army, which after conquering Burma almost succeeded in invading the tribal areas on India's eastern border. Ursula was an anthropologist who had been living in Nagaland before the war where she had in her own words 'an embarrassing reign as a divinity' and become known to the outside world as 'The Queen of the Nagas'. So she seemed an ideal V Force officer although she had no previous military experience. Tim was a naturalist also serving in V Force. Fascinated by Ursula's reputation he went to see her, saying he was looking for butterflies. Within one month the two were engaged to be married.

Ursula wrote a book called *The Hidden Land* about her stay in Arunachal. Writing graphically, and sometimes in a manner which might not be considered politically correct today, she describes a way of life which was certainly not idyllic. Slaves were still bought and sold, and putting someone in a mobile stock – clamping one foot to a bulky one-yard-long log – was a common punishment. Although the tribals were considered peaceful by the British there were plenty of disputes between them. Settling those disputes was one of the functions they expected a representative of the government to perform. Apparently those who came to Tim to settle their disputes thought a government representative would be so ignorant of their ways that he could be tricked into taking their side.

Once Tim and Ursula established a small settlement, tribals 'flooded in, gate-crashing the great hall and screaming complaints at him in the middle of breakfast. They sat in clumps wherever it was most inconvenient, orating over lines of tally-sticks, rehearsing nightmare crimes, tracing hideous webs of murder, kidnapping and theft. When Tim and the interpreters tried to bring the opposing parties together, both threw up a smoke screen of lies, evasions, and wilful misunderstandings to prevent it. For as long as they still hoped for some wrongfully gained advantage peace was the last thing they wanted.'

By no means all the disputes were settled. Ursula witnessed a brutal attack that resulted from a twenty-five-year-old quarrel. Raiders surrounded two long houses, set them on fire and hacked to death anyone who managed to escape. There was also a brief all-out war between villages.

But often disputes were ended, after much argument, by a comparatively simple and inexpensive settlement. This could well involve the payment of a *mithun*, a semi-domesticated *gaur* or Indian bison, looking like a buffalo with white socks. One man who had promised to pay a *mithun* to ransom his wife reneged on the settlement. Tim saw this as serious because the settlement had been made by the government, whose word must not be gainsaid otherwise his authority would crumble away. When the man remained adamant Tim's Gurkha soldiers arrested him and he quickly changed his mind. Tim had a quiet laugh when he heard that the guilty party had eventually handed over a *mithun* but it was one he had stolen.

Each tribe in the area to which Tim was posted dressed in a particular way. A headman of the Apatani tribe who paid an official call on Tim and Ursula when they first arrived was nearly six feet tall. 'His lids were heavy and drooped over full eyes, giving him a reptilian look. There was a blue tattoo mark under his lower lip; his skin was fair and the mark showed up clearly. His hair was black and long and plaited in a horn on his forehead, and a foot-long brass skewer was thrust through it. He was formidably armed; a dagger hung round his neck on a string, he carried a Tibetan sword on a baldric ornamented with a tiger's jawbone and he wore a hairy black palm-fibre rain cape.' Fortunately for Tim and Ursula, whose small party was far outnumbered by the Apatanis accompanying their headman, the call passed off well.

Less important Apatani men wore very few clothes. The women wore handwoven skirts and quilted jackets. Their necks were adorned with row after row of blue beads and their nostrils were pierced and stretched to accommodate large black resin nose-plugs.

When India became independent Tim and Ursula returned to London, never to work in India again. Travelling by train through the English countryside, where everything seemed on such a small scale after the Eastern Himalayas, Ursula said, 'The wound ached unceasingly. People talked kindly, couldn't understand, and were bewildered. We had come home; what could be the matter? How could one explain that home was no longer home, that it was utterly foreign, that home was in the Assam hills and that there would never be any other, and that for the rest of our lives we should be exiles?'

The first Prime Minister of independent India, Jawaharlal Nehru, took a very enlightened view of the legacy of the Raj in the Eastern Himalayas. He realised there was a danger that isolating the tribals might turn them into an ethnographic museum. But at the same time he feared that pushing ahead with development, as he was trying to in the rest of India, could undermine the culture of the tribals and deracinate them. The area that is now Arunachal Pradesh was named the North East Frontier Agency, or NEFA, in the early days of Independence. In his foreword to a book called *A Philosophy for NEFA*, Nehru said, 'We cannot allow matters to drift in the tribal areas or just not take interest in them. In the world of today that is not possible or desirable. At the same time we should avoid over-administering these areas and in particular sending too many outsiders into tribal territory. It is between these two extreme positions that we have to function.'

Nehru then went on to spell out five fundamental principles. The last one was particularly relevant to the debate on development in India today, with its headlong rush to achieve ever higher GDP growth. Nehru said, 'We should judge results not by statistics or the amount of money spent but by the quality of human character that is evolved.'

A Philosophy for NEFA was written by Verrier Elwin, a most unusual Englishman whom Nehru had appointed as his advisor for tribal affairs. Elwin had a profound knowledge of tribal life in India and sympathy for tribals. The son of an Anglican clergyman, he first came to India as a celibate priest to join a new Christian community, Christa Seva Sangh. But he quickly came under the influence of the Independence movement and was close to Gandhi for some time. This led to Elwin having doubts about Christianity and the missionary ambition to convert Indians. Eventually he wrote to the Bishop of Calcutta, known as the Metropolitan because of the seniority of his diocese, formally renouncing his priesthood and his membership of the Church of England.

In 1932 Elwin went to live in the tribal villages of central India and study their way of life, becoming an anthropologist whose unorthodox methods, perhaps not surprisingly, did not meet with professional acclaim from academia. He married twice, both times tribal women. A man of many parts he has been described as 'a poet, translator, social worker, explorer and ethnologist'. His biographer, the historian Ramachandra Guha, has suggested, 'We might remember Elwin as Gandhian Christian or anthropologist. Elwin would want to be remembered most of all as the defender of the aboriginal.'

Guha also implies that Elwin's defence has been in vain in the tribal areas of central India where he lived and worked. The biographer says, 'The tribals' forests have been encroached upon by paper mills, their lands inundated by dams or destroyed by mines.' He points out that economic progress has taken a particularly heavy toll on the tribals of central India because they have the misfortune to be living in places where the very resources needed for economic development are to be found in abundance. But Guha does say that Arunachal Pradesh is one place where Elwin's policies 'have been followed to some degree'.

Elwin and Nehru, following his advice, advocated what might be called the golden mean. Elwin certainly did not favour total isolation of the tribals. In *A Philosophy for NEFA*, he refuted those who criticised the government for going too far down the isolation route, saying that if anything the government was 'bringing them a little too quickly into the mainstream of life'. He quoted several examples of government efforts to bring the tribals into the mainstream, including building roads, encouraging the teaching of the national language Hindi and of Assamese so that they could speak to their neighbours in the plains, and taking school children on tours to see how other parts of India lived.

On the other hand Elwin was strongly opposed to the policy known as detribalisation, which he said was popular with 'Christian missionaries, social reformers and village up-lifters'. They, according to Elwin, 'make the tribesman ashamed of his own culture and religion and so create that inferiority complex which is a political as well as a social danger'. Elwin went on to say, 'All over the world it has been noted that the break-up of tribal society leads to a loss of the tribal virtues and rapid acquisition of the vices of civilisation.'

It's now more than sixty years since Elwin's philosophy for NEFA was published, and inevitably things have moved on. But maintaining a degree of isolation has protected the tribes' land and this undoubtedly is an important cause of the peace Arunachal has enjoyed compared with the other North Eastern states. The government did breach its own inner line policy once. In the mid-sixties Chakma and Hajong tribals fled from persecution into what was then East Pakistan, and India resettled them in Arunachal. The indigenous tribes of Arunachal resented and still do resent this. They have resisted all efforts to grant the settlers citizenship, and their resentment has on occasions boiled over in attacks on settlers' villages. But as Subir Bhaumik says, 'The conflict between the indigenous tribes of Arunachal Pradesh and the Chakma and Hajong refugees has been simmering but has not exploded into a bloody feud.'

The people of Arunachal are happy that they have been able to keep their state to themselves. Looking down onto the plains, they see all the problems created in Assam by Bengali migration and they want to avoid that. They want to protect their land and their culture. But at the same time they are not happy that their infrastructure is even less well developed than the rest of the North East.

The day after the inauguration of the Buddhist Pagoda we set off for Mamang's home town of Pasighat, travelling along the beginnings of a new West–East Highway that was being constructed to run across Arunachal. Much of the rough track had been cut through thick forest, and the charred earth and foliage along it showed that the road-builders had resorted to 'slash and burn' to force their way through. Wild banana plantains, gigantic bamboos and dense undergrowth were already beginning to reclaim the road, Orchids and creepers embraced trees forty metres high. The SUV slithered and slid along the mud track, made precarious by recent rain. It was tempting to stop and examine the jungle more closely, but the dark clouds were getting lower and Mamang was anxious that we at least reached the halfway point in our journey before the rain came. The car didn't have four-wheel drive, there was no mobile phone connectivity, and there would be no one in this remote area to help us if we got stuck.

So I sat back and enjoyed the wind whipping through the windows, and the intense green of the forest. I wondered how long it could survive. The Indian government has drawn up ambitious plans for a network of roads to make Arunachal's border with China easier to defend. Then there are the roads being built to construct hundreds of dams to generate power. Roads in India, on the whole, spell disaster for forests. They open the way for corrupt contractors in collusion with corrupt officials to reap a rich harvest of timber. I remembered one Chief Minister of the Western Himalayan state of Himachal Pradesh who was known by the sobriquet of 'Lakri Chor' – 'Wood Thief'. Roads also encourage settlements, with the new residents using local timber to build their homes and fuel their fires. And yet, I told myself, without roads people say there can be no development.

One answer to this dilemma is to combine community participation with law enforcement by the government that will prevent roads causing the destruction of forests. The Arunachal Pradesh government has started a movement called Apna Van, which means 'Your Forest', to encourage communities to protect the forests around them. But if the example of the rest of India is anything to go by, there will also need to be effective law enforcement as villagers on their own cannot be a match for the timber mafia, as they are known.

For part of our journey there was no visible road, not even a track that I could see. We bumped along the dry beds of rivers that only filled with water during the monsoon. When I asked the driver whether this really was a road, he said, 'Oh yes. It's national highway number fifty-two.' In the riverbeds I saw activity that didn't give me much room for optimism about the law enforcement machinery in Arunachal Pradesh. Truck after truck was filling up with stones. In some places the riverbed had already been denuded. There were no stones, just grit and mud. It was quite clear that one or perhaps several stone 'mafias' were at work and that no effort was being made to check them. The pristine Arunachal Pradesh was being raped.

By the time we reached the halfway point of Roing, one of the longest established settlements in Arunachal, what Mamang had feared had indeed come to pass. It was now raining torrents and we got drenched just trying to get from the car to the dining room of the rest house where we stopped for lunch. As we sat making polite conversation with an official from the Idu tribe about his home deep in the Mishmi Hills beyond Roing, a long lost 'brother' of Mamang appeared.

'How wonderful to see you. I totally forgot you were here or I would have told you we were coming,' she greeted him.

For all her convent education and sophistication, tribal traditions remain very important to Mamang. She is a member of the Pasi clan of the Adi tribe and we found that wherever we went we ran into people she introduced as 'brothers and sisters' who turned out to be more distant relatives known as 'clan brothers and sisters'. This gentleman was one of them. He and Mamang went into detailed discussions about the journey. His brow furrowed and he was clearly worried by our plans.

'I will get my vehicle,' he told Mamang. 'Better to have two, and I don't think I could relax if I didn't know for sure you had arrived. This rain will make it very difficult.'

After lunch, he climbed into the front seat of our SUV beside the young driver, who we now discovered was new to his job and had never attempted a journey remotely on this scale, and began to give him encouragement and advice. His own Jeep followed behind as we set off down a straight but more or less underwater track through ramrod straight trees. With his guidance we managed to reach the banks of one of the perennial rivers of Arunachal, the Dibang, down whose valley the Chinese had advanced in their 1962 invasion. There was a small queue of cars standing on the bank in the cold wind waiting for the ferry. Dark clouds glowered over the hills upstream where it was obviously raining hard. The river seemed to swell as we watched.

I was alarmed to see that the ferry carrying two cars consisted of a pair of traditional wooden boats lashed together to form a makeshift catamaran that required constant bailing to keep it afloat. It was being propelled by six men with bamboo poles. I couldn't see how the crew would control their vessel and prevent it being swept away downstream. But no. Just before the ferry reached midstream, where the river was flowing very rapidly, the crew hurriedly exchanged their poles for oars, rowed for all they were worth and managed to edge the ferry into the far bank. Then they struggled to tow it up to the landing point, which was just two planks. When it came to our turn I noticed with trepidation that all three waiting cars were being loaded, not just two. The crew obviously doubted whether the rising river would make it possible for them to make any more crossings and they didn't want to leave anyone stranded.

We all decided we felt safer outside rather than inside the SUV, so we stood in the rain. Approaching midstream I looked down anxiously at the dark foaming water which I could see through the gaps in the planks beneath my feet. The ferry started to roll and veer round in the current but once again the crew's drill was immaculate. They were at the oars in no time, rowed feverishly, controlled the ferry, and brought it safely to the other bank. The only casualty was one passenger's hat that flew into the river. Even that a crew member rescued by fishing it out with his punting pole.

Once away from the river we were back in the jungle, with the car skidding along the uneven muddy track until we reached the hills that Mamang said were the prettiest section of our journey. Although she was anxious to get as near as possible to Pasighat before dark, we stopped to look down on the thatched houses-on-stilts of an Adi village still famous for taking up arms against the might of the British Raj. Soon we were in complete darkness pierced only by our headlights. Eventually we made out the scattered lights of Pasighat ahead of us and crossed a new concrete bridge over the Siang river, as the Brahmaputra is called in its upper reaches.

The Pasighat bridge is one obvious sign of the development of infra-structure now beginning in Arunachal. But past lack of development isn't the only reason that Arunachal Pradesh has conserved more of its natural richness than other parts of India. The state is more sparsely populated than any other in India. The density of population in Arunachal, when the 2001 census was conducted, was thirteen inhabitants to every square kilometre. In neighbouring Assam the figure was three hundred and forty people per square kilometre.

The next morning Mamang took us to a unique Arunachal event rarely witnessed by outsiders – a *kebang*, or tribal council meeting. We drove into the hills above Pasighat to a clearing in the forest where some fifty people had gathered. Although the government has now introduced courts in Arunachal Pradesh and there is a police force, tribals still usually prefer to sort out their differences by holding kebangs.

On this occasion the kebang was being held on some disputed land. The dispute appeared to have been going on for a long time because a middle-aged, balding man, wearing a flak jacket and unlike the elders no hat, was shouting, 'I must have a decision this time. I must have a decision. This is now the fifth time we have met without a decision.' Mamang told us he was one of her cousins called Akem Dai. He was claiming the land we were standing on but someone else had cleared the forest and so maintained the land was his.

I have to say I was a bit disappointed that no one was wearing anything like the traditional garb that Ursula had described, but the men did all carry the tribe's traditional *dhaos*, long, broad, double-edged knives that looked to me like straight versions of the famous curved Nepali *kukri*. There was only one woman present. Some of the elders wore the red jackets that had been the uniform of interpreters in the days of the British. One was wearing an interpreter's sash with a large circular metal badge of office on it. I was interested to note that there were young men too at the *kebang*, but they squatted in silence most of the time. The speaking was done by the two rivals for the land, more senior members of the community and the elders.

One elder, his cheeks sunken, his face deeply lined and covered down to the eyebrows by an over-large felt hat, an imitation of what used to be called a trilby, said, 'This is a decision you all have to make. So no one should hide their knowledge but come forward and speak plainly.'

The man who had cleared the land then spoke and his opponent had to be restrained to prevent him interrupting. The main point of the argument he put forward was that he wouldn't have been able to clear the land if it hadn't been his.

Then another elderly man stood up. The bobble on the top of his knitted hat bounced in synchronisation with his agitation. 'One claim I know is false,' he said. 'It's not true that this land was not cleared by the party who has got it. The other part of the story I don't have any knowledge of. I can't smell the truth.'

No one else seemed any clearer. I asked Mamang what would happen if there were no decision again.

'Well, it might be referred to the courts. But they will be reluctant to touch it and will probably refer it back to the *kebang*. There are no land records in Arunachal so it would be difficult for the court to reach a decision anyhow.'

The man who had cleared the land sat with his head in his hands. The irrepressible Akem Dai pointed at him and shouted, 'If you want to be a thief, come openly as a thief and I will give you land!' Then, poking someone in the back who had given evidence against his claim, he shouted again, 'You are a liar! If you want to come as liar and take land, I will give you land.'

Things threatened to get nasty when the man who had cleared the land challenged his opponent to *peki*, a trial by ordeal which could involve among other things putting a hand in boiling water or holding a burning coal. Mamang's cousin accepted. His supporters tried to restrain him, saying, 'Don't provoke him.' But he replied, 'I'm using his tactics. Let me scratch and provoke him, and then he'll hit me first and lose the case.'

But instead of getting hotter, tempers cooled and eventually yet again no decision was reached. That didn't seem to bother Mamang's clan. We all repaired for a feast to the traditional bamboo house of the cousin who claimed he had been robbed. Some of the men sat in the middle of the main room of the house around the open hearth on which the food was being cooked, drinking glasses of freshly brewed rice beer, while the women of the house prepared dishes of pork and liver, wrapped portions of steamed rice in *ekam* leaves, boiled spinach and kept the supply of their home-brew going. The beer was whitish with a pleasant, slightly bitter taste. Mamang explained, 'This beer is a vital part of social life. You can't have any social occasion without it. There is an old saying among the Miri tribe: "Before rice beer was invented life was very dull. Men sat about feeling bored: they had nothing to talk about, they did not hold councils or tell stories."'

Akem Dai and some of his friends were sitting outside under a tree. At the *kebang*, Akem Dai had been accused of being a drunkard. He certainly kept the women busy filling his glass but the beer didn't seem to have any adverse effect beyond helping him to get over his disappointment and join in the conversation without any of the agitation he had shown at the *kebang*. He was joined by the family dog, cat, tame mynah bird and a strange black hen whose feathers were permanently ruffled. The cat didn't try to catch the mynah bird, the dog didn't chase the cat, the hen was allowed to peck away happily, all was peace and harmony until a pig tried to muscle in and get his share of the scraps from the feast. That was too much for the dog, who showed his teeth and snapped viciously, sending the pig away squealing.

Eventually we repaired to our rest house to sleep off the feast and in my case the rice beer too.

The next day I set off with Mamang to visit a clan family who lived in a remote village called Bizari. The drive over dried riverbeds and along tracks through the jungle took more than two hours. In the jungle we came across a group of young men with guns slung over their shoulders. 'Hunters,' Mamang explained. 'Hunting is very much a part of our traditional culture. In modern times gun licences have been issued indis-criminately and so we haven't been as good as we should have been at preserving our wildlife.'

Her clan uncle and his family lived in a traditional village house, built of bamboo and standing on stilts, with a sloping roof of palm frond thatch. The village was not cramped. The houses, one hundred and twenty of them, were not crammed into every available inch of space, as they tend to be in villages in the plains. Set in a clearing in the jungle there was more than enough space between each house to allow the dogs and other family animals their freedom and to store grain. It was much cleaner than a plains village too.

The head of the family, Mori Dai, was sitting on the extended verandah in front of the main room that is a feature of all Adi houses. He wore a green jacket made of cloth woven by the women of his family, and shorts. All the eight people living in the house turned out to greet us. There was a pile of knobbly ginger roots, the main cash crop, in one corner. The villagers grow their own maize and rice, which is the backbone of their largely self-sufficient economy. Unfortunately, porcupines have a taste for ginger and wild pigs for rice shoots. The villagers' diet is supplemented by hunting. Mori Dai showed me how a bamboo device that looked like a fragile crossbow should be set for catching squirrels. In the market in Pasighat we had seen skewered dried squirrels on sale as a delicacy.

The Adis, like many other tribals, had a tradition of sending their boys and girls to sleep in dormitories, in some cases mixing the sexes and sometimes keeping them apart in separate dormitories. I asked whether this was still practised in Bizari. 'Yes,' Mori Dai replied, 'the dormitories are still there, separate ones for girls and boys but the young people are allowed to visit each other. They don't sleep in the dormitories any longer but they do still go there from the age of ten until they get married. And in case you are wondering, we do allow love marriages,' he added with a smile.

I told Mori Dai that I was reminded of a time when a BBC crew had been filming tribals in a village in central India and a row had blown up over allegations that they were filming boys and girls having sex in the dormitory. The allegations were untrue but a national Hindi paper had published an absurd report saying that the BBC team was using special cameras which began filming automatically when a couple started to have sex, and lights which flashed on and off so that the boys and girls would think they were lightning.

Mori Dai laughed and said, 'That just shows we should stay remote and keep away from people like journalists.'

Mamang said, 'But Mark is a journalist.'

'Ah yes, but he has come with you so he must be all right,' Mori Dai replied.

The villagers didn't have television. There were two mobile phones but there was no signal. Communications by road were not much better. Villagers had to stay overnight if they went by the one bus of the day to the nearest town. They were cut off during the rainy season. Mori Dai has never been to the state capital of Itanagar. But this isolation didn't seem to worry him very much.

'There have been changes,' he said. 'We do have a higher secondary school in the village but all the educated boys who left the village have come back because they couldn't get jobs. So it's not surprising that the teachers don't take their job all that seriously and tend to say, "Oh, it's a nice day, let's go to the fields."' Apparently all the teachers are Adis.

Lunch was very similar to the meal I'd had the day before at the feast. This time the rice beer was darker but as far as I could remember seemed to taste quite similar. When I asked about the difference in colour Mamang explained that there is more than one method of brewing. For the darker beer, burnt paddy husk is sprinkled over the cooked rice before it is left to ferment.

*

On the way from Pasighat to the capital Itanagar, a dull drive because we had to come down from the mountains and travel along the flat plain of Assam, I said to Mamang, 'Your clan relatives seem so much happier, if that isn't a rather naïve word, than the tribals of central India. There people seem in some way to be crushed, hopeless, and full of a sense of grievance. I don't get any sense of that here and yet you couldn't say the village of Bizari has had much benefit from what the government calls development.'

'I think it's our sense of place in the land, in relation to the rest of the environment,' she replied. 'We realise how important that is, but also how fragile, how responsible we should be. It was there in olden times and it is still very much there in the rural areas.'

'But with development won't all this change?'

'I think there will be change. Customs, behaviour, dress – everything has already changed to some extent.'

'What seems to me particularly important is the clan system. Can that survive?' I asked.

'Yes, if there is judicious and enlightened leadership. It all depends on leadership. Local leaders are important. But I think customs will survive, including the clan system, if a good pace is set and there is judicious development.'

Mamang went on to explain what she meant by judicious development.

'We need simultaneous development on all fronts – health, education and employment. At the moment the development being crammed down our throats is agriculture-based, and things like eco-tourism. But that is rather patronising. We need to increase options so that people have more choice. Obviously not everybody will be working in rice fields and planting ginger all the time. With choice, people will make their own brilliant success stories. Society develops like that, but it has to be facilitated.'

My mind went back to the stormy but magnificent and pristine Dibang river that we had just managed to cross. 'What about plans to harness the rivers of Arunachal Pradesh, doesn't that worry you?' I asked.

'There are plans to sell hydro-electricity to the rest of India by building dams, and I am quite worried about this. But no one is really in the know about what is happening, so we should go slowly, cautiously. There's no need to rush into signing MoUs. People are arguing that we are sitting on a bed, not of oil, but of hydro-electric power and we'll be rich like Kuwait if we develop it, but I'm not convinced that it's right to treat our rivers like that.'

We arrived in Itanagar to find a modern town whose architecture is not worthy of the beautiful state of which it is the capital. Despite all the talk in Arunachal Pradesh and among economic planners back in Delhi about the income tourism could bring to a place with such magnificent scenery, the government hotel in Itanagar is almost the only one worth the name in the state. Mamang's family home was just below the hotel.

Mamang insisted that we came to dinner. As we entered the large rambling house we were greeted by her parents, and taken into a spacious living room, filled with mementos of her father's long career in the Arunachal civil service. We sat with Mamang's father and mother and other members of the family in front of a wood fire. Gilly was presented with a sarong and jacket, and I was given a shawl woven in their home on a 'loin-loom'. Mamang's mother showed us the loom in the next room. One end was tied to the window, and she explained that the other end was held in place by a strap behind the weaver's back. Weaving is a popular leisure activity for the women of the family. Mamang herself had chosen the colours of my orange and lepricorn green shawl. It consisted of two strips of checked cloth sewn together because the loin-loom is too narrow to weave a shawl in one piece.

While we were in Itanagar, Mamang arranged for me to meet some student activists, who had concerns about plans to build dams and generate electricity. Students had played a major role in the ethnic disturbances in Assam, and the central government feared that they might disturb the peace of Arunachal.

As Mamang said, there is much talk about Arunachal's potential for generating hydro-electricity. In his book *Troubled Periphery*, Subir Bhaumik writes, 'With several power projects on the anvil this sparsely populated state is well on the way to being one of the nation's major sources of hydro-electric power.' But this won't happen, or at least it will be severely delayed, unless the government can take the people with it when it builds the dams.

Already plans to build a large dam in the lower reaches of the Siang river have been scrapped. The fact that Arunachal Pradesh is so sparsely populated does mean that the problem of removing people from their homes and their land and relocating them won't be on the same scale as the dam builders in the plains have faced. As the dams are all run-of-the-river they will not require land for large reservoirs. But there is a special difficulty about relocation in Arunachal. Many of the tribes are very small and if half of a tribe, which could be as few as two thousand people, is relocated some distance away, the tribe feels its identity has been taken away.

The students I met included the General Secretary of the All Arunachal Pradesh Students' Union, Tujum Poyom. A slight young man with Tibetan features, he had just returned from Delhi where he had presented a list of demands to opposition leaders. He was not wholly opposed to dams but he did say, 'Hydro-electric projects have to be properly implemented. The public should be consulted.'

'But aren't they?' I asked.

'No, not in a proper way, not so that those really affected are listened to. Anyhow, you know it's not just removing people from their homes. There is all the damage to the ecology that will be done if the dams are not properly implemented. Then there are all the outsiders who will come to work on the dams. Will they go home?'

Tujum Poyom's main concern was that Arunachal would be swamped by Indians from other parts of the country who would dominate them and destroy their culture. That of course was the fear Nehru and Elwin had sixty years earlier.

'We still demand that the inner line restrictions should be there until we feel secure,' the student leader told me. 'We have a fear that we will be overcrowded by outsiders. We don't want to see that. The inner line is very important, very necessary.'

'What do you mean by "secure"?'

'We are lacking when compared with other states. Sometimes we feel we are living in very primitive times. We don't have any special skills. Even in agriculture the system we follow is very old. They will come and exploit us and take away our land. We can see how the original people of Assam are having such problems.'

'Do you feel part of India?'

'We were never ruled by the British and we have been compelled to say we are Indians. Not that I am against India but I'm made to be against Indians, because they look on us as foreigners. Looking at us, they say so many things like "chinki eyes" – slit eyes – words we daren't say, unparliamentary language. In that way it's mental torture. We never comment on Indians from other parts. They make a mockery of us.'

'Do they imply that you are backward and they are superior, is that why you feel so insulted?'

'Yes. They are saying we are different and so inferior. We have the same trouble with Christians. The trouble is that we are innocent, we can be moved by any person. That's why so many go to the churches who say they are right and our worship is wrong. But this is our worship, given to us by our ancestors, and I feel we should practise this.'

The student leader was referring to the Donyi-Polo faith. It is a loose grouping of animistic faiths manifesting itself in different ways in different tribes. Donyi means sun, and Polo moon, and so many have come to believe that followers of the faith worship the sun and moon. But Mamang Dai in her book, also called *The Hidden Land*, points out that this is wrong. She says, 'The sun and moon are the symbolic power through which the supreme spiritual being is revealed. This practice holds that all life is sacred and that the universal spirit resides in every being and in rocks and stones and trees.'

Alarmed at the success of Christian missionaries' efforts to spread their religion, an organisation was set up in 1986 to give the Donyi-Polo faith a more formal shape and institutionalise it. Inevitably politics got mixed up in this with one Chief Minister, Gegong Apang, actively promoting the faith, and attacking his opponents for being supporters of the Christian missionaries. He was backed by the Rashtriya Swayamsevak Sangh, or RSS, the powerful nationalist organisation that promotes the concept of a Hindu India. It is the hard core of the right-wing Hindu nationalist party the BJP. The RSS tries to persuade the tribes of Arunachal that Donyi-Polo is a form of Hinduism. So in an understandable attempt to protect their religion, the advocates of Donyi-Polo are in danger of being subsumed by a militant pan-Indian form of Hinduism. The Christian missionaries by their active evangelisation are in danger of creating a damaging religious divide.

Clearly there are tensions in Arunachal Pradesh that need to be addressed. The central government must not come in and deliver development on its own terms and in its own way. The future of Arunachal Pradesh and indeed the whole North East depends on development which is honest and sensitive. The pace and manner of the development should be chosen by the tribals or at least have their approval. Back in Delhi an interview with the Minister in the previous government's Department for the Development of the North East, Mani Shankar Aiyar, made me aware it was unlikely India's cumbersome bureaucracy could deliver development like this.

Mani Shankar Aiyar is a great talker, a skill he demonstrated as an undergraduate in the debates in the Cambridge Union. I knew that I would be going to listen to a lecture rather than conduct an interview. Sure enough I just pressed the button on the recorder, asked a blunt question – 'Is it true that most of the money allocated to the North East has been squandered?' – and the words came flowing out.

'I wouldn't say squandered but there haven't been the results there should have been. One problem is that the relationship between the state governments and the central government has been bad. The state governments don't have the manpower to implement development schemes and the central government agencies which could help don't try to. They don't take any action, they are content just to sneer. Then again there is the same problem as there is elsewhere in India – failure to push decisions down to where they should be taken. There has to be heavy decentralisation and there hasn't been. Just look at the North East Council. It was given the mandate to be the planning authority for the region but the central Planning Commission won't accept this, it won't devolve its powers.'

Mani went on to answer my usual question about the inefficiency of the bureaucracy without my asking it:

'Of course there is the usual problem of bureaucracy. Would you believe it, every central government scheme has its own delivery system and there are about one hundred and twenty schemes, that means all the ministries operating these schemes are isolated from each other. They are acting in an atomised manner. But don't just blame the government, the private sector has let the North East down. Do you realise just 0.5 per cent of India's total capital formation has taken place in the North East? This means there is a chronic shortage of managers, entrepreneurs and technicians. They have failed to invest there, blaming the security situation. This is rubbish, there is only one of the states where there is still a problem and that is Manipur, which I admit is in a mess.'

Eventually I managed to get another word in and asked, 'So what about the future?'

Mani sped off again. 'You know the Prime Minister is always talking about the need for inclusive growth to narrow the gap between rich and poor. Well, when I was a minister I managed to get Manmohan Singh to say in one of his Independence Day speeches, "You have to have inclusive government to get inclusive growth." Until we do something about that we won't have the growth we ought to have and can have either in the North East or in the rest of India. Inclusive government means including the people in the decisions about development.'

If there is to be any hope of Arunachal Pradesh developing without its society breaking up, leading, in the word's of Verrier Elwin to 'a loss of the tribal virtues and rapid acquisition of the vices of civilisation', the clumsy and corrupt Indian democracy will have to develop a delicate touch. This would be quite alien to the bureaucratic culture, as described by Mani. The Christian missionaries will also need to show respect to the traditional religion of Arunachal Pradesh. That is difficult for them in view of their belief in the innate superiority of Christianity. So if development does go ahead there could be troubled days in one of the more remote and most beautiful areas of the world. One of the North East's most prominent human rights campaigners, Babloo Loitongbam, has said, 'If India tries to force the dams on Arunachal without consulting the people, Arunachal will no longer be peaceful.'

10 | SAVING THE TIGER

In the previous chapter I raised the question of development versus environment. If India cannot protect its environment, all the development I have been discussing could well eventually prove in vain. The tiger is the national animal of India, considered by the government to be of 'incomparable value'. According to the conservation zoologist and leading tiger expert Ullas Karanth, the tiger is also the emblem of the health of India's environment. He has said: 'Wild tigers are the warning lights that indicate how healthy landscapes continue to remain in the face of our onslaught.' So if India cannot preserve its wild tigers, in spite of making a special effort to do so, that says a great deal about its ability to preserve its environment, which is already showing signs of being under severe stress. India's Centre for Science and Environment has reported most of the country's fourteen major, fifty-five minor, and several hundred small rivers have been degraded to 'sewage flowing drains'. Waterborn diseases are the leading cause of India's high child mortality. No one who lives in any of India's big cities can be in any doubt about air pollution, and in the countryside the land is polluted by excessive use of agricultural chemicals. The loss of forests may have been arrested, but it will take more than that to re-establish a healthy proportion of the land covered with diverse natural forest.

Tigers are magnificent animals revered here in India and in lands where they have never lived. They have long been potent symbols of power and strength. The flawless Goddess Durga is mounted on a tiger as she slays the buffalo demon, a victory that is celebrated by Hindus every year throughout India. Hers is not simply a victory of good over evil. Philosophically the three figures can be seen to represent the three *gunas*, or qualities of Nature, including human nature. The Goddess stands for *sattva*, light and clarity, the tiger for *rajas*, raw energy and anger – forces that are important for us to have under our control – and the demon for *tamas*, dullness, stupidity and sloth – traits that are worth slaying.

In the coastal districts of the southern Indian state of Karnataka, to celebrate Durga's victory, troupes of tiger dancers, dressed only in underpants and covered from head to toe in elaborate black, yellow and white body paint, dance in the streets and lanes during Durga's festival, and on the last day accompany the images of the Goddess as they are carried in procession to be submerged in rivers or temple ponds. The dancers are not only made up to look like tigers, they also mimic their behaviour, from the way they walk and lick their paws to the way a female tiger protects her cubs.

This is the most famous but by no means the only tiger dance in India, and not all the dancers are Hindu. Near Umaria in the central state of Madhya Pradesh, which has some of the best tiger habitat in the country, I have watched Muslim dancers, similarly painted, and with long false claws attached to their fingernails, leaping and jumping to the rhythm of drums. These dancers, many of them enthusiastic children, perform in the first ten days of the Muslim month of Muharram, the anniversary of the martyrdom of the Prophet's grandson, Hussain, who died fighting against insuperable odds in distant Iraq. No one can say exactly how the tradition began but perhaps local people, living in tiger territory, associated the courage of their neighbour the tiger with the courage of their hero Hussain.

Tiger deities are still worshipped in certain parts of India and tigers of flesh and blood can inspire reverence even in death. I remember watching the most moving footage, shot by the wildlife film-makers Naresh and Rajesh Bedi, of a man-eater that had been killed by the Forest Department. The magnificent animal lay lifeless, strapped across the bonnet of a Jeep with villagers crowding around it, making offerings of flowers, bowing before it and reaching out to gently touch its paws.

Internationally the tiger's reputation was established hundreds of years before the first wildlife documentary. There was Shakespeare's famous version of Henry V's address to his army on the eve of the crucial battle of Agincourt:

> But when the blast of war blows in our ears
> Then imitate the action of the tiger;
> Stiffen the sinews, summon up the blood,
> Disguise fair nature with hard-favour'd rage;
> Then lend the eye a terrible aspect.

The mystic poet William Blake found in the tiger a symbol of the mystery of creation. He asked:

> Tiger tiger burning bright,
> In the forests of the night;
> What immortal hand or eye
> Could frame thy fearful symmetry?

Because we have allowed this magnificent, awe-inspiring animal, to become an endangered species, the biologist George Schaller has warned, 'Future generations would be truly saddened that this century had so little foresight, so little compassion, such lack of generosity of spirit for the future that it would eliminate one of the most beautiful and dramatic animals that the world has ever seen.' George Schaller was speaking in 1993. Sadly the warning has not been heeded and there is no certainty that the wild tiger will survive the twenty-first century.

There are some prophets of doom who believe the battle to save the tiger is already lost. But Ullas Karanth said in his book *The Way of the Tiger*: 'Mere doomsday prophecies, however well intentioned, discourage rational conservation action, and may be harming rather than helping the tiger cause.' The tiger scientist believes that 'on the basis of biological facts and historical background the tiger is not yet a lost cause.'

A secure tiger population indicates that a forest is healthy because tigers cannot survive if the water supply is depleted. They must also have prey, such as deer and wild boar. The prey needs vegetation, and so it goes on down to the smallest insect in the ecological chain. If that chain is intact tigers survive and so do forests.

It's not just environmentalists and tiger experts who appreciate how essential the health of India's forests is to the health of India's environment. In his book *Awakening Giants, Feet of Clay: Assessing the Economic Rise of China and India*, Pranab Bardhan, who is Professor of Economics at the University of California, Berkeley, has warned that the environmental conditions in both India and China are alarming, and he has focused his attention on forests and local environmental resources, blaming land degradation and deforestation for flooding and the expansion of deserts in both countries. So it might not be too fanciful to say that if India can't save its tigers it cannot stave off the environmental crisis facing it.

But Bardhan does see some grounds for hope. He points out that the activist environmental movement is more vigorous in India than in China. Indian activists have been in the vanguard of the campaign to save the tiger, and without them the Indian tiger would almost certainly have already disappeared. However, all the activist movements' carefully researched warnings have not moved the central or the state governments to take perhaps the most important action of all if the tiger is to be saved – reform of the Forest Service.

While I was researching this chapter it was suggested I should meet Prashant Sen, a highly respected forester and conservationist, to discuss the need for reforming the Forest Service. Sen himself spent forty-five years in that service and led the prestigious national conservation programme, Project Tiger, for five years. After his retirement he worked for the Worldwide Fund for Nature and supervised the successful transfer of rhinoceroses from a wildlife reserve where the rhino population was multiplying to a reserve where they had been eliminated by poachers. His passion for wildlife was still not spent and so now he was running an NGO working in Ranthambore, one of India's best-known national parks.

Sitting in the living room of Sen's small flat in Delhi, surrounded by much enlarged photographs of tigers, I started the conversation, as conversations do so often start in India, by finding out which part of the country he was from. 'You are, I suppose, Bengali,' I suggested. It wasn't just his name, Sen, which gave me that idea. His round face and broad forehead also seemed very Bengali to me.

But the burly forester replied, 'I am an out-and-out Bihari. Yes, my family is Bengali but we came to Ranchi in 1858, and have been established there ever since. I have spent all my working life in the Bihar cadre of the Forest Service.'

'Of course Bihar has now been split and Ranchi is the capital of the new state of Jharkhand,' I pointed out.

Sen roared with laughter and said, 'Yes, I suppose I should say I am an out-and-out Jharkhandi.'

Moving on to the Forest service, I asked, 'Many people blame your service for the plight of the tiger. Is that justified?'

'It's not really the fault of the officers, it's the fault of the system. If you can properly train foresters, and give them full support – political, financial and all the rest of it – then there will be no poaching, no trade in tiger parts, and you will save the tiger. But you can't do that unless you change the Forest Service. It is completely unreformed.'

'Have there been no attempts to change it?'

'None worth the name. In fact things have got worse in some ways. The dedication has gone. When I joined the service I was told to walk round the whole of our forest checking whether the pillars marking the boundary were intact. That took three and a half months. Then I had to repeat the whole process after the monsoon. I also used to walk through the forest marking trees and bamboo for felling. During my training I stayed in a tent for six months. All that's completely forgotten. Forest officers go around in vehicles now.'

The state governments' Forest Departments are responsible for managing the tiger reserves. These departments were established during the British Raj to manage the forests as commercial enterprises, and meet the strategic needs of the Raj, including satisfying the railways' huge demand for sleepers. Many foresters were dedicated naturalists but preserving wildlife was not part of their official duties. They were responsible for ensuring that trees were not stolen, and that all the laws that made it difficult for the tribals who lived in the forests to pursue their traditional way of life were obeyed. Preserving tigers requires qualities that are alien to a colonial law-enforcing institution, but that legacy lives on in the Indian Forest Departments.

Inevitably there is a tendency for Forest Departments, which have inherited a colonial ethos, to regard forests as their preserve and resent any outside intrusion in their management. So instead of taking advantage of all the knowledge and the energy that the environmental movement can provide, the Forest Departments tend to regard activists as intruders in their domain. The tragic story of the disappearance of tigers from one of India's most beautiful national parks, the Panna forest in the central Indian state of Madhya Pradesh, is a tale of obstinate and obstructive forest officials who refused to accept the findings of scientists and conservationists when they were staring them in the face – brutal poachers, traders with no fear of the law, and China's voracious appetite for products made from the parts of tigers, even down to their whiskers and their penises.

The Panna forest was the hunting ground for the local maharaja before India became independent in 1947 and the princely states were merged with the rest of the country. The large number of teak trees with their leaves the size of elephants' ears indicate that the forest was also a money-spinner for the maharaja. For more than twenty years after Independence, hunting continued in Indian forests. Those who had the money to rent a forest block for a shoot were allowed to kill tigers or any other animal. Shooting tigers was eventually banned in 1969 and in 1972 a national census revealed that they were an endangered species.

It's often said that there were 40,000 tigers in India at the beginning of the century, but that is just one naturalist's opinion. The 1972 survey maintained there were one thousand eight hundred and twenty-seven tigers left. Experts have pointed out that the accuracy of the census figure also cannot be guaranteed, but at the same time no one doubted there was a precipitous fall in the tiger population in the first seventy years of the twentieth century.

Alarmed by the 1972 survey, the government launched Project Tiger, which established Tiger Reserves. They were large areas of the forest where the tiger reigned, supposedly free of any of the threats humans posed, in an environment that supported plenty of prey. The project had the energetic backing of the formidable Prime Minister at the time, Indira Gandhi.

When Alasdair Milne, the Director-General of the BBC, visited India I took him to meet Indira Gandhi. He told her he was going to Corbett Park, a national park named after the legendary hunter of man-eating tigers, Jim Corbett, and she said, 'Oh, I would love to go there, but I am afraid that my security apparatus and all the rest of the activities which go with a Prime Minister would disturb the animals.' Rajiv Gandhi, who succeeded his mother, also took a keen interest in Project Tiger, but after he was defeated in an election his successors did not regard the project as a top priority. Without the stimulus only a Prime Minister can provide, the lethargy which is so common in the implementation of government schemes overtook Project Tiger.

*

The tiger scientist Raghu Chundawat, himself the son of a Forest Officer, was one of many independent experts who realised that, although Project Tiger had been in place for twenty-two years, and the number of reserves had increased from nine to twenty-seven, the tiger was still endangered. One reason for this was lack of scientific knowledge about the way tigers lived. So Raghu set up camp in Panna to undertake a lengthy research project, using the radio-collaring of tigers, to find out why they are most vulnerable in the dry forests that constitute their largest habitat in India.

Raghu's project was to be the first long-term study of Indian tigers, and the first study of any sort in a dry tropical forest. He had managed to accomplish the not inconsiderable task of obtaining all the clearances he needed from the central government and the government of Madhya Pradesh. Furthermore his project originated from the Wildlife Institute of India, a government educational and research institute.

The project was remarkably successful at first. There was, in Raghu's words, 'One of the finest recoveries of a tiger population documented in recent history.' But then the park management changed, his monitoring suffered and the tiger population started to dwindle. When Raghu pointed out that poaching was becoming a major problem, the Madhya Pradesh Forest Department turned against him, and refused to accept his evidence of an alarming decline in Panna's tiger population. Eventually the Madhya Pradesh Minister of Forests had to admit there were no longer any tigers left in Panna.

To find out more about this story, I went to visit Raghu and his wife Joanna Van Gruisen at their home next to a group of beautiful, thatched, mud-build cottages they had just built and named the Sarai at Toria. Joanna, who has given up writing, photographing, and making films about wildlife to run the Sarai, explained that Toria was the name of the nearby village. As for Sarai, it was an Urdu word for a place where travellers used to stay in Mughal times. She and Raghu had chosen the name because they felt that words like hotel, hostel, resort or camp were not apt for what they wanted to create. The Sarai is set high above the Ken river. It is surrounded by the flame of the forest trees and grassland, home to small birds such as colourful munias, button quails and shrikes or butcher birds with their distinctive black bandit-like eye stripes. As I was talking to Joanna she pointed out a crocodile basking in the sun on a rock and another swimming sedately between rocks in the river below the Sarai.

The Forest Department had recently brought two tigresses and a tiger from other reserves and released them in Panna. Although one of the tigresses had given birth to four cubs, two of which were still surviving, Raghu wasn't convinced that this move to repopulate Panna had been properly thought through. He was keeping an eye on the tigers, and suggested that we went for a drive in the reserve on the next morning to see whether we could find one of them.

We entered the park at six o'clock in the morning, before sunrise, the coldest time of the night. I sat in the front of the open vehicle while Raghu stood at the back. Lean and apparently as fit as he was in his younger days when he played first-class cricket and wasn't 'much interested in studies', Raghu was now a naturalist with a PhD to his credit. Driving along the jungle tracks he spotted a large, shaggy deer with handsome antlers rolling in mud. 'Sambar,' he said. 'It's the mating season and the females like their males to be covered in mud.' Sambar are India's largest deer species and therefore the tiger's favourite prey. Just round the corner another sambar stag stood obligingly while photographs were taken, while a group of does stood behind him and the youngest members of the group chased one another up and down a muddy slope.

We soon saw our first herd of the smaller, brown and white spotted cheetal, the commonest of India's deer, and for me the most delicate. Like all the deer in the park they were used to vehicles like ours so they continued grazing.

'You seem to have plenty of food here for the tiger,' I said.

'Yes, we have adequate prey,' Raghu replied. 'There should be forty-five animals to the square kilometre for a good prey ratio and I don't think we fall far short of that. Apart from deer, tigers are very fond of wild boar and we are bound to see them.'

Sure enough it wasn't long before Raghu pointed out a black boar with a line of grey bristle running down his spine and armed with two ferocious tusks. Rootling in the undergrowth with his long snout firmly to the ground, the boar was far too busy searching for his breakfast to be bothered with us.

Coming out of the thicker forest into open land where the dew on the grass was glittering in the thin early morning sun, we heard a varied and very noisy squawking which we traced to two black birds with long forked tails perched on the branch of a dead tree. 'Drongo crows,' Raghu said. 'Small birds nest around a drongo's nest because the drongo protects them. I have even seen a bulbul feeding drongo chicks.' Red-vented bulbuls, with their black crests and patches of red beneath their tails, are very common in Panna.

Back in the forest near a river we stopped at a tall, stately arjun tree to examine the scratches a bear had left on its pale, almost white trunk. The Indian dry tropical forest is not very dense but in Panna the undergrowth was very high, which made seeing animals and birds that are usually ground-dwelling quite difficult, so I was particularly pleased when a spurfowl scuttled across the track in front of us.

After two hours or so we arrived at the top of a high escarpment and stopped for a tea break. A long way below us the Ken river flowed on its wandering way. It meanders for fifty-five kilometres through the park. Looking down into the gorge, Raghu said, 'This is the gorge where the translocated tigress gave birth to her cubs. Yesterday a tiger, perhaps her, was sighted just below where we are standing.'

As he drank his tea Raghu remembered how he came to this park: 'I was told don't go to Panna, there are too few tigers to study there. But my thinking was that there was no point studying tigers where they were doing fine. I wanted to study tigers where they are vulnerable, in places like Panna, to understand what factors make these populations so vulnerable.

'I monitored one breeding female and her four litters. Her cubs had cubs too and so that one female was responsible for more than twenty-five tigers within seven years. This was possible to a large extent because of our presence and regular monitoring, especially monitoring of kills. People knew that we would come to kills and that we could trace anyone who had visited them. Any kill where we saw a human footprint we investigated in detail. So the possibility of poisoning and trapping at kill sites stopped.

'When our movements were restricted by the new management, the decline set in because of poaching. Initial warnings were ignored and later the decline was denied by a special census they conducted. The entire responsibility for what happened should be put on the Forest Department. After all, they own and run the tiger's home, and they refused to accept there was a problem of poaching.'

'But the forest officers in the reserves are the victims of an outdated colonial system,' I suggested. 'Surely you can't blame them.'

'Yes, you do have a point. They play catch-up games with the poachers, and they don't play very successfully. You have to be ahead, and how can you when the forest system of beats and patrolling hasn't changed since colonial times? In private parks in South Africa guards are hidden, but here they are out in the open. Then they have no incentive to catch poachers. In fact there is a disincentive. If a forester makes an arrest he will have a headache for years, having to make futile appearances in courts where his never-ending case will be heard. Now there's another headache. The Madhya Pradesh government seems to have decided that the emphasis should be more on tourism than on conservation. But we can talk more about that when we get back to the Sarai; let's go and look for that tiger.'

We never did see the tiger, nor did we hear the alarm call of monkeys warning that there was a tiger in the vicinity, but we did see tiger pugmarks. We also saw the imprints of a bear's flat-footed paw, but sadly no bear. In all my times in Indian tiger reserves I have only once seen a bear, a very scruffy one at that, sitting covered with dust under a tree in another Madhya Pradesh reserve looking distinctly bad-tempered.

Back in the Sarai we returned to the fate of that remarkable recovery of the Panna tiger population.

In 1996, shortly after Raghu started his research, it was estimated that in Panna there were two to three tigers for every one hundred square kilometres. In 2002 camera traps showed that the population density had probably increased to seven. In 2009 it was officially admitted that there were no tigers in Panna. The last tiger pugmark, a male's, was seen in January of that year.

The problem, according to a report written by Raghu and Joanna, started with a new management taking over the Panna National Park. It was then that the concentration on tourism began. One consequence of this was that the park's elephants spent their time giving rides to visitors and were no longer available for monitoring and protection. The elephants were crucial to Raghu's work because they provided the only safe way to visit a kill while the tiger was still lying up nearby. Kills were no longer being effectively monitored, and poachers realised that.

Raghu said to me, 'If we had been able to visit the kills the decline in population might never have taken place. We lost our first tiger in October 2002 and our second in December. When I reported on this to the Field Director of the park and the Director of Project Tiger, my troubles started. I provided photographs to show that the tigress had been caught in a snare placed for a deer and a dead deer was also found near her. These photos were clear evidence that poachers were at work. What was the reaction of the officials? To shoot the messenger and ignore the message.

The roll of film was confiscated. Our team was accused of what they called 'causing negative effect on the park management'. Our patrolling at night was curtailed, and that is particularly important because the tiger normally moves at night.'

As the tragedy of Panna developed, officials closed ranks to intensify the pressure on Raghu. At one stage Raghu was warned that he would never get the pension from the government's Wildlife Institute which was his due. The state government's intelligence agency was also roped in to question him. The Forest Department seized some of his equipment and a vehicle, claiming he had entered the reserve illegally after dark. He was presented with a magisterial order demanding payment of a bill for the equivalent of more than two thousand pounds for using elephants. I asked Raghu how he felt about this harassment.

'I thought it was typical of the officials who work the system in this country,' he replied. 'They gang up against anyone who challenges them, and misuse government institutions, police, investigation bureaus, tax and excise departments to threaten, pressurise and humiliate anyone who dares to criticise them. But that wouldn't be so bad if they paid attention to the criticism. In the case of Panna, instead of investigating my warnings they rubbished me. The Chief Wildlife Warden of Madhya Pradesh said the issue of missing tigers had been "blown out of proportion by one individual and his claims are baseless". The Madhya Pradesh Forest Minister wrote me off as "a disgruntled researcher". The most senior official in the Ministry of Environment and Forests in Delhi said that I and others who had warned about Panna were "so-called experts who are not scientists but seeking publicity". If our warnings had been heeded Panna wouldn't have lost its tigers.'

'It seems the heart of the matter was the Forest Department's refusal to admit that tigers were being poached, so poachers were able to clean out the reserve,' I suggested.

'Well, yes, that was certainly crucial,' Raghu replied. 'We had hard evidence of trapping, and one poacher was arrested. He admitted to trading in the body parts of eight tigers and over thirty leopard skins, most of which came from Panna. When all was almost lost the National Tiger Conservation Authority sent a special team to Panna and they confirmed that poaching was going on. But to the end the State Forest Department refused to accept this. Two years before the department was forced to admit there were no tigers, a very senior official, Dr H.S. Pabla, reported that there was no need to worry about Panna and denied that poaching was a problem. One year later in an article in the magazine *Sanctuary* he said we were "dead wrong" to warn that Panna was about to lose all its tigers because of mismanagement and heavy poaching.'

'Why were Pabla and the rest of the Madhya Pradesh Forest Department so reluctant to admit poaching was a problem?'

'I can only assume because it reflected badly on them. The end result, the loss of all the tigers, reflected a lot worse on them. But maybe I too was partly to blame. Perhaps I was too pushy and antagonised them more than I should have done, but I pushed hard because it was a desperate situation.'

'So what needs to be done to prevent another Panna – after all, this is the second tiger reserve to have lost all its tigers?'

'To put it succinctly, establish a new system for managing reserves and increase the conviction rate for those arrested for poaching. Trials drag on while the guilty are out on bail, and there is also the problem of witnesses being suborned. But actually courts are not so much the problem as the Forest Department not doing enough to ensure conviction.

'I am suggesting proper forensic investigation of the evidence that is already presented in the court. Courts will accept forensic evidence if it is from a recognised forensic lab. The trouble is that the Wildlife Institute of India's lab is not recognised and so its evidence is merely taken as expert opinion. Then of course the relationship between the Forest Department and the villagers living outside the reserves needs to become one of cooperation rather than coercion. You can't save tigers unless villagers cooperate.'

While in Panna I decided to visit some of the villages surrounding the park to discover just how bad the relationship between the Forest Department and villagers really was. In Madla, on the opposite bank of the river Ken to the Sarai, a group had gathered at the village meeting place – benches surrounding a large stone table. One man stood out from the rest. Smartly dressed in brand-new trainers, a mobile clipped to the belt of his neatly pressed trousers, and hair reddened by henna, he had the appearance and airs of a town-dweller. He introduced himself as Hamid Khan, the *panchayat* Secretary, saying with pride that he owned the land on which we were meeting. As a government official I expected him to defend his fellow officials in the Forest Department but he started off the discussion by saying, 'People here don't trust the Forest Department because there's a big difference between what they say they're going to do and what they actually do.'

Dhan Singh, a farmer who with his grey stubble, bedraggled hair and paan-stained teeth, was as unkempt as Hamid Khan was kempt, became the spokesman for the small group of villagers who had gathered. He took up the *panchayat* Secretary's theme. 'The Forest Department said that mahua trees were free, then they didn't allow us to go into the forest to collect the flowers which we cook and eat as well as use to make liquor. They used to allow us to collect wood for cooking – now we can't do that. Our cattle used to be allowed in, there were areas of land where that was allowed, now we can't even cut fodder, so now my cow and buffalo don't produce milk. In everything we have been deceived.'

'Do you have anyone you can appeal to?' I asked.

'No,' replied Dhan Singh. 'What they say goes, and if we disobey them we get punished. If we complain the department calls the police and they beat us.'

One of the principles of wildlife conservation is that villagers like Dhan Singh should benefit from reserved forests. In today's management jargon they should be stake-holders. So I asked the farmer whether he benefited in any way from the forest being a tiger reserve.

'No,' Dhan Singh replied. 'It has just caused us a lot of difficulties. Animals come into our crops and destroy them. If we set off crackers to keep them away the Forest Department fines us. Wild boar come in daily and they cause a lot of damage. As for me there is now a fence right next to my house so I can't even do latrine in the forest.'

The villagers of Hinota were even less enthusiastic about the reserve because they were now completely surrounded by it. It's a substantial village with a nursery for infants, primary and middle level schools, a community school and, for some reason I couldn't fathom, an office of the Registrar of Births and Deaths. The villagers had given up hope of getting any benefit from the national park. With nowhere to graze their cattle, no land to cultivate, nowhere even to 'freshen up' (none of the houses had toilets), all they wanted was to be relocated. As one villager put it, 'better to die once than every day'. But so far no one had told the villagers of Hinota when or where they could move.

Had the Forest Department been more light-handed in its dealings with villagers they might have given more information about the activities of the traditional hunting communities who live all around the reserve. Poachers from one of theses communities, the Baheliyas, virtually cleaned out the tigers of Panna between 2004 and 2007. They were helped by the fact that from May 2006 to December 2007 the Forest Department lost effective control of much of the forest to a gang of *dacoits* or bandits. The Thokia gang was always described as 'dreaded' in the press and by officials but they let the Baheliyas get on with their work.

*

It is a non-governmental organisation, the Wildlife Protection Society of India, that has pieced together the chronology of the poaching that killed the tigers of Panna. The society's main objective is to provide information and other support to the government's campaign against poaching and trading in wildlife products, particularly the products of wild tiger. The society has provided intelligence that has led to the arrests of hundreds of traders as well as poachers and it has pursued their cases through the courts.

The network of the society's field investigators is spread throughout India. In its confidential report on Panna the society even published photographs of ten suspected poachers and the probable locations of thirteen. The report warned that these poachers were still active and ended saying 'at the very least sustained surveillance of these individuals will go a long way to saving wild tigers'. The report was published in June 2009, not long before the Madhya Pradesh Forest Minister finally admitted that tigers had been eliminated from Panna.

Belinda Wright, a remarkable Englishwoman, founded the Wildlife Protection Society of India in 1994 and is still its Executive Director. Eighteen months after the Panna report was published I went to the house where she lives with her mother just outside Delhi and asked her whether Forest Departments in different states had taken the society's advice about surveillance to heart. 'The answer has to be no,' she replied. 'There were eighty-five cases of tiger mortality last year.'

Among the many awards Belinda has received in recognition of her work is the OBE given by Queen Elizabeth II for 'services to the protection of wildlife and endangered species in India'. English but born in Calcutta, Belinda has lived virtually all her life in India. She did go to school in England but didn't ever want to stay on there. She said to me, 'I left school as soon as possible and came back to Calcutta. It wasn't that I was unhappy, although the other girls did think I was boasting when I talked about the jungle camps I had been to with my parents, and the pet tiger and other animals we had at home. The thing was that I wanted to get home and start the career I had chosen.'

'What was that?' I asked.

'Since the age of fourteen I knew what I wanted to be – a wildlife photographer. But when I came home from school and told my father, he said scornfully, "That's not a job, it's a hobby."'

Her father, Bob Wright, was the last of the tribe of British businessmen in Calcutta who were responsible for the city's commercial importance under the Raj. After a career in which he became chairman of the Indian Mining Association, Bob went on to be the Managing Member of the city's most prestigious sports club at Tollygunge, always known as Tolly. There he saved the club from the clutches of successive state governments who, being communists, regarded it as an elitist eyesore and thought the green acres of its golf course should be public land.

Unfazed by her formidable father's opposition, Belinda went off to Hong Kong and got a job as a secretary in a bank that soon paid her enough money to buy the photographic equipment she needed. Showing the initiative that has characterised her later career as a protector of wildlife, she returned to India and managed to get a job as an assistant to a photographer working for *National Geographic*, and graduated to being a photographer for the same magazine. When I asked whether she had any training, she replied, 'No. It's much more important to be a good naturalist than a photographer. I found that to be equally true when I moved on to films.'

For fifteen years Belinda and the Australian wildlife film-maker and writer Stanley Breeden criss-crossed the subcontinent travelling to as wide a variety of habitats as they could. Each wrote part of their book, *Through the Tiger's Eyes*, and in it Stanley Breeden describes the Belinda he first met as 'cheerful, intelligent and quick-witted. Twenty years old with an engaging manner and an air about her that suggests she is afraid of nothing'.

Courage has been the hallmark of Belinda since she gave up film-making and writing in order to protect the tiger. She has shown courage not just in challenging dangerous gangs of poachers and ruthless traders in wildlife products, but also in fighting against the bureaucracy. Although the bureaucracy bitterly resents outside interference, particularly interference by a foreigner, Belinda has been appointed to the highest level wildlife committees of both the central and several state governments.

When I suggested that it had been a big sacrifice to give up her career as a film-maker and writer to found the Wildlife Protection Society of India Belinda replied, 'I felt it had to be done because nobody was taking the trouble to find out any of the facts about the losses of tigers which were taking place. Without those facts what was the hope of stemming those losses? Now we have built up one of the largest databases on wildlife crime in the world. We also have investigators going from forest range to forest range to collect the details of known tiger deaths. When tigers die naturally they make every effort to go to some remote place to die where you won't find them. So if a tiger is found dead for instance on an open pathway or near a waterhole, you know there is something odd about the death.'

'Poaching is continuing, as you yourself have said, so what have you achieved?'

Without a moment's thought Belinda said, 'A tiger no longer dies in vain and unheralded. Now we know why it has been killed and where the products go.'

Where the products go is particularly important because if there was no market for the bones and other parts of tigers there would be no poaching. Belinda was a member of a team that went to Tibet in 2005 and exposed the large-scale trade in tiger, leopard and otter skins there. She has tried to work with the Chinese authorities to curb the trade in tiger parts, which are used in manufacturing traditional medicines. On a visit to China in 2007 she was horrified to see tigers being bred in captivity in so-called 'tiger farms'.

*

Belinda and her colleagues managed to gather such detailed information about the Panna poachers by planting informers in the Baheliya community. They are a close-knit tribal community who live by hunting. When I was making a programme for BBC Radio 4 on the tiger crisis in India Belinda arranged for me to meet one of the community. We met on condition that I would not broadcast or write anything which might identify him because that would endanger his life.

The Baheliya described his community as: 'People who don't farm even if they have land, their life is wherever they find animals to kill them and eat them.'

'Now that all hunting is illegal how can they continue with their traditional lives? Surely the police must be after them all the time?' I suggested.

'Even though all hunting is illegal, how much will the police chase them? The police have been driven crazy catching them, but they will not give up hunting.'

'You say they drive the police crazy, but do the police sometimes catch them?'

'They are caught time and time again, and get out time and time again. Ever since this business started, they've been arresting them, lots get off and lots are still in jail. And then they start the same business again, it's not as if they get off and start doing something else. They go back to hunting.'

'How do they get off?'

'They employ a lawyer, give him ten thousand, fifty thousand rupees, and they get out on bail.'

The Baheliya told me his community had only started killing tigers four or five years ago. They had only killed small animals until some tiger hunters from a different community came to the Panna forest and the Baheliyas assisted them. When the Baheliyas picked up the technique they sidelined the other hunters and took over the poaching for themselves. That prompted me to suggest that it must have been a very difficult technique to learn.

He seemed surprised.

'Why difficult?' he asked. 'No, it's not difficult for these people. It's very light work for them. Like if you are an airline pilot it's very easy for you to fly a plane. And for those whose profession is killing animals, it's very easy for them.'

The Baheliyas set traps on paths the tigers use regularly. Sometimes they use the carcass of a cow, bullock or buffalo to attract the tiger. The traps are made of iron. They weigh about four or five kilos, and are made locally. At one stage the Baheliya said there was no way an animal could get out once it was trapped. At another stage, however, he told me tigers did sometimes escape and kill or wound hunters. 'Over the years a lot of men have been killed or maimed,' he said, 'and you can find them limping around, but for the sake of their stomachs these people are never going to stop hunting.' Apparently the last of the Panna tigers managed to escape from a trap but he lost all the skin off one of his paws.

I went on to ask how the tiger was killed once it was caught in the trap.

'They use all the force they have,' he explained. 'They hit it with staffs and spears, and hit it with so much force that a big tiger is dead in five or ten minutes. If a tiger is making too much noise, they hit its mouth with staffs, and stuff the ends of a lump of wood into its mouth and then two or three kilos of earth into its mouth, then it doesn't make any noise any more. When those people are killing the tiger, then it's a question of life and death. If they are going to die in the struggle they will die, so they will kill it, they won't let it live. And then when they've killed it in their hearts they are very happy, very happy indeed that they are going to get two, three, four lakh rupees.'

'Don't they feel this is cruel?' I asked.

'What will they feel? They do it to fill their stomachs. It's their profession. They're doing it as a profession and so they don't think about it. They just think we are going to get money – one lakh, two lakhs, three lakhs, four lakhs. And however difficult it is, they will find a tiger and kill it. They don't fear the government or the police.'

But where were the Forest Department in all this? Forest officials patrol regularly and have outposts inside the forest where they live. So how did a large gang of poachers always escape their attention, and why were they not alerted by the roaring of any of the Panna tigers that were caught in traps? The Baheliya gave me a detailed answer to that question.

'The hunters go into the jungle at four in the morning and they know that the Forest Department people will get up, have a bath, have something to eat, and they won't set out until ten in the morning. By that time the hunters will have gone round the jungle and come out again, and worked out where the animals are moving. So they are out of the jungle by ten.

'And then when they have found where there are one or two animals, then a group of up to eight men get a team together, and if there is a village which is good to them, they camp in the village itself. And if it's a bad place where the Forest Department is more active they set up house at a distance, somewhere in the town or city, and then they set out after eight pm with their traps. It's dark then and no one can see what they're doing, where they are going. They check the traps from two in the morning until four and if they catch something they kill it, otherwise they pack up their traps and take them away.

'Then the next evening they lay out the traps again. And if they get an animal they kill and butcher it, and take its skin and bones out of the forest and back to their house while it is still dark. So this entire business goes on at night. So neither the villagers nor the Forest Department have any idea they've been there.'

'But don't forest officials ever hear the roar of a trapped tiger?'

'If it even happens that a forest guard comes when a tiger is killed then as well as the tiger he will be killed and his body thrown into the forest,' the Baheliya replied in a matter-of-fact manner.

But the Baheliyas don't have it all their own way. They were caught taking a tiger skin or leopard skin to a trader in a bag, so then they tried using a suitcase but again there were arrests. When dressing their women in burqas and wrapping skins round their waists did not prove safe they said the traders would have to send their men to the forest to collect the skins.

During the making of the Radio 4 programme I went to meet the officer of the Madhya Pradesh Forest Department with the impressive title of Additional Principal Chief Conservator of Forests (Wildlife), Dr H.S. Pabla. Only one year earlier he had had this to say about Panna when writing in the magazine *Sanctuary*: 'I would like to assure the world that the tiger density in the park has never been better. I dare say this out of my rather unique position of having known this park since its inception.' Even when Pabla had to accept that the situation was so serious that it had become necessary to transfer two tigers to Panna, he wrote to the National Tiger Conservation Authority in Delhi, saying that Raghu should not be involved in supervising the introduction of the two tigresses because he had 'biased perceptions' about Panna and had filed cases against the state government in the Supreme Court.

I had thought that Dr Pabla would be hostile or at least defensive after the claim he had made in the magazine *Sanctuary* had been shown to be, to put it mildly, incorrect, but he wasn't. His equanimity was remarkable. An engaging Sikh, he admitted that at best there was only one tiger left in Panna. But he still wouldn't agree that poachers were responsible for this debacle. He had an alternative explanation: 'One thing we have to keep in mind,' he said, 'is that all small tiger populations are extremely vulnerable to random movements, random events. What may have happened in Panna, which normally people blame on poaching, is not essentially one hundred per cent poaching. It's mainly a biological problem. We haven't seen sufficient breeding of tigers in that area for quite some time because tiger population is basically controlled by high birth rate and high mortality rate. What has happened is that high mortality hasn't come down but birth rate has.'

'What are these random movements and events?'

'We still haven't got a handle on these things,' Dr Pabla replied.

This didn't seem very convincing. Why was the mortality rate high – what, other than poaching, could have been the movements or events which had decimated the tiger population? So I asked, 'Why don't you accept that poaching is a major problem?'

Here the senior official of the Forest Department did do something of a row-back. 'I don't say we don't accept there hasn't been poaching,' he said and then added, 'but we haven't had any evidence of poaching there.'

But I later learnt that there was an explanation for the decline in the birth rate in Panna, and it wasn't a biological explanation. The poachers appear to have gone first for the tigresses rather than the tigers. Tigresses' movement is limited so they are easier to kill. When a mother has cubs she has to carry each of them individually in her mouth. That means she might have to cover the same ground three or maybe even four times.

Although Dr Pabla insisted that poaching in Panna was not proven he did admit there was a problem with the traditional hunting communities like the Baheliyas. He believed the problem lay in the low status of hunters in traditional Indian society.

'It's very difficult for them,' he said. 'I asked a young man what it would take to check him. His answer was, "Put your hand on my shoulder, and I'll give it all up."'

Dr Pabla is one of the most senior officials in the Madhya Pradesh Forest Department and is aware of the problems posed by the Baheliyas and similar communities, but the fact remains that he still denied the evidence of poaching in Panna collected by Belinda and her team, and the research carried out by Raghu. But in spite of the sorry tale that evidence and research tells, Belinda and Raghu don't despair.

When I asked Belinda about the future for the wild tiger in India she was despondent at first: 'In my heart, privately, I feel it's all downhill. We are losing the big picture.'

But when I went on to suggest that meant we might be approaching the end of the road, she replied, 'Not necessarily and we certainly shouldn't be. There is still hope because tigers are not difficult to save. They breed well and flourish if they have protection, food – that is, prey – water and relatively undisturbed habitat. I can name you three reserves in India and one in Nepal where small populations with four to five breeding tigers, doomed to extinction by any decent predictive model, recovered and expanded.'

When I asked Belinda to comment specifically on Panna she showed me a statement she had issued in which she had described the loss of the tigers as 'a very sad and shameful chapter'. The Forest Department was accused of 'a failure of management in a system where the field staff are not allowed to be open and honest'. The statement ended with an outright condemnation: 'There is no accountability in our present system of wildlife management – the system has failed under a defensive cloud of denial, that would not accept the facts or any outside criticism.'

'So it's a bleak picture?' I suggested.

'Well, not entirely. The central government has now greatly increased funding and is making a sincere effort to be proactive. Various steps are now being taken to improve the protection and management of our tiger reserves and to secure their boundaries. What we need now is the same acceptance and political will from the state governments. Sadly they still seem to be more concerned about projects that produce financial gains rather than tiger conservation.'

When I asked Raghu about the future he replied, 'There is no reason why the tiger should not survive in the wild here in India. We need two things – courts which convict those caught poaching, and a new system of managing the forest. I have been very critical of the Forest Department but most of their officers and lower ranks are good people. It's just that the system doesn't allow them to function.'

'What changes would you like to see?' I asked.

'Above all, I think, more openness. The department should invite everyone who has anything to offer with open arms. At present, officers feel threatened by outsiders. Then accountability is a huge problem. All the effort goes into fudging responsibility for anything which has gone wrong, or hiding it. There should be space for outsiders to point a finger at what is wrong, and there should be an effective system to discover the problem and punish the responsible officer.

'There is a problem also with the junior ranks who patrol the forests. They have too many different jobs, one day they are cutting grass, another the are building a bridge, they are responsible for enforcing the law and have to patrol, and they have to deal with the public, a big problem now that tourism has become so important.'

I have always felt it's symptomatic of the bureaucratic character of the Forest Service that the senior officers who manage reserves don't live in them. They have large office compounds, complete with the full panoply all senior Indian government servants are armed with – peons, or messengers, clerks, minor officials and all the rest of them. These compounds are often located many miles away from the reserves the Directors are meant to be managing. The Director of Panna National Park is comfortably ensconced in the District Headquarters twelve miles away. This to me indicates that keeping files in order matters more than saving the tiger.

Raghu agreed, saying, 'In my experience in Panna, where I had my camp inside the park, the Director very rarely spent a night there. Messages were sent before he visited so everyone knew he was coming, and all that might have been revealed by a surprise visit was put right or hidden before he arrived.'

*

Prashant Sen probably has more direct experience of managing tigers than anyone else in India. His long career in the government forest service was spent entirely in wildlife management and conservation. He too still has hope for their future. At the end of our conversation, he said to me, 'We must not despair. We must remember that in its heyday Project Tiger was widely regarded as the world's most successful tiger preservation project. That just shows that India can do it. The tiger population recovered then and it can recover now. But it does, as I said earlier, need full political support.'

'So India has to put its heart into saving the tiger,' I said.

'Yes,' he replied, 'but heart alone is not enough. The other day there was this day-long programme on a television channel with India's biggest film star Amitabh Bachchan appealing for money to save the tiger. It was fine, educated a lot of people and raised fifty or sixty million rupees. But how can you save the tiger by raising that sort of money when the government is already spending six thousand five hundred million and that is not saving the tiger?

'We only need two per cent of India's land to save the tiger, the elephant, and the rhino. India must give us that and the money, the men and the political support to manage it.'

'That means allow you to reform your own service, the Forest Service?'

'Yes, of course. We must train our staff in modern methods of patrolling and preventing poaching, in gathering intelligence and detecting tiger trading. I wasn't trained in any of these and young officers are still not trained in them.'

So it appears that all the efforts of Indian activists, and all the money contributed around the world, will not guarantee that India remains the land of the tiger unless the Forest Service sheds its colonial past, and becomes a modern, well-equipped, and specifically trained guardian of wildlife.

CONCLUSION

On the day of the deadline my editors had set for this book, I still hadn't decided what to say in this brief conclusion when the *Journal of the Royal Society for Asian Affairs* arrived in the post. Being a believer in the significance of coincidences, I looked at the contents to see whether there was any article that would give me an idea for the conclusion. I knew what I wanted to say, but that is not the same thing as knowing how to say it. Inside was an article by an old friend of mine, Bal Mundkur, one of the doyens of the Indian advertising world. His article was called 'Incredible India: The Inconvenient Truth'. As soon as I read the first page I knew what I needed to write.

'Incredible India' is the long-running slogan of the Indian tourist industry. Bal Mundkur maintains that it helps to conceal 'the basic flaws' of India, and is 'a myth and an insult to India's 950 million poor'. He then goes on to list the flaws. They include: the divide between India's haves and have-nots which he says is growing alarmingly; discrimination based on colour, religion and caste; population growth out of control; endemic corruption; and incompetent administration.

Pessimism like this seems to me as dangerous as 'the culture of short-sighted optimism' William Bissell criticised in the introduction. Short-sighted optimism tends to produce blindness, blindness to faults. Hopeless pessimism tends to produce fatalism, a fatalism which undermines efforts to put things right. But I have to be fair to Bal. In his epilogue he does say, 'Growth over the next three decades will provide the biggest opportunity for India's youth to meet the challenges ahead.' The main challenge, he believes, is 'the calamitous failings of the system which left to itself will keep India in reverse gear'.

I hope that I have steered a middle course between William Bissell and Bal Mundkur. But the failures of the system are a theme which does recur throughout the stories I have told. I recall another friend, Ram Agarwala, warning in the introduction against blaming all India's problems on governance, the failure of the system. But it does seem to me that the most important task for India is to reform the system, to make proper use of the institutions which are in place, and prevent the dishonest from obstructing the many honest men and women in those institutions, not allowing them to function as they should. That can best be done by following the advice of Gopalakrishnan in the Tata story – having rules and clear policies. The policies must be adhered to, and the rules obeyed. This means that the dreaded discretionary powers which enable bureaucrats and politicians to diverge from policies and disobey rules must be removed. Then businessmen and women will not be able to offer inducements to get politicians and civil servants to use their discretionary powers. The government must not be allowed to send agencies such as the police and Income Tax authorities to harass those it wants to cow, then the business community will have the courage, hopefully, to campaign for good governance. Much else needs to be done. A new ethos needs to be created in government departments so that people who work there think of themselves as civil servants, not relics of the Raj like the forest officers who see themselves as rulers. The courts need drastic reforms so that the old adage of justice delayed is justice denied becomes one of the basic principles of the legal system. And, as Seva Mandir has shown, the poor of India have to realise they too must help to build just communities. In spite of all that still needs to be done much has changed for the better over the last twenty years. Corruption scandals are now coming out of the woodwork because of a more alert media and so there is, as Gopalakrishnan says, every hope this will lead to lancing the cyst, and to a demand for reform no government can resist. Twenty years ago I wrote a book called *No Full Stops in India*, and I am confident that there won't be any full stops to halt progress over the next twenty years. Maybe it's also not too much to hope that there will be fewer commas.

SELECT BIBLIOGRAPHY

Abley, Mark, *Spoken Here: Travels Among Threatened Languages*, London: Arrow Books, 2003

Bagchi, Amitabha, *Above Average*, New Delhi: Harper Collins, 2007

Bardhan, Pranab, *Awakening Giants, Feet of Clay*, New Delhi: OUP, 2010

Bhaumik, Subir, *Troubled Periphery: Crisis of India's North East*, New Delhi: Sage Publications, 2009

Bissell, William Nanda, *Making India Work*, New Delhi: Viking Penguin, 2009

Chakravarti, Sudeep, *Red Sun, Travels in Naxalite Country*, New Delhi: Penguin, 2009

Dai, Mamang, *Arunachal Prades: The Hidden Land*, New Delhi: Penguin Enterprise, 2009

Das, Gurcharan, *The Difficulty of Being Good: On the Subtle Art of Dharma*, New Delhi: Allen Lane, 2009

Elwin, Verrier, *A Philosophy for NEFA*, Itanagar: Directorate of Research, Government of Arunachal Pradesh, 2006

Ghosh, Amitav, *Sea of Poppies*, New Delhi: Viking Penguin, 2008

Guha, Ramachandra, *India After Gandhi*, New Delhi: Picador India, 2007

Hazarika, Sanjoy, *Strangers of the Mist, Tales of War and Peace from India's Northeast*, New Delhi: Viking Penguin, 1994

Ilaiah, Kancha, *Post-Hindu India*, New Delhi: Sage Publications, 2009

Jadhav, Narendra, *Untouchables: My Family's Triumphant Journey Out of the Caste System in Modern India*, New York: Scribner, 2003

Jaffrelot, Christophe, *The Hindu Nationalist Movement and Indian Politics*

1925 to the 1990s, Strategies of Identity Building, Implantation and Mobilisation, New Delhi: Viking Penguin, 1996

Karanth, K. Ullas, *The Way of the Tiger*, Bangalore: Centre for Wildlife Studies, 2002

Nilekani, Nandan, *Imagining India: Ideas for the New Century*, New Delhi: Allen Lane, 2008

Panagariya, Arvind, *India: The Emerging Giant*, New Delhi: OUP, 2008

Prahalad, C. K., *The Fortune at the Bottom of the Pyramid: Eradicating Poverty through Profits*, Philadelphia: Wharton School Publishing, 2005

Putnam, Robert D., *Making Democracy Work: Civic Traditions in Modern Italy*, Princeton University Press, 1992

Singh, Narendra, *Once a Prince in Sarila: of Palaces and Tiger Hunts, Nehrus and Mountbattens*, London: IB Tauris, 2008

Singh, Prakash, *The Naxalite Movement in India*, New Delhi: Rupa & Co., 1995

Stiglitz, Joseph, *The Roaring Nineties, Seeds of Destruction*, London: Allen Lane, 2003

Wright, Belinda and Stanley Breeden, *Through the Tiger's Eyes, A Chronicle of India's Wildlife*, Berkeley: Ten Speed Press, 1996

INDEX